AIR FRYER COOK

Top 550 Amazingly Easy and Delicious Air Fryer Recipes For The Everyday Home

By

Robert Wilson

TABLE OF CONTENTS

Introduction

This cookbook is comprised of a delicious collection of recipes that are suitable for all tastes. Each recipe is simple to make, full of flavor, and offers a healthier alternative to traditionally fried foods. This book is made to help ensure you get the most out of your Air Fryer.

With an air fryer, you end up with healthier, low-fat dishes that make use of little to no oil. As for the flavor and texture, you have to be the judge of it. Most people say they can't taste any difference between deep-fried foods and air-fried foods. On top of all this, the device is easy to use and clean up.

Throughout the pages of this book, you will discover a variety of sweet, savory, salty, citrusy, and other delicious recipes. These flavorful dishes are hand-picked to ensure you have a hearty collection of the best recipes on hand at all times. As a result, this cookbook is the ultimate companion book to any Air Fryer. You are guaranteed to find a wonderful selection of traditional, modern and alternative recipes inside to suit any palette. There is certainly something here for everyone.

Enjoy cooking!

Air fryer and How It works.

Air Fryer is a versatile and intelligent kitchen machine with patented technology that utilizes super-heated air to cook food. The machine heats up in a minute, hot air circulates in the specialized chamber so the food is cooked evenly, using a limited amount of oil.

This game changer kitchen appliance has the rapid air circulation technology which enables heated air to move through the food ingredients at high speed to develop the crispy food we all crave for. On top of the delicious crunchy food, little oil is used in the process which makes it a guilt-free delicacy!

Choosing air frying doesn't mean skimping on flavor. In fact, it means aiming for the healthier versions of our favorite fried foods! For instance, vegetables are one of the healthiest and most nutritious foods.

The same cannot be said for deep fried vegetables - they are linked to heart diseases, obesity, diabetes, cancer and other serious health problems.

When it comes to crispy, flavorful and healthy food, it's hard to beat an Air Fryer. You will be able to prepare an entire meal with just one kitchen device.

You will be pleasantly surprised what this incredible machine can do for you! Therefore, to put it in a nutshell, if you like your food fried and healthy, an Air Fryer is worth investing in.

Benefits of Using Air Fryer

Air Fryers have many perks to offer when it comes to improving quality of life. It helps in maintaining your wellness and fitness.

1. Time Saving

With only 24 hours to complete everyday routine tasks, the time has become a genuinely luxury in our fast-paced lifestyle. Air Fryers are designed to save your precious cooking time by serving you crunchy snacks and fried cuisines in a matter of minutes. If you are always on a tight schedule, Air Fryer is no less than a time savior.

2. Superfast Heating

Unlike traditional frying method, Air Fryers takes only a few minutes to heat and prepare foods. They are always ready to make meals whenever you crave for fried foods.

Most Air Fryer models get ready in only 3 minutes to heat up properly and they can also go as high as 400 degrees F to make you crispy meals.

3. Versatile Options

Air Fryer allows you cook a diverse range of foods, be it chicken tenders, mushrooms, crispy fries, fried shrimp, mozzarella sticks, or grilled vegetables. You want to grill, fry, roast, or bake your foods? Air Fryers are there to prepare them in real quick time. Specific ultra-modern range of Air Fryers also allow you make many recipes in a single cooking session.

4. Natural Food Taste

It's quite common for anyone to worry about their food's ability to delight them with their mouthwatering flavors. When it comes to Air Fryers, things are no different. Air Fryers prepare meals without compromising on their taste profile. As far as the taste is concerned, they can easily be compared with deep-fried foods.

5. Space Saver and Ease of Cleaning

Cleaning after cooking foods is also very easy as they are designed for effortless cleaning. On top of that, they don't take up much of your counter space and require quite less space to store.

How to Use an Air Fryer.

Take it easy It is Very simple to use an Air Fryer just follow these steps

STEPS:

1: The first step is to prepare the air fryer. For this, start by picking the right attachment to be used. You have to place the attachment the right way in order for the air fryer to work

2: Preheat the air fryer so that it reaches the right temperature for your food. You can look up the instructional manual provided with your machine to check which temperature suits what food the best. Generally speaking, meats and hard vegetables require the highest temperature to cook

3: Brush a little oil over the food and place it inside the attachment before fixing it on to the air fryer.

4: Choose the right timing and wait patiently. Once done, you can serve the dish hot

Tips to Prepare Healthy Foods in Your Air Fryer

1. Re-heating leftovers: There's no hard and fast rule for time and temperature when re-heating leftovers because leftovers vary so significantly. I suggest re-heating in the air fryer at 350 degrees Fahrenheit and doing so for as long as it takes for the food to be re-heated to a food safety temperature of 165 degrees Fahrenheit. This is especially important for any potentially hazardous foods like chicken and beef

2. Vegetables are one of the easiest foods to cook in Air Fryer. A wide variety of plants can be cooked, be it delicate beans to root vegetables. For the best cooking experience, firstly, soak the vegetables, especially the harder ones, in cold water for 15 - 20 minutes. Then after, dry them using a clean kitchen towel

3. Keep in mind that you should always aim to cook your food to desired doneness because the recipes are flexible and they are designed for all Air Fryer models

If you feel that the food needs more cooking time then adjust it and cook for a few more minutes. It is not a thumb rule to stick to recipe time only as certain ingredients can vary in their size and firmness from one country to another

4. Flip foods over halfway through the cooking time; Just as you would if you were cooking on a grill or in a skillet, you need to turn foods over so that they brown evenly

5. Roasting with air is a new cooking trend you have to try because you can finally prepare your winter favorites

6. You can bake your favorite recipes in your Air Fryer but always check with the machine's manual before using new baking ware with Air Fryer

7. When it comes to the cooking time, it changes depending on particular Air Fryer model, the size of food, food pre-preparation and so on. For shorter cooking cycles, you should preheat Air Fryer for about 3 - 4 minutes. otherwise, if you put the ingredients into the cold cooking basket, the cooking time needs to be increased to 3 additional minutes

8. Use a good quality oil spray to brush food and cooking basket, it is also helpful for easy cleanup

Measurements & Conversions

Unit of Measurement:		= Equals:	Ounces to Grams
Pinch or dash	=	Less than 1/8 teaspoon	1 oz = 29 g
3 teaspoons	=	1 tablespoon	2 oz = 57 g
2 tablespoons	=	1 fluid ounce	3 oz = 85 g
4 tablespoons	=	1/4 cup	4 oz = 113 g
5 tablespoons plus 1 teaspoon.	=	1/3 cup	5 oz = 142 g
12 tablespoons	=	3/4 cup	6 oz = 170 g
16 tablespoons	=	1 cup	7 oz = 198 g
1 cup	=	8 fluid ounces	8 oz = 227 g
2 cups	=	1 pint or 16 fluid ounces	10 oz = 283 g
2 pints	=	1 quart or 32 fluid ounces	20 oz = 567 g
4 quarts	=	1 gallon	30 oz = 850 g
			40 oz = 1133 g

Breakfast Recipes

1. Fluffy Egg Breakfast

Prep + Cook Time: 25 minutes   **Servings:** 2

Ingredients:

- 2 cups flour [all-purpose]
- 1 cup pumpkin puree
- 2 tablespoon oil
- 2 tablespoon vinegar
- 2 teaspoon baking powder
- 1/2 cup milk
- 2-eggs
- 1 teaspoon baking soda
- 1 tablespoon brown sugar
- 1 teaspoon cinnamon powder

Instructions:

1. Preheat the Air Fryer to 300 - degrees Fahrenheit
2. Whisk eggs into a bowl. Add milk, pumpkin puree, flour, baking powder, baking soda, and brown sugar and cinnamon powder.
3. Mix well and add milk. Grease the baking tray with oil and pour the mixture. Place it in the Air Fryer and cook for 10 minutes.

2. Toasties and Sausage

Prep + Cook Time: 30 minutes   **Servings:** 2

Ingredients:

- 1/4 cup milk or cream
- 2 sausages; boiled
- three eggs
- 1 piece of bread; sliced lengthwise
- 4 tablespoon grated cheese
- sea salt to taste
- chopped fresh herbs and steamed broccoli [optional]

Instructions:

1. Preheat the Air Fryer to 360 - degrees Fahrenheit. Set the timer for 5 minutes. Meanwhile; break the eggs into a bowl, scramble them, adding milk.
2. Take 3 muffin cups and grease them with a cooking spray. Pour the equal amount of egg mixture into each of them.
3. Arrange sliced sausages with bread slices in muffin cups, sinking them deeply into the egg and milk mixture. Sprinkle it with cheese and add a bit of salt to taste.
4. Put the muffin cups into the Air Fryer and set the timer for 15 – 20 minutes, depending on the consistency you prefer. When the meal is done, you may season it with fresh herbs and add steamed broccoli.

3. Parsley and Spinach Baked Omelet

Prep + Cook Time: 15 minutes   **Servings:** 1

Ingredients:

- 3 tablespoon ricotta cheese
- 1 tablespoon chopped parsley
- 1 teaspoon olive oil
- 3-eggs
- 1/4 cup chopped spinach
- salt and pepper; to taste

Instructions:

1. Preheat your Air Fryer to 330 - degrees Fahrenheit and heat the olive oil in it. Beat the eggs and season with some salt and pepper.
2. Stir in the ricotta, parsley, and spinach. Pour the egg mixture in your Air Fryer. Cook for 10 minutes. Serve and enjoy.

4. Cheesy Omelet

Prep + Cook Time: 30 minutes   **Servings:** 2

Ingredients:

- 1 large onion; chopped
- 2 tablespoon cheddar cheese; grated
- 3-eggs
- 1/2 teaspoon soy sauce
- salt to taste
- pepper powder to taste
- cooking spray

Instructions:

1. Whisk together eggs, salt, pepper, and soy sauce.
2. Spray a small pan, which fits inside the Air Fryer with cooking spray. Add onions and spread it all over the pan and place the pan inside the Air Fryer. Air fry at 355 - degrees Fahrenheit for 6 - 7 minutes or until onions are translucent.
3. Pour the beaten egg mixture all over the onions.
4. Sprinkle cheese all over it. Air fry for another 5 – 6 minutes.
5. Remove from the Air Fryer and serve with toasted multi grain bread.

5. Delicious Muffins

Prep + Cook Time: 25 minutes   **Servings:** 4

Ingredients:

- 4 small eggs; whisked
- 4 tablespoon vegetable oil
- 1/2 cup milk
- 1 cup plain flour
- 1 tablespoon baking powder
- 1/2 teaspoon of mustard powder
- 2 ounces. Parmesan; grated
- 1 teaspoon Worcestershire sauce
- 2 tomatoes; for garnishing
- A Handful of basil leaves; garnishing

Equipment: 8 paper muffin cases

Instructions:

1. Preheat the Air Fryer to 390 - degrees Fahrenheit.
2. Combine two muffin cases to form one. Take a large bowl and whisk the egg in it.
3. Then add milk and oil. Add in the baking powder and flour. Combine it to form a smooth paste.
4. Add the cheese, mustard powder and Worcestershire sauce.
5. Mix well and then fill the muffin cups with the mixture.
6. Cook in Air Fryer for about 15 minutes. Then arrange the muffins in the muffin tray and garnish with slices of tomato and basil leaves.

6. Cheesy Risotto

Prep + Cook Time: 40 minutes   **Servings:** 2

Ingredients:

- 1 onion; diced
- 2 cups chicken stock; boiling
- 1/2 cup parmesan cheese or cheddar cheese; grated
- 1 clove garlic; minced
- 3/4 cup Arborio rice
- 1 tablespoon olive oil
- 1 tablespoon butter; unsalted

Instructions:

1. Preheat the Air Fryer to 390 - degrees Fahrenheit and adjust the time to 5 minutes.
2. Take round baking tin; grease it with oil and add stirring the butter, onion, and garlic.
3. When the fryer is hot; adjust the time to 8 minutes.
4. Place the tin into the Air Fryer and cook for 4 minutes. Then add rice and cook for another 4 minutes.

5. Stir three times during the cooking time.
6. Reduce the heat to 320 - degrees Fahrenheit and set the timer to 22 minutes. Pour in the chicken stock and stir gently.
7. Do not cover the Air Fryer and cook for 22 minutes as have been set. Add in the cheese, stir once again and serve.

7. Coffee Doughnuts

Prep + Cook Time: 20 minutes   **Servings:** 6

Ingredients:

- 1 cup white all-purpose flour
- 1/4 cup coconut sugar
- 1/2 teaspoon salt
- 1 teaspoon baking powder
- 2 tablespoon aquafaba
- 1 tablespoon sunflower oil
- 1/4 cup coffee

Instructions:

1. In a mixing bowl; mix together the dry ingredients flour, sugar, salt, and baking powder.
2. In another bowl; combine the aquafaba, sunflower oil, and coffee. Mix to form a dough. Let the dough rest inside the fridge.
3. Preheat the Air Fryer to 400 - degrees Fahrenheit. Knead the dough and create doughnuts.
4. Arrange inside the Air Fryer in single layer and cook for 6 minutes. Do not shake so that the donut maintains its shape.

8. Taco Crisp Wraps

Prep + Cook Time: 30 minutes   **Servings:** 4

Ingredients:

- 1 tablespoon water
- 4 pieces commercial vegan nuggets; chopped
- 1 small yellow onion; diced
- 1 small red bell pepper; chopped
- 2 cobs grilled corn kernels
- 4 large tortillas mixed greens for garnish

Instructions:

1. Preheat the Air Fryer to 400 - degrees Fahrenheit.
2. In a skillet heated over medium heat; water sauté the vegan nuggets together with the onions, bell peppers, and corn kernels. Set aside.
3. Place filling inside the corn tortillas. Fold the tortillas and place inside the Air Fryer and cook for 15 minutes until the tortilla wraps are crispy. Serve with mix greens on top.

9. Tasty Shrimp Toasts

Prep + Cook Time: 30 minutes   **Servings:** 4

Ingredients:

- 3/4-pound raw shrimps; peeled and deveined
- 4 – 5 white bread slices
- One Egg white
- 3 garlic cloves; minced
- 2 tablespoon cornstarch
- salt and black pepper; to taste
- 2 tablespoon olive oil

Instructions:

1. In a medium bowl combine chopped shrimps, egg white, minced garlic, cornstarch, salt and pepper. Stir to combine.
2. Spread shrimp mixture over bread slices with a knife. Sprinkle each slice with olive oil.

3. Preheat the Air Fryer to 370 - degrees Fahrenheit and place bread slices in the basket. Cook for 10 minutes or less; until crispy and lightly brown.

10. Cheesy Potato Wedges

Prep + Cook Time: 20 minutes   **Servings:** 4

Ingredients:

- 1-pound fingerling potatoes; cut into wedges
- 1 teaspoon extra virgin olive oil
- 1/2 teaspoon garlic powder
- salt and pepper to taste
- 1/2 cup raw cashews; soaked in water overnight

- 1/2 teaspoon ground turmeric
- 1/2 teaspoon paprika
- 2 tablespoon nutritional yeast
- 1 teaspoon fresh lemon juice
- 2 tablespoons to 1/4 cup water

Instructions:

1. Preheat the Air Fryer to 400 - degrees Fahrenheit.
2. Place the potatoes in a bowl and add the olive oil, garlic powder, salt and pepper. Toss to coat the potatoes.
3. Place the potatoes inside the fryer basket and cook for 10 minutes.
4. Meanwhile; make the cheese sauce by mixing the remaining ingredients in a blender. Pulse until well combined.
5. Adjust the consistency of the cheese sauce by adding less or more water.
6. Once the potatoes are done; transfer in a bowl that will fit inside the Air Fryer. Pour the cheese sauce on top and air fry again for another 3 more minutes.

11. Spinach Balls

Prep + Cook Time: 20 minutes   **Servings:** 4

Ingredients:

- 1 carrot; peeled and grated
- 1 package fresh spinach; blanched and chopped
- 1/2 onion; chopped
- One Egg; beaten
- 1/2 teaspoon garlic powder
- 1 teaspoon garlic; minced

- 1 teaspoon salt
- 1/2 teaspoon black pepper
- 1 tablespoon nutritional yeast
- 1 tablespoon corn flour
- 2 slices bread; toasted and made into bread crumbs

Instructions:

1. In a mixing bowl; combine all the ingredients except the bread crumbs.
2. Create small balls and roll over the bread crumbs. Place the spinach balls inside the Air Fryer and cook at 390 - degrees Fahrenheit for 10 minutes.

12. Vegetable Pasta Salad

Prep + Cook Time: 30 minutes   **Servings:** 6

Ingredients:

- 1 zucchini; sliced into semicircles
- 3 bell peppers of different colors; roughly chopped
- 1 squash; sliced into semicircles
- 1 cup mushrooms; sliced
- 1 cup cherry tomatoes; cut in halves

- 1 red onion; sliced into semicircles
- 1/2 cup kalamata olives; pitted and halved
- 1 Pound. rigatoni pasta or penne rigate; boiled
- 2 + 2 tablespoon olive oil [separately]
- 3 tablespoon balsamic vinegar

- 1 teaspoon Italian seasoning
- a handful of fresh basil; minced
- sea salt and black pepper to taste

Instructions:
1. Preheat the Air Fryer to 380 - degrees Fahrenheit for 5 minutes.
2. Meanwhile; mix bell peppers, mushrooms, squash, zucchini and onion with salt, black pepper, Italian herbs in a pan.
3. Pour 2 tablespoons of olive oil over the vegetables and stir well to combine.
4. Put the vegetables into a basket and roast in the Air Fryer for 12 – 14 minutes, shaking the basket halfway cooked.
5. Transfer the roasted vegetables to a bowl. Combine them with cooked pasta, cherry tomatoes, and olives, pouring in balsamic vinegar and the remaining 2 tablespoons of the olive oil. Toss well.
6. Sprinkle the salad with fresh basil, salt, and black pepper.
7. Stir well and you are ready to serve.

13. Cheese and Chicken Sandwich

Prep + Cook Time: 15 minutes **Servings:** 1

Ingredients:
- 1/3 cup cooked and shredded chicken
- 2 mozzarella slices
- 1 hamburger bun
- 1/4 cup shredded cabbage
- 1 teaspoon mayonnaise
- 2 teaspoon butter
- 1 teaspoon olive oil
- 1/2 teaspoon balsamic vinegar
- 1/4 teaspoon smoked paprika
- 1/4 teaspoon black pepper
- 1/4 teaspoon garlic powder
- pinch of salt

Instructions:
1. Preheat your Air Fryer to 370 - degrees Fahrenheit.
2. Brush the outside of the bun with butter.
3. Combine the chicken with garlic powder, paprika, pepper, and salt.
4. Cut the bun in half and add the chicken. Place the mozzarella slices over.
5. In a small bowl combine the cabbage, mayonnaise, olive oil, and balsamic vinegar.
6. Top the chicken with the coleslaw. Close the sandwich and place it in the Air Fryer. Cook for 5 – 7 minutes.

14. Bacon, Brussels Sprouts, And Horseradish Cream

Prep + Cook Time: 1 hour 40 minutes **Servings:** 4

Ingredients:
- 1/2 Pound. thick cut bacon; diced
- 2 tablespoon butter
- 2 shallots; sliced
- 1/2 cup milk
- 1 ½ Pounds. Brussels sprouts; halved
- 2 tablespoon all-purpose flour
- 1 cups heavy cream
- 2 tablespoon prepared horseradish
- 1/2 tablespoon fresh thyme leaves
- 1/8 teaspoon ground nutmeg
- 1 tablespoon olive oil
- 1/2 teaspoon sea salt
- ground black pepper to taste
- 1/2 cup water

Instructions:
1. Preheat the Air Fryer to 400 - degrees Fahrenheit.
2. Cover the Brussels sprouts with olive oil and season it with pepper and salt. Cook for 30 minutes; stirring halfway. Remove and set aside.
3. Put the bacon into the Air Fryer basket. Add the water to the drawer below in order to catch the grease. Set the timer to 10 minutes and cook stirring 2 – 3 times throughout the process.

4. Add shallots and cook for another 10 – 15 minutes. The shallots should become soft enough and the bacon should become brown. Then season the ingredients with pepper and let it drain on paper towels.
5. Meanwhile; melt the butter. Then combine it with the flour and whisk well. Pour in heavy cream with milk slowly and whisk again.
6. The sauce should be thick enough, so continue whisking it for 3 – 5 minutes. Add horseradish, thyme, salt, and nutmeg, stirring well again.
7. Prepare the 9" x 13" baking dish and preheat the oven to 350 - degrees Fahrenheit.
8. Spread the Brussels sprouts over this dish; cover it with horseradish cream sauce, layer bacon, and shallots on top. Bake in the oven for 30 minutes and serve hot.

15. Vegetables on Toast

Prep + Cook Time: 25 minutes   **Servings:** 4

Ingredients:

- 4 slices French or Italian bread
- 1 red bell pepper; cut into strips
- 1 cup sliced button or cremini mushrooms
- 1 small yellow squash; sliced
- 2 green onions; sliced
- 1 tablespoon olive oil
- 2 tablespoon softened butter
- 1/2 cup soft goat cheese

Instructions:

1. Sprinkle the Air Fryer with olive oil and preheat the appliance to 350 - degrees Fahrenheit.
2. Add red pepper, mushrooms, squash, and green onions, mix well and cook for 7 minutes or until the vegetables are tender, shaking the basket once during cooking time.
3. Transfer vegetables to a plate and set aside.
4. Spread bread slices with butter and place in the Air Fryer; butter-side up. Toast for 2 to 4 minutes or until golden brown.
5. Spread the goat cheese on the toasted bread and top with the vegetables. Serve warm and enjoy!

16. Banana Cookies

Prep + Cook Time: 45 minutes   **Servings:** 6

Ingredients:

- 3 ripe bananas
- 2 cups rolled oats
- 1 cup dates; pitted and chopped
- 1/3 cup vegetable oil
- 1 teaspoon vanilla

Instructions:

1. Preheat the Air Fryer to 350 - degrees Fahrenheit.
2. In a bowl; mash the bananas and add in the rest of the ingredients. Let it rest inside the fridge for 10 minutes.
3. Drop a teaspoonful on cut parchment paper.
4. Place the cookies on parchment paper inside the Air Fryer basket. Make sure that the cookies do not overlap. Cook for 20 minutes or until the edges are crispy.
5. Serve with almond milk.

17. Cinnamon Toasts

Prep + Cook Time: 15 minutes   **Servings:** 4

Ingredients:

- 10 medium bread slices
- 1 pack salted butter
- 4 tablespoon sugar
- 2 teaspoon ground cinnamon

- 1/2 teaspoon vanilla extract

Instructions:
1. Place salted butter to a mixing bowl and add sugar, cinnamon, and vanilla extract. Mix well and spread the mixture over bread slices.
2. Preheat the Air Fryer to 380 - degrees Fahrenheit and place bread slices to a fryer. Cook for 4 – 5 minutes and serve hot!

18. Toasted Cheese

Prep + Cook Time: 20 minutes   **Servings:** 2

Ingredients:

- 2 sliced white bread
- 4 ounces. cheese; grated
- little piece of butter

Instructions:

1. At first; toast the bread in the toaster.
2. Once toasted spread the butter on bread pieces. Cover with grated cheese.
3. Preheat the Air Fryer to 350 - degrees Fahrenheit.
4. Place covered bread slices into the Fryer and cook for 4 - 6 minutes.
5. Serve and enjoy!

19. Peanut Butter Bread Breakfast

Prep + Cook Time: 15 minutes   **Servings:** 3

Ingredients:

- 1 tablespoon oil
- 2 tablespoon peanut butter
- 4 slices bread
- 1 banana [slices]

Instructions:

1. Get the slices of bread and on one side add the peanut butter. Place slices of banana and cover with the other slice.
2. Grease the Air Fryer with oil. Place the bread in it and cook for 5 minutes on 300 - degrees Fahrenheit.

20. Easy English Breakfast

Prep + Cook Time: 35 minutes   **Servings:** 2

Ingredients:

- 1 cup sliced and diced potatoes
- 2 cups beans in tomato sauce
- two eggs
- 1 tablespoon olive oil
- 1 sausage
- salt to taste

Instructions:

1. Preheat your Air Fryer to 390 - degrees Fahrenheit. Crack the eggs onto an oven safe dish.
2. Sprinkle with salt if desired. Place the beans next to the eggs.
3. In a separate container; place the potatoes, and 1 tablespoon of olive oil, combine well. Sprinkle with salt if desired.
4. First place the potatoes in the Air Fryer. Cook for 10 minutes.
5. Then place the form with the eggs and the beans. Cover the potatoes with parchment paper to separate. Cook for an additional 10 minutes.
6. Cut the sausage into pieces and add to the dish with the beans and eggs. Cook for another 5 minutes. Serve with toast and coffee for a big and hearty breakfast.

21. Avocado Eggs

Prep + Cook Time: 15 minutes

Servings: 4

Ingredients:

- 2 large avocados; sliced
- 1 cup of panko bread crumbs
- 1/2 cup of flour
- two eggs; beaten
- 1/4 teaspoon of paprika
- black pepper to taste
- salt to taste

Instructions:

1. Preheat the Air Fryer 400 - degrees Fahrenheit for 5 min.
2. Season the avocado slices with some salt and pepper.
3. Dust the avocados with some flour and dip them in the eggs then roll them in the breadcrumbs. Place the avocado slices in the Air Fryer then fry for 6 min.

Tip: To make it tastier; add in 1/2 teaspoon of dry oregano to the breadcrumbs.

22. Avocado Tempura

Prep + Cook Time: 20 minutes

Servings: 4

Ingredients:

- 1/2 cup panko breadcrumbs
- 1/2 teaspoon salt
- 1 pitted Haas avocado; peeled and sliced
- liquid from 1 can white beans or aquafaba

Instructions:

1. Preheat the Air Fryer at 350 - degrees Fahrenheit.
2. In a shallow bowl, toss the breadcrumbs and salt until well combined.
3. Dredge the avocado slices first with the aquafaba then in the breadcrumb mixture. Place the avocado slices in a single layer inside the Air Fryer basket. Cook for 10 minutes and shake halfway through the cooking time.

23. Potato and Kale Nuggets

Prep + Cook Time: 25 minutes

Servings: 4

Ingredients:

- 1 teaspoon extra virgin olive oil
- 1 clove of garlic; minced
- 4 cups kale; rinsed and chopped
- 2 cups potatoes; boiled and mashed
- 1/8 cup almond milk
- salt and pepper to taste
- vegetable oil for spraying

Instructions:

1. Preheat the Air Fryer to 390 - degrees Fahrenheit.
2. In a skillet; heat the olive oil over medium heat and sauté the garlic until golden brown. Add in the kale and cook for another 3 minutes. Set aside.
3. In a mixing bowl; combine the mashed potatoes and kale mixture. Add milk and season with salt and pepper to taste.
4. Spray vegetable oil on the surface of the nuggets. Place inside the Air Fryer basket and cook for 15 minutes.
5. Be sure to give the fryer basket a shake halfway through the cooking time for even cooking.

24. Potato Bread Rolls

Prep + Cook Time: 30 minutes

Servings: 5

Ingredients:

- 5 large potatoes; boiled
- salt and pepper to taste
- 1 tablespoon olive oil
- 1/2 teaspoon mustard seeds
- 2 small onions; chopped
- 1/2 teaspoon turmeric
- 2 sprigs; curry leaves
- 8 slices of vegan wheat bread; brown sides discarded
- 2 green chilies; seeded and chopped
- 1 bunch coriander; chopped

Instructions:

1. In a bowl; mash the potatoes and season with salt and pepper to taste. Set aside.
2. Heat olive oil in a skillet over medium low flame and add the mustard seeds. Stir until the seeds sputter.
3. Then add the onions and fry until translucent. Stir in the turmeric powder and curry leaves. Continue to cook for 2 more minutes until fragrant.
4. Remove from heat and add to the potatoes. Stir in the green chilies and coriander.
5. This will be the filling. Wet the bread and remove the excess water.
6. Place a tablespoon of the potato mixture in the middle of the bread and gently roll the bread in so that the potato filling is completely sealed inside the bread.
7. Brush with oil and place inside the Air Fryer.
8. Cook in a 400 - degrees Fahrenheit preheated Air Fryer for 15 minutes. Make sure to shake the Air Fryer basket gently halfway through the cooking time for even cooking.

25. Veg Frittata

Prep + Cook Time: 35 minutes   **Servings:** 2

Ingredients:

- 1/4 cup milk
- 1 zucchini
- 1/2 bunch asparagus
- 1/2 cup mushrooms
- 1/2 cup spinach or baby Spinach
- 1/2 cup red onion; sliced
- four eggs
- 1/2 tablespoon olive oil
- 5 tablespoon Feta cheese; crumbled
- 4 tablespoon cheddar; grated
- 1/4 bunch Chives; minced
- Sea salt and pepper to taste

Instructions:

1. Combine eggs, salt, pepper and milk in a hollow dish.
2. Slice zucchini, asparagus, mushrooms and red onion, tear spinach with hands.
3. Heat the non-stick pan, greased with olive oil and put vegetables into it. Stir-fry for 5 - 7 minutes over medium heat.
4. Cover the baking tin with parchment paper. Transfer vegetables into it and pour in the egg mixture.
5. Cover the contents of the baking dish with feta and sprinkle with grated cheddar.
6. Preheat the Air Fryer to 320 – degrees Fahrenheit, setting the timer to 5 minutes.
7. As soon as the Air Fryer is preheated; put in the baking tin. Set the timer to 15 minutes.
8. When the time is over; take frittata out of the Air Fryer and let it chill for 5 minutes.
9. Sprinkle it with minced chives and enjoy.

26. Maple Cinnamon Buns

Prep + Cook Time: 1 hour 55 minutes   **Servings:** 9

Ingredients:

- 3/4 cup tablespoon unsweetened almond milk
- 4 tablespoon maple syrup
- 1 ½ tablespoon active yeast
- 1 tablespoon ground flaxseed

- 1 tablespoon coconut oil; melted
- 1 cup wholegrain flour; sifted
- 1 ½ cup plain white flour; sifted
- 2 teaspoon cinnamon powder
- 1/2 cup pecan nuts; toasted
- 2 ripe bananas; sliced
- 4 Medjool dates; pitted
- 1/4 cup icing sugar

Instructions:

1. Heat the 3/4 cup almond milk to lukewarm and add the maple syrup and yeast. Allow the yeast to activate for 5 to 10 minutes.
2. Meanwhile; mix together flaxseed and 3 tablespoons of water to make the egg replacement. Allow flaxseed to soak for 2 minutes.
3. Add the coconut oil. Pour the flaxseed mixture to the yeast mixture.
4. In another bowl; combine the two types of flour and the 1 tablespoon cinnamon powder.
5. Pour the yeast-flaxseed mixture and combine until dough forms.
6. Knead the dough on a floured surface for at least 10 minutes.
7. Place the kneaded dough in a greased bowl and cover with a kitchen towel. Leave in a warm and dark area for the bread to rise for 1 hour.
8. While the dough is rising; make the filling by mixing together the pecans, banana slices, and dates. Add 1 tablespoon of cinnamon powder.
9. Preheat the Air Fryer to 390 - degrees Fahrenheit. Roll the risen dough on a floured surface until it is thin. Spread the pecan mixture on to the dough.
10. Roll the dough and cut into nine slices. Place inside a dish that will fit in the Air Fryer and cook for 30 minutes.
11. Once cooked; sprinkle with icing sugar.

27. Fried Tofu

Prep + Cook Time: 40 minutes   **Servings:** 4

Ingredients:

- 1 block firm tofu; pressed and cut into 1-inch thick cubes
- 2 tablespoon of soy sauce
- 2 teaspoon sesame seeds; toasted
- 1 teaspoon rice vinegar
- 1 tablespoon potato starch

Instructions:

1. Preheat the Air Fryer to 400 - degrees Fahrenheit.
2. In a mixing bowl; mix all ingredients except the cornstarch until the tofu cubes are well combined. Toss the tofu in the cornstarch and place inside the Air Fryer basket.
3. Cook for 25 minutes and shake every five minutes of cooking time.

28. Rice Paper Bacon

Prep + Cook Time: 30 minutes   **Servings:** 4

Ingredients:

- 3 tablespoon soy sauce or tamari
- 2 tablespoon cashew butter
- 2 tablespoon liquid smoke
- 2 tablespoon water
- 4 pieces rice paper; cut into 1-inch thick strips

Instructions:

1. Preheat the Air Fryer to 350 - degrees Fahrenheit.
2. In a large mixing bowl; combine together the soy sauce, cashew butter, liquid smoke, and water.
3. Soak the white rice paper for 5 minutes. Place the rice paper in the Air Fryer making sure that they do not overlap.
4. Air fry for 15 minutes or until crispy. Serve with steamed vegetables.

29. Tasty Soufflé

Prep + Cook Time: 25 minutes   **Servings:** 4

Ingredients:

- 1/4 cup all-purpose flour
- 1/3 cup butter
- 1 cup milk
- 1/4 cup brown sugar
- 4 egg yolks
- 1 teaspoon vanilla extract
- 6 egg whites
- 1 ounce. of white sugar
- 1 teaspoon cream of tartar

Instructions:

1. Preheat the Air Fryer to 320 - degrees Fahrenheit.
2. Take a bowl and combine flour and butter until smooth.
3. Heat milk in a saucepan and add brown sugar. Cook to dissolve the sugar. Bring to a boil.
4. Next; add the flour mixture to the milk. Remember to beat vigorously to ensure that no lumps formed simmer for 7 minutes until the mix thickens.
5. Remove from the heat and cool for 15 minutes. Meanwhile; take 6 soufflé dishes and coat it with oil spray.
6. Take a separate mixing bowl and beat egg yolks and vanilla extract.
7. Add in the cooling milk Mix all ingredients well.
8. Now; in a small bowl, beat egg whites, white sugar, and cream of tartar.
9. Fold this into soufflé base and pour the prepared flour mixture on top.
10. Place soufflé dishes into the Air Fryer and cook for 15 minutes. Once done serve.

30. Egg and Bacon Muffin Sandwich

Prep + Cook Time: 15 minutes   **Servings:** 1

Ingredients:

- One Egg
- 2 slices of bacon
- 1 English muffin

Instructions:

1. Preheat your Air Fryer to 395 - degrees Fahrenheit.
2. Spray a ramekin with cooking spray and crack the egg into it. Place the muffin, ramekin, and bacon slices in the Air Fryer.
3. Cook for 6 minutes. Let cool a minute or two. Cut the muffin in half.
4. Place the egg on top of one half, arrange the bacon slices over it, and close the sandwich with the other muffin half

31. Pea Protein Delight

Prep + Cook Time: 25 minutes   **Servings:** 2 – 4

Ingredients:

- 1 cup almond flour
- 1 teaspoon baking powder
- three eggs
- 1 cup coconut milk
- 1 cup cream cheese
- 3 tablespoon pea protein
- 1/2 cup chicken or turkey strips
- 1 pinch of sea salt
- 1 cup mozzarella cheese

Instructions:

1. Preheat your Air Fryer to 390 - degrees Fahrenheit.
2. Combine all the ingredients in a large mixing bowl. Stir by hand using a large wooden spoon ideally. Fill muffin cups with the mixture. Bake for 15 minutes.

32. Choco Cherry Bars

Prep + Cook Time: 30 minutes   **Servings:** 8

Ingredients:

- 2 cups old-fashioned oats
- 1/2 cup quinoa; cooked
- 1/2 cup chia seeds
- 1/2 cup almonds; sliced
- 1/2 cup dried cherries; chopped
- 1/2 cup dark chocolate; chopped
- 3/4 cup almond butter
- 1/3 cup honey
- 2 tablespoon coconut oil
- 1/4 teaspoon salt
- 1/2 cup prunes; pureed

Instructions:

1. Preheat the Air Fryer to 375 - degrees Fahrenheit.
2. In a mixing bowl; combine the oats, quinoa, chia seeds, almond, cherries, and chocolate.
3. In a saucepan; heat the almond butter, honey, and coconut oil.
4. Pour the butter mixture over the dry mixture.
5. Add salt and prunes. Mix until well combined.
6. Pour over a baking dish that can fit inside the Air Fryer. Cook for 15 minutes. Let it cool for an hour before slicing into bars.

33. French Toast Sticks

Prep + Cook Time: 25 minutes   **Servings:** 2

Ingredients:

- 4 slices of your bread of choice
- 2 tablespoon soft butter
- Two eggs; lightly beaten
- pinch of salt
- pinch of cinnamon
- pinch of ground nutmeg
- pinch of ground cloves
- nonstick cooking spray
- confectioners' sugar or maple syrup for serving

Instructions:

1. Combine the eggs, salt, and spices in a shallow bowl. Spread both sides of the bread with butter and cut the bread into strips. Alternatively, use cookie cutters to make fun French toast shapes.
2. Briefly preheat your Air Fryer to 350 - degrees Fahrenheit.
3. Dip each strip of bread in the egg mixture and place in the Fryer; cooking for 2 minutes or until golden brown.
4. Remove the cooking tray, spray the tops of the bread strips with cooking spray, turn, and cook for an additional 4 minutes. Dust the finished French toast sticks with confectioners' sugar [or drizzle with maple syrup] and serve.

34. Cheddar and Bacon Mini Quiche

Prep + Cook Time: 30 minutes   **Servings:** 4

Ingredients:

- 3 tablespoon. Greek yogurt
- 1/2 cup grated cheddar cheese
- 3 ounces chopped bacon
- four eggs; beaten
- 1/4 teaspoon garlic powder
- pinch of black pepper
- 1 shortcrust pastry
- 1/4 teaspoon onion powder
- 1/4 teaspoon sea salt
- some flour for sprinkling

Instructions:

1. Preheat the Air Fryer to 330 - degrees Fahrenheit. Grease 8 ramekins and coat them with a little bit of flour. Tap the excess flour off.

2. Divide the shortcrust pastry into 8 pieces.
3. Place each shortcrust piece at the bottom of each ramekin.
4. Place all of the remaining ingredients in a bowl and mix to incorporate them well.
5. Pour the filling over the shortcrust pastry.
6. Place the ramekins in your Air Fryer and bake for 20 minutes. Serve and enjoy!

35. Mushroom and Chorizo Risotto Balls

Prep + Cook Time: 1 hour 20 minutes   **Servings:** 4

Ingredients:

- 1/4 cup milk
- 1/2 cup plain flour
- 4 ounces. bread crumbs
- 4 ounces. chorizo; sliced
- 1 serve mushroom risotto rice
- One Egg
- sea salt to taste

Instructions:

1. Mix the mushroom risotto rice with finely sliced chorizo, add salt to taste and let it cool in the refrigerator.
2. Preheat the Air Fryer to 390 - degrees Fahrenheit and set the time to 5 minutes. Create a rice ball.
3. Take 2 tablespoons of risotto and roll it in the plain flour.
4. Break the egg into a bowl; whisk it with milk and dip the rice ball into it. Then roll the rice ball in bread crumbs.
5. Repeat the same procedure with the remaining risotto mass.
6. Fill the baking dish of the Air Fryer with the rice balls; arranging them in such way, so there must be some distance between them. Bake the rice balls for 20 minutes or until the crispy golden crust will appear.
7. Serve warm. It tastes great with fresh vegetables and garden salad.

36. Zucchini and Carrot Muffins

Prep + Cook Time: 25 minutes   **Servings:** 4

Ingredients:

- 1 tablespoon yogurt
- 1/2 cup shredded zucchini
- 1/4 cup shredded carrots
- 1 ½ cups all-purpose flour
- 2 tablespoon cream cheese
- three eggs
- pinch of salt
- 2 tablespoon butter; melted
- 2 tablespoon sugar
- 2 teaspoon baking powder
- 1 cup milk
- pinch of black powder

Instructions:

1. Preheat the Air Fryer to 350 - degrees Fahrenheit.
2. Beat the eggs along with the milk, baking powder, salt, pepper, sugar, and yogurt. Whisk in the flour gradually. Fold in the carrots and zucchini.
3. Grease your muffin tins and pour the muffin batter into the tins. Cook for about 12 – 14 minutes; depending on the density you prefer.

37. Choco Zucchini Bread

Prep + Cook Time: 30 minutes   **Servings:** 12

Ingredients:

- 1 tablespoon flax egg [1 tablespoon flax meal + 3 tablespoon water]
- 1 cup zucchini; shredded and squeezed
- 1/2 cup sunflower oil
- 1/2 cup maple syrup

- 1 teaspoon vanilla extract
- 1 teaspoon apple cider vinegar
- 1/2 cup almond milk
- 1 cup oat flour
- 1 teaspoon baking soda
- 1/2 cup unsweetened cocoa powder
- 1/4 teaspoon salt
- 1/3 cup chocolate chips

Instructions:
1. Preheat the Air Fryer to 350 - degrees Fahrenheit.
2. Line a baking dish that will fit the Air Fryer with parchment paper.
3. In a bowl; combine the flax meal, zucchini, sunflower oil, maple, vanilla, apple cider vinegar and milk.
4. Stir in the oat flour, baking soda, cocoa powder, and salt.
5. Mix until well combined. Add the chocolate chips.
6. Pour over the baking dish and cook for 15 minutes or until a toothpick inserted in the middle comes out clean.

38. Springs Rolls

Prep + Cook Time: 45 minutes

Servings: 6

Ingredients:
- 7 cups of minced meat
- 1 small onion; diced
- 1 packet spring rolls
- 2 ounces. Asian noodles
- 3 cloves garlic; crushed
- 1 cup mixed vegetables
- 1 tablespoon sesame oil
- 2 tablespoon water
- 1 teaspoon soy sauce

Instructions:
1. Prepare the noodles: let them soak in the hot water. When they are soft enough, cut them and set aside.
2. Take the wok and grease it with sesame oil and heat. When it is hot; add minced meat, vegetables, onion, and garlic.
3. Cook over medium high heat stirring often until the mince is cooked through.
4. It may take 3 – 5 minutes if you are using wok, and 7 – 10 minutes if you are using a regular frying pan.
5. Add soy sauce to the prepared mince, and set it aside. Stir through the noodles. Leave it and wait for the juices to be absorbed.
6. Take a spring roll sheet; add a strip of filling diagonally across. Fold the top point over the filling. Then fold in both the side points.
7. Before rolling the spring roll over the final point brush it with cold water to seal it.
8. Do the same to all other spring roll sheets.
9. Prepare the Air Fryer by preheating it to 360 - degrees Fahrenheit.
10. Cover spring rolls with a little amount of oil. It will provide a more familiar traditional taste of spring rolls.
11. However, you may not use oil at all if you want a healthier meal.
12. Put the rolls into the Air Fryer in layers and cook for 8 minutes in batches. Serve.

39. Chia and Oat Porridge

Prep + Cook Time: 15 minutes

Servings: 4

Ingredients:
- 4 cups milk
- 2 tablespoon peanut butter
- 2 cups oats
- 1 cup chia seeds
- 4 tablespoon honey
- 1 tablespoon butter; melted

Instructions:
1. Preheat the Air Fryer to 390 - degrees Fahrenheit.
2. Whisk the peanut butter, honey, butter, and milk in a bowl. Stir in oats and chia seeds.

3. Pour the mixture into an oven-proof bowl that can fit in the Air Fryer. Cook for 5 minutes. Stir before serving. Enjoy.

40. Tofu Frittata

Prep + Cook Time: 65 minutes   **Servings:** 4

Ingredients:

- 1 and 3/4 cups brown rice; cooked
- 1 flax egg [1 tablespoon flaxseed meal + 3 tablespoon cold water]
- 1 tablespoon olive oil
- 1/2 onion; chopped
- 4 cloves garlic; crushed
- 1 yellow pepper; chopped
- 3 big mushrooms; chopped
- 1/2 cup kale; chopped
- 1/2 cup baby spinach; chopped
- 4 spring onions; chopped a handful of basil leaves; chopped
- 1 package firm tofu
- 2 teaspoon Dijon mustard
- 1/2 teaspoon turmeric
- 2 tablespoon soy sauce
- 3 tablespoon nutritional yeast
- 2/3 cup almond milk
- 2 teaspoon arrowroot powder

Instructions:

1. Preheat the Air Fryer to 375 - degrees Fahrenheit.
2. Grease a pan that will fit inside the Air Fryer. Prepare the frittata crust by mixing the brown rice and flax egg.
3. Press the rice onto the baking dish until you form a crust.
4. Brush with a little oil and cook for 10 minutes. Meanwhile; heat olive oil in a skillet over medium flame and sauté the garlic and onions for 2 minutes.
5. Add the pepper and mushroom and continue stirring for 3 minutes.
6. Stir in the kale; spinach, spring onions, and basil. Remove from the pan and set aside.
7. In a food processor; pulse together the tofu, mustard, turmeric, soy sauce, nutritional yeast, vegan milk and arrowroot powder.
8. Pour in a mixing bowl and stir in the sautéed vegetables. Pour the vegan frittata mixture over the rice crust and cook in the Air Fryer for 40 minutes.

41. Breakfast Donuts

Prep + Cook Time: 1 hour 20 minutes   **Servings:** 6

Ingredients:

- 1 cup white all-purpose flour
- 1/4 cup coconut sugar
- 1 teaspoon baking powder
- 1/2 teaspoon salt
- 1/4 teaspoon cinnamon
- 1 tablespoon coconut oil; melted
- 2 tablespoon aquafaba or liquid from canned chickpeas
- 1/4 cup almond milk

Instructions:

1. In a mixing bowl; mix the flour, sugar, and baking powder. Add the salt and cinnamon and mix well.
2. In another bowl; mix together the coconut oil, aquafaba, and almond milk.
3. Gently pour the dry ingredients to the wet ingredients. Mix together until well combined or until you form a sticky dough.
4. Place the dough in the refrigerator to rest for at least an hour.
5. Preheat the Air Fryer to 370 - degrees Fahrenheit.
6. Create small balls of the dough and place inside the Air Fryer and cook for 10 minutes.
7. Do not shake the Air Fryer. Once cooked; sprinkle with sugar and cinnamon.
8. Serve with your breakfast coffee.

42. Tofu Scramble

Prep + Cook Time: 40 minutes

Servings: 3

Ingredients:

- 2 ½ cups red potato; chopped
- 1 tablespoon olive oil
- 1 block tofu; chopped finely
- 1 tablespoon olive oil
- 2 tablespoon tamari
- 1 teaspoon turmeric powder
- 1/2 teaspoon onion powder
- 1/2 teaspoon garlic powder
- 1/2 cup onion; chopped
- 4 cups broccoli florets

Instructions:

1. Preheat the Air Fryer to 400 - degrees Fahrenheit.
2. Combine the potatoes and olive oil.
3. Place the potatoes in a dish that can fit inside the Air Fryer and cook for 15 minutes. Shake once for even frying.
4. In a mixing bowl; toss the tofu, olive oil, tamari, turmeric, onion powder, and garlic powder. Stir in the chopped onions. Add the broccoli florets.
5. Pour the tofu mixture on top of the air fried potatoes and cook for another 15 minutes. Serve warm.

43. Spinach Quiche

Prep + Cook Time: 1 hour 15 minutes

Servings: 4

Ingredients:

- 3/4 cup whole meal flour a pinch of salt
- 1/2 cup cold coconut oil
- 2 tablespoon cold water
- 2 tablespoon olive oil
- 1 onion; chopped
- 4 ounces mushrooms; sliced
- 1 package firm tofu; pressed to remove excess water then crumbled
- 1-pound spinach; washed and chopped
- 1/2 tablespoon dried dill
- 2 tablespoon nutritional yeast
- salt and pepper
- a sprig of fresh parsley; chopped

Instructions:

1. Preheat the Air Fryer to 375 - degrees Fahrenheit.
2. Create the pastry by sifting the flour and salt together. Add the coconut oil until the flour crumbles. Gradually add water to bind the dough or until you form a stiff dough.
3. Wrap with a cling film and leave inside the fridge to rest for 30 minutes. Heat olive oil in a skillet over medium heat and sauté the onion for 1 minute.
4. Add the mushroom and tofu. Add the spinach, dried dill, and nutritional yeast.
5. Season with salt and pepper to taste. Throw in the parsley last. Set aside.
6. Roll the dough on a floured surface until you form a thin dough.
7. Place the dough in a greased baking dish that fits inside the Air Fryer.
8. Pour the tofu mixture and cook for 30 minutes or until the pastry is crisp.

44. Delicious Spring Onion Pancake

Prep + Cook Time: 45 minutes

Servings: 6

Ingredients:

- 1 cup flour [plain]
- 1/4 cup water [cold]
- 1/4 cup water [boiling]
- olive oil
- 1 teaspoon salt
- 1/2 cup spring onion [chopped]

Instructions:

1. Knead flour by adding hot water and then cool it until it smoothens.

2. Add 1 tablespoon oil. Let it rest for an hour.
3. Cut the kneaded flour into four equal parts and make it into rolls.
4. Spray oil in the pan and add onions and salt to it. Let it cook till golden brown. Cover the rolls with aluminum film and rest them for another hour, then flatten the rolls.
5. Preheat Air Fryer to 350 - degrees Fahrenheit and cook them in it for 15 minutes. Serve with any fresh juice and enjoy the taste.

45. Breakfast Pull Apart Bread

Prep + Cook Time: 40 minutes   **Servings:** 2

Ingredients:

- 1 large vegan bread loaf
- 2 tablespoon olive oil
- 2 tablespoon garlic puree
- 2 tablespoon nutritional yeast
- 2 teaspoon chives
- salt and pepper to taste

Instructions:

1. Preheat the Air Fryer to 375 - degrees Fahrenheit.
2. Slice the bread loaf making sure that you don't slice through the bread.
3. In a mixing bowl; combine the olive oil, garlic puree, and nutritional yeast. Pour over the mixture on top of the slices you made on the bread. Sprinkle with chopped chives and season with salt and pepper.
4. Place inside the Air Fryer and cook for 10 minutes or until the garlic is thoroughly cooked.

46. Fried Cabbage Patties

Prep + Cook Time: 20 minutes   **Servings:** 3

Ingredients:

- 2 cups shredded purple cabbage
- four eggs; beaten
- 1 cup cornmeal
- 1 pinch sea salt
- 1 tablespoon onion powder
- 1 teaspoon black pepper
- 1 tablespoon olive oil

Instructions:

1. Preheat your Air Fryer to 390 - degrees Fahrenheit. Combine all of the ingredients except the olive oil in a mixing bowl.
2. Grease a heat safe dish using the olive oil.
3. Spoon the mixture onto the dish and form patties but pushing down with a spoon. Cook for 15 minutes. Serve with bread as a vegetarian burger; or with salad as a vegetable based light meal.

47. Mushroom and Feta Frittata

Prep + Cook Time: 35 minutes   **Servings:** 4

Ingredients:

- 1 red onion; thinly sliced
- 4 cups button mushrooms; thinly sliced
- 2 tablespoon olive oil
- 6 medium eggs salt nonstick cooking spray
- 6 tablespoon feta cheese; crumbled

Instructions:

1. Sauté the onion and mushroom in the olive oil over medium heat until the vegetables are tender.
2. Remove from the pan and drain on a paper towel-lined plate.
3. In a medium bowl; whisk the eggs with the salt.
4. Lightly coat the bottom and sides of an 8-inch baking dish with nonstick spray.
5. Briefly preheat your Air Fryer to 325 – degrees Fahrenheit.

6. Assemble the frittata; pour the beaten eggs into the prepared pan and scatter the sautéed vegetables and crumbled feta on top.
7. Bake in the Fryer for 30 minutes.
8. Let cool slightly and serve.

48. Toffee Apple Upside Down Cake

Prep + Cook Time: 45 minutes   **Servings:** 9

Ingredients:

- 1/4 cup almond butter
- 3/4 cup + 3 tablespoon coconut sugar
- 3 baking apples; cored and sliced
- 1 cup plain flour
- 1 teaspoon baking soda
- 1 ½ teaspoon mixed spice

- 1/4 cup sunflower oil
- 3/4 cup water
- 1 teaspoon vinegar
- 1 lemon; zest
- 1/2 cup walnuts; chopped

Instructions:

1. Preheat the Air Fryer to 390 - degrees Fahrenheit.
2. In a skillet; melt the almond butter and 3 tablespoons sugar.
3. Pour the mixture over a baking dish that will fit in the Air Fryer.
4. Arrange the slices of apples on top. Set aside.
5. In a mixing bowl; combine flour, 3/4 cup sugar, and baking soda. Add the mixed spice.
6. In another bowl; mix the oil, water, vinegar, and lemon zest. Stir in the chopped walnuts.
7. Combine the wet ingredients to the dry ingredients until well combined.
8. Pour over the tin with apple slices. Bake for 30 minutes or until a toothpick inserted comes out clean.

49. Cornish Pasties

Prep + Cook Time: 55 minutes   **Servings:** 4

Ingredients:

- 1 ½ cups plain flour
- 3/4 cup cold coconut oil
- a pinch of salt
- cold water for mixing the dough
- 1 tablespoon olive oil
- 1 onion; sliced
- 1 stick celery; chopped

- 1 medium carrot; chopped
- 1 medium potato; diced
- 1/4 cup mushrooms; chopped
- 1 teaspoon oregano
- salt and pepper to taste
- 1 tablespoon nutritional yeast

Instructions:

1. Preheat the Air Fryer to 400 - degrees Fahrenheit.
2. Prepare the dough by mixing the flour, coconut oil, and salt in a bowl. Use a fork and press the flour to combine everything.
3. Gradually add a drop of water to the dough until you achieve a stiff consistency of the dough.
4. Cover the dough with a cling film and let it rest for 30 minutes inside the fridge. Roll the dough out and cut into squares. Set aside.
5. Heat olive oil over medium heat and sauté the onions for 2 minutes. Add the celery, carrots and potatoes.
6. Continue stirring for 3 to 5 minutes before adding the mushrooms and oregano. Season with salt and pepper to taste. Add nutritional yeast last. Let it cool and set aside.
7. Drop a tablespoon of vegetable mixture on to the dough and seal the edges of the dough with water. Place inside the Air Fryer basket and cook for 20 minutes or until the dough is crispy.

50. Carrot Mix Salmon

Prep + Cook Time: 25 minutes   **Servings:** 2

Ingredients:

- 4 bread slices
- 1 Pound. salmon [chopped]
- 1 carrot [shredded

- 2 cucumber [slices]
- 2 cups feta crumbled
- 3 tablespoon pickled red onion

Instructions:

1. Put salmon with feta into a bowl. Add carrot, cucumber and red onion. Mix well.
2. Make a layer of bread in the oven safe tray and then pour the mixture over it. Let it cook in the Air Fryer for 15 minutes on 300 – degrees Fahrenheit.

51. Shell Spaghetti

Prep + Cook Time: 25 minutes   **Servings:** 3

Ingredients:

- 1 tablespoon oil
- 2 skinless chicken breast [boneless]
- 2 cloves garlic [minced]
- 2 tablespoon chile paste
- 1/2 cup soy sauce
- 1 tablespoon canola oil
- 2 pounds shell spaghetti

- salt to taste
- 2 carrots [cut]
- 1 onion [sliced]
- 1/2 cabbage [chopped]
- ginger to taste
- broccoli to taste [optional]

Instructions:

1. Grease oil in the round baking tray. Add chicken with garlic. Mix Chile paste, soy sauce, salt, carrots, cabbage, ginger and broccoli.
2. Place the tray in the Air Fryer for 15 minutes on 300 - degrees Fahrenheit. Meanwhile; boil the shell spaghetti. When the mixture is ready; pour it in the cooked spaghetti and enjoy the meal!

52. Pecan and Pumpkin Breakfast Muffins

Prep + Cook Time: 20 minutes   **Servings:** 4

Ingredients:

- 4 tablespoons cake flour
- 1/3 teaspoon baking powder
- 1/4 cup oats
- A pinch of salt
- 1/4 cup ghee; at room temperature
- 1/4 cup caster sugar

- 2 tablespoons pecans; ground
- 1/4 cup pumpkin puree
- 1/2 teaspoon freshly grated nutmeg
- 1/4 teaspoon crystalized ginger
- 1/4 teaspoon ground cinnamon

Instructions:

1. Mix the first 4 Ingredients in a bowl.
2. In another bowl; beat the ghee with sugar, fold in the pecans and pumpkin puree, and stir again.
3. Add this mixture to the dry flour mixture. Add the nutmeg, ginger and cinnamon, and mix again using a wide spatula.
4. You can add a little water to make a batter. Then; prepare the muffin moulds by adding muffin liners to each of them.
5. Bake the muffins at 320 - degrees Fahrenheit for 10 minutes.
6. Let them stay for 10 to 12 minutes before removing from the moulds.

53. Amazing Apricot French Toast

Prep + Cook Time: 10 minutes   **Servings:** 6

Ingredients:

- 6 slices of French bread
- 2 tablespoons butter; at room temperature
- 1/3 cup milk
- three eggs; whisked
- A pinch of ground allspice
- A pinch of kosher salt
- 1/4 cup dried apricots; chopped
- Confectioners' sugar; for garnish

Instructions:

1. Start by preheating your Air Fryer to 380 - degrees Fahrenheit.
2. Coat the bread slices with butter on both sides. In a mixing bowl; whisk the milk, eggs, allspice, and salt.
3. After that; soak buttered bread slices in the milk mixture for about 10 minutes.
4. Transfer the bread slices to an Air Fryer baking dish.
5. Scatter chopped apricots over the top of each slice of bread.
6. Spritz with a non-stick cooking spray.
7. Air-fry them for 2 minutes. Now; flip each bread slice over, spritz with the cooking spray, and cook for additional 3 minutes.
8. Afterward; dust with confectioners' sugar and serve.

54. Scallion and Corn Cakes

Prep + Cook Time: 15 minutes   **Servings:** 6

Ingredients:

- 1 and 1/4 cups all-purpose flour
- 1/2 teaspoon baking soda
- 1 teaspoon baking powder
- 1/4 teaspoon sugar
- A pinch of kosher salt
- A pinch of freshly grated nutmeg
- 1 teaspoon paprika
- 1/4 teaspoon white vinegar
- 1/2 cup milk
- 1 and 1/2 tablespoons melted butter
- 1 whole egg
- 1 and 1/4 cups corn kernels
- 1/4 cup cilantro, chopped
- 1/4 cup scallions, chopped

Instructions:

1. In a mixing bowl, combine the flour, baking soda, baking powder, sugar, salt, nutmeg, and paprika.
2. In another bowl, combine the vinegar along with the milk, butter and egg.
3. Add this mixture to the dry mixture.
4. Preheat the Air Fryer to 380 - degrees Fahrenheit. Stir in the corn kernels, cilantro, and the scallions.
5. Then, shape the batter into the rounded fritters. Chill them in your freezer for 6 to 7 minutes.
6. Air-fry them for about 5 minutes and serve warm with mayonnaise.

Lunch & Dinner Recipes

55. Sriracha Cauliflower

Prep + Cook Time: 25 minutes   **Servings:** 4

Ingredients:

- 1/4 cup vegan butter; melted
- 1/4 cup sriracha sauce
- 4 cups cauliflower florets
- 1 cup panko bread crumbs
- 1 teaspoon salt

Instructions:

1. In a mixing bowl; combine together the vegan butter and sriracha sauce. Pour over the cauliflower florets and toss to coat. In another bowl; mix the bread crumbs and salt.
2. Dip the cauliflower florets in the panko mixture and place inside the Air Fryer. Cook for 17 minutes in a 375 - degrees Fahrenheit preheated Air Fryer.

56. Easy Ratatouille

Prep + Cook Time: 30 minutes   **Servings:** 4

Ingredients:

- 1 sprig of basil
- 1 sprig flat-leaf parsley
- 1 sprig mint
- 1 tablespoon coriander powder
- 1 teaspoon capers
- 1/2 lemon; juiced
- salt and pepper to taste
- 2 eggplants; sliced crosswise
- 2 red onions; chopped
- 4 cloves of garlic; minced
- 2 red peppers; sliced crosswise
- 1 fennel bulb; sliced crosswise
- 3 large zucchinis; sliced crosswise
- 5 tablespoon olive oil
- 4 large tomatoes; chopped
- 2 teaspoon herb de Provence

Instructions:

1. In a blender, combine basil, parsley, mint, coriander, capers and lemon juice. Season with salt and pepper to taste. Pulse until well combined.
2. Preheat the Air Fryer to 400 - degrees Fahrenheit. Toss the eggplant, onions, garlic, peppers, fennel, and zucchini with olive oil.
3. In a baking dish that can fit in the Air Fryer; arrange the vegetables and pour over the tomatoes and the herb puree. Season with more salt and pepper and sprinkle with herbs de Provence.
4. Place inside the Air Fryer and cook for 25 minutes.

57. Pesto Stuffed Bella Mushrooms

Prep + Cook Time: 25 minutes   **Servings:** 6

Ingredients:

- 1 cup basil
- 1/2 cup cashew nuts; soaked overnight
- 1/2 cup nutritional yeast
- 1 tablespoon lemon juice
- 2 cloves of garlic
- 1 tablespoon olive oil
- salt to taste
- 1-pound baby
- Bella mushroom; stems removed

Instructions:

1. Preheat the Air Fryer to 400 - degrees Fahrenheit. Place the basil, cashew nuts, nutritional yeast, lemon juice, garlic and olive oil in a blender.

2. Pulse until well combined; Season with salt to taste.
3. Place the mushrooms cap-side down and spread pesto on the underside of the cap.
4. Place inside the Air Fryer and cook for 15 minutes.

58. Cauliflower Veg Burger

Prep + Cook Time: 25 minutes   Servings: 8

Ingredients:

- 1/2-pound cauliflower; steamed and diced
- 2 teaspoon coconut oil melted
- 2 teaspoon garlic; minced
- 1/4 cup desiccated coconut
- 1/2 cup oats
- 3 tablespoon plain flour
- 1 flax egg [1 flaxseed egg + 3 tablespoon water]

- 1 teaspoon mustard powder
- 2 teaspoon thyme
- 2 teaspoon parsley
- 2 teaspoon chives
- salt and pepper to taste
- 1 cup bread crumbs

Instructions:

1. Preheat the Air Fryer to 390 - degrees Fahrenheit.
2. Place the cauliflower in a tea towel and ring out excess water.
3. Place in a mixing bowl and add all ingredients except the bread crumbs. Mix well until well combined.
4. Form 8 burger patties with the mixture using your hands. Roll the patties in bread crumbs and place in the Air Fryer basket. Make sure that they do not overlap.
5. Cook for 10 to 15 minutes or until the patties are crisp.

59. Roasted Mushrooms and Asparagus

Prep + Cook Time: 20 minutes   Servings: 6

Ingredients:

- 1 bunch fresh asparagus; trimmed and cleaned
- 1/2-pound fresh mushroom; quartered

- 2 sprigs of fresh rosemary; minced
- 2 teaspoon olive oil
- salt and pepper to taste

Instructions:

1. Preheat the Air Fryer to 450 - degrees Fahrenheit.
2. Place the asparagus and mushrooms in a bowl and pour the rest of the ingredients. Toss to coat the asparagus and mushrooms.
3. Place inside the Air Fryer and cook for 15 minutes.

60. Fried Chili Potato Wedges

Prep + Cook Time: 50 minutes   Servings: 4

Ingredients:

- 1-pound fingerling potatoes; washed and cut into wedges
- 1 teaspoon olive oil
- 1 teaspoon salt

- 1 teaspoon black pepper
- 1 teaspoon cayenne pepper
- 1 teaspoon nutritional yeast
- 1/2 teaspoon garlic powder

Instructions:

1. Preheat the Air Fryer to 400 - degrees Fahrenheit.
2. Place all ingredients in a mixing bowl and toss to coat all ingredients. Place inside the Air Fryer basket and cook for 16 minutes. Shake the Air Fryer basket halfway through the cooking time.

61. Fried Brussels Sprouts

Prep + Cook Time: 20 minutes   **Servings:** 2

Ingredients:

- 2 cups Brussels sprouts; halved
- 1 tablespoon olive oil
- 1 tablespoon balsamic vinegar
- 1 tablespoon maple syrup
- 1/4 teaspoon sea salt

Instructions:

1. Preheat the Air Fryer to 375 - degrees Fahrenheit
2. Mix all ingredients in a bowl and make sure that the Brussels sprouts are coated evenly.
3. Place all ingredients in the Air Fryer basket and cook for 5 minutes first then shake the fryer basket. Cook again for 8 minutes at 400 - degrees Fahrenheit.

62. Crispy Fried Spring Rolls

Prep + Cook Time: 25 minutes   **Servings:** 4

Ingredients:

- 1 cup shiitake mushroom; sliced thinly
- 1 celery stalk; chopped
- 1 medium carrot; shredded
- 1/2 teaspoon ginger; finely chopped
- 1 teaspoon coconut sugar
- 1 tablespoon soy sauce
- 1 teaspoon nutritional yeast
- 8 spring roll wrappers
- 1 teaspoon corn starch + 2 tablespoon water

Instructions:

1. In a mixing bowl; mix together the celery stalk, carrots, ginger, coconut sugar, soy sauce and nutritional yeast.
2. Get a tablespoon of the vegetable mixture and place at the center of the spring roll wrappers. Roll and seal the edges of the wrapper with the cornstarch mixture.
3. Cook in a preheated Air Fryer to 400 - degrees Fahrenheit for 15 minutes or until the spring roll wrapper is crisp.

63. Fried Cucumber and Eggplant Pickle Rice Bowl

Prep + Cook Time: 55 minutes   **Servings:** 4

Ingredients:

- 1/4 cup cucumber; sliced
- 1 teaspoon salt
- 1 tablespoon coconut sugar
- 7 tablespoon Japanese rice vinegar
- 3 medium-sized eggplants; sliced
- 3 tablespoon sweet white miso paste
- 1 tablespoon mirin rice wine
- 4 cups sushi rice; cooked
- 4 spring onions
- 1 tablespoon sesame seeds; toasted

Instructions:

1. Prepare the cucumber pickles by mixing the cucumber, salt, sugar, and rice wine vinegar.
2. Place a dish on top of the bowl to weight it down completely. Preheat the Air Fryer to 400 – degrees Fahrenheit.
3. In a mixing bowl; combine the eggplants, miso paste, and mirin rice wine. Marinate for 30 minutes.
4. Place the eggplant slices in the Air Fryer and cook for 10 minutes. Assemble the rice bowl by placing eggplants and pickled cucumbers on top of the rice. Garnish with spring onions and sesame seeds.

64. Fried Asian Tofu Bites

Prep + Cook Time: 20 minutes
Servings: 4

Ingredients:

- 1 packaged firm tofu; cubed and pressed to remove excess water
- 1 tablespoon soy sauce
- 1 tablespoon ketchup
- 1 tablespoon maple syrup
- 1/2 teaspoon vinegar
- 1 teaspoon liquid smoke
- 1 teaspoon hot sauce
- 2 tablespoon sesame seeds
- 1 teaspoon garlic powder
- salt and pepper to taste

Instructions:

1. Preheat the Air Fryer to 375 - degrees Fahrenheit.
2. Spray a baking dish that will fit in the Air Fryer.
3. In a mixing bowl; mix all ingredients and allow to marinate for 30 minutes. Place the tofu in the baking dish and bake for 15 minutes. Turn the tofu after the cooking time is done and cook for another 15 minutes more.

65. Fried Chickpeas

Prep + Cook Time: 20 minutes
Servings: 4

Ingredients:

- 1 15-ounce can chickpeas; drained but not rinsed
- 2 tablespoon olive oil
- 1 teaspoon salt
- 2 tablespoon lemon juice

Instructions:

1. Preheat the Air Fryer to 400 - degrees Fahrenheit. Combine all ingredients in a mixing bowl and place inside the Air Fryer basket. Cook for 15 minutes until the chickpeas are crisp.

66. Fried Cauliflower Cheese Tater Tots

Prep + Cook Time: 25 minutes
Servings: 12

Ingredients:

- 1-pound cauliflower; steamed and chopped
- 1/2 cup nutritional yeast
- 3 tablespoon oats
- 1 flax egg [1 tablespoon 3 tablespoon desiccated coconuts flaxseed meal + 3 tablespoon water]
- 1 onion; chopped
- 1 teaspoon garlic; minced
- 1 teaspoon parsley; chopped
- 1 teaspoon oregano; chopped
- 1 teaspoon chives; chopped
- salt and pepper to taste
- 1/2 cup bread crumbs

Instructions:

1. Preheat the Air Fryer to 390 – degrees Fahrenheit.
2. Place the steamed cauliflower on a paper towel and ring to remove excess water.
3. Place in a mixing bowl and add the rest of the ingredients except the bread crumbs. Mix until well combined and form balls using your hands.
4. Roll the tater tots on the bread crumbs and place in the Air Fryer basket. Cook for 6 minutes. Once done; increase the cooking temperature to 400 - degrees Fahrenheit and cook for another 10 minutes.

67. Fried Sweet Onions and Potatoes

Prep + Cook Time: 30 minutes   **Servings:** 6

Ingredients:

- 2 large sweet potatoes; peeled and cut into chunks
- 2 medium sweet onions; cut into chunks
- 3 tablespoon olive oil
- 1 teaspoon dried thyme
- salt and pepper to taste
- 1/4 cup sliced almonds; toasted

Instructions:

1. Preheat the Air Fryer to 425 - degrees Fahrenheit. Toss all ingredients except the sliced almonds in a mixing bowl.
2. Place in a ramekin that will fit inside the Air Fryer and cook for 20 minutes. Top with almonds.

68. Crispy Cauliflower Peanut and Tofu

Prep + Cook Time: 45 minutes   **Servings:** 2

Ingredients:

- 2 cloves of garlic; minced
- 1 tablespoon sesame oil
- 1/4 cup low sodium soy sauce
- 1/4 cup brown sugar
- 1/2 teaspoon chili garlic sauce
- 2 ½ tablespoon almond butter
- 1 package extra firm tofu; pressed to release extra water and cut into cubes
- 1 small head cauliflower; cut into florets

Instructions:

1. Place the garlic, sesame oil, soy sauce, sugar, chili garlic sauce, and almond butter in a mixing bowl. Whisk until well combined.
2. Place the tofu cubes and cauliflower in the marinade and allow to soak up the sauce for at least 30 minutes.
3. Preheat the Air Fryer to 400 - degrees Fahrenheit.
4. Meanwhile; place the remaining marinade in a saucepan and bring to a boil over medium heat. Adjust the heat to low once boiling and stir until the sauce thickens.
5. Pour the sauce over the tofu and cauliflower. Serve with rice or noodles.

69. Tasty Mushroom Pizza Squares

Prep + Cook Time: 20 minutes   **Servings:** 10

Ingredients:

- 1 vegan pizza dough
- 1 cup oyster mushrooms; chopped
- 1 shallot; chopped
- 1/4 red bell pepper; chopped
- 2 tablespoon parsley
- salt and pepper

Instructions:

1. Preheat the Air Fryer to 400 - degrees Fahrenheit. Slice the pizza dough into squares. Set aside.
2. In a mixing bowl; mix together the oyster mushroom, shallot, bell pepper and parsley. Season with salt and pepper to taste.
3. Place the topping on top of the pizza squares. Place inside the Air Fryer and cook for 10 minutes.

70. Tofu and Sweet Potatoes

Prep + Cook Time: 50 minutes   **Servings:** 8

Ingredients:

- 8 sweet potatoes; scrubbed
- 2 tablespoon olive oil
- 1 large onion; chopped
- 2 green chilies; deseeded and chopped
- 1/2-pound tofu; crumbled

- 2 tablespoon Cajun seasoning
- 1 cup tomatoes
- 1 can kidney beans; drained and rinsed
- salt and pepper to taste

Instructions:

1. Preheat the Air Fryer to 400 - degrees Fahrenheit.
2. Prick the potatoes with knife on several places and cook in the Air Fryer for 30 minutes until soft. Set aside.
3. In a skillet; heat the oil over medium heat and sauté the onions and chilies for 2 minutes until fragrant.
4. Add the tofu and Cajun seasoning and continue cooking for 3 more minutes. Add the tomatoes and kidney beans.
5. Season with salt and pepper to taste. Pour the tofu mixture on top of a sweet potato halve.

71. Cheesy Risotto

Prep + Cook Time: 40 minutes   **Servings:** 2

Ingredients:

- 1 onion; diced
- 2 cups chicken stock; boiling
- 1/2 cup parmesan cheese or cheddar cheese; grated

- 1 clove garlic; minced
- 3/4 cup arborio rice
- 1 tablespoon olive oil
- 1 tablespoon butter; unsalted

Instructions:

1. Preheat the Air Fryer to 390 - degrees Fahrenheit and adjust the time to 5 minutes.
2. Take round baking tin; grease it with oil and add stirring the butter, onion, and garlic. When the fryer is hot, adjust the time to 8 minutes.
3. Place the tin into the Air Fryer and cook for 4 minutes.
4. Then add rice and cook for another 4 minutes. Stir three times during the cooking time.
5. Reduce the heat to 320 - degrees Fahrenheit and set the timer to 22 minutes.
6. Pour in the chicken stock and stir gently. Do not cover the Air Fryer and cook for 22 minutes as have been set.
7. Add in the cheese; stir once again and serve.

72. Cauliflower Chickpea Flatbread with Avocado Mash

Prep + Cook Time: 30 minutes   **Servings:** 4

Ingredients:

- 1 medium-sized head of cauliflower; cut into florets
- 1 can chickpeas; drained and rinsed
- 1 tablespoon extra-virgin olive oil

- 2 tablespoon lemon juice
- salt and pepper to taste
- 4 flatbreads; toasted
- 2 ripe avocados; mashed

Instructions:

1. Preheat the Air Fryer to 425 - degrees Fahrenheit.

2. In a mixing bowl; combine the cauliflower, chickpeas, olive oil, and lemon juice. Season with salt and pepper to taste. Place inside the Air Fryer basket and cook for 25 minutes.
3. Once cooked; place on half of the flatbread and add avocado mash. Season with more salt and pepper to taste. Serve with hot sauce.

73. Special Fried Potatoes

Prep + Cook Time: 55 minutes   **Servings:** 1

Ingredients:

- 1 medium russet potatoes; scrubbed and peeled
- 1 teaspoon olive oil
- 1/4 teaspoon onion powder
- 1/8 teaspoon salt
- a dollop of vegan butter
- a dollop of vegan cream cheese
- 1 tablespoon Kalamata olives
- 1 tablespoon chives; chopped

Instructions:

1. Preheat the Air Fryer to 400 - degrees Fahrenheit.
2. Place the potatoes in a mixing bowl and pour in olive oil, onion powder, salt, and vegan butter.
3. Place inside the Air Fryer basket and cook for 40 minutes. Be sure to turn the potatoes once halfway.
4. Serve the potatoes with vegan cream cheese, Kalamata olives, chives, and other vegan toppings that you want.

74. Fried French Green Beans

Prep + Cook Time: 20 minutes   **Servings:** 4

Ingredients:

- 1 ½ pound French green beans; stems removed and blanched
- 1 tablespoon salt
- 1/2 pounds shallots; peeled and cut into quarters
- 1/2 teaspoon ground white pepper
- 2 tablespoon olive oil
- 1/4 cup slivered almonds; toasted

Instructions:

1. Preheat the Air Fryer to 400 - degrees Fahrenheit.
2. Mix all ingredients in a mixing bowl. Toss until well combined. Place inside the Air Fryer basket and cook for 10 minutes or until lightly browned.

75. Fried Black Bean Chili

Prep + Cook Time: 25 minutes   **Servings:** 6

Ingredients:

- 1 tablespoon olive oil
- 1 medium onion; diced
- 3 cloves of garlic; minced
- 1 cup vegetable broth
- 3 cans black beans; drained and rinsed
- 2 cans diced tomatoes
- 2 chipotle peppers; chopped
- 2 teaspoon cumin
- 2 teaspoon chili powder
- 1 teaspoon dried oregano
- 1/2 teaspoon salt

Instructions:

1. In a large sauce pan; heat oil over medium heat and sauté the onions and garlic for 3 minutes.
2. Add the rest of the ingredients and scrape the bottom to remove the browning.
3. Pour the mixture in a heat-resistant dish that will fit in the Air Fryer. Cover the top with aluminum foil. Place in an Air Fryer preheated to 400 - degrees Fahrenheit and cook for 20 minutes.
4. Serve with chopped cilantro, diced avocado, and chopped tomatoes.

76. Spicy Fried Cauliflower

Prep + Cook Time: 20 minutes

Servings: 4

Ingredients:

- 1 head cauliflower; cut into florets
- 1 tablespoon extra-virgin olive oil
- 2 scallions; chopped
- 5 cloves of garlic; sliced
- 1 ½ tablespoon tamari
- 1 tablespoon rice vinegar
- 1/2 teaspoon coconut sugar
- 1 tablespoon sriracha

Instructions:

1. Preheat the Air Fryer to 400 – degrees Fahrenheit. Place the cauliflower florets in the Air Fryer and sprinkle oil on top. Cook for 10 minutes.
2. Turn the cauliflower after 10 minutes and add the onions and garlic. Give a stir and cook for another 10 minutes.
3. In a mixing bowl; combine the remaining ingredients.
4. Take the cauliflower out and pour them in the sauce.
5. Toss to coat and place inside the Air Fryer to cook for 5 more minutes. Serve with rice and enjoy!.

77. Tasty Peanut Tofu Bites

Prep + Cook Time: 65 minutes

Servings: 3

Ingredients:

- 2 tablespoon sesame oil
- 1/4 cup maple syrup
- 3 tablespoon peanut butter
- 1/4 cup liquid aminos
- 3 tablespoon chili garlic sauce
- 2 tablespoon rice wine vinegar
- 2 cloves of garlic; minced
- 1-inch fresh ginger; peeled and grated
- 1 teaspoon red pepper flakes
- 1 block extra firm tofu; pressed to remove excess water and cut into cubes
- toasted peanuts; chopped
- 1 teaspoon sesame seeds
- 1 sprig cilantro; chopped

Instructions:

1. Place the first 9 ingredients in a mixing bowl and whisk until combined.
2. Pour in a Ziploc bag and add the tofu cubes. Marinate for at least 30 minutes.
3. Preheat the Air Fryer to 425 – degrees Fahrenheit.
4. Save the marinade for the sauce and place the marinated tofu cubes in the Air Fryer. Cook for 15 minutes. Pour the marinade in a sauce pan and heat over medium flame until reduced in half.
5. Place the cooked tofu on top of steaming rice and pour over the sauce. Garnish with toasted peanuts; sesame seeds and cilantro.

78. Air Fried Faux Rice

Prep + Cook Time: 60 minutes

Servings: 8

Ingredients:

- 1 head of cauliflower; medium to large
- 1/2 lemon; juiced
- 4 garlic cloves; minced
- 2 cans mushrooms; 8 oz. each
- 1 can water chestnuts; 8 oz.
- 3/4 cup peas
- 1/2 cup egg substitute; or one egg beat together
- 4 tablespoon soy sauce
- 1 tablespoon peanut oil
- 1 tablespoon sesame oil
- 1 tablespoon ginger; fresh and minced
- high quality cooking spray

Instructions:

1. In a bowl; combine: sesame oil, peanut oil, soy sauce, minced garlic, minced ginger, and lemon juice. Mix together until thoroughly blended.
2. Peel the cauliflower and thoroughly wash it. Then; cut the head into smaller florets.
3. Don't leave the florets too large. In a food processor, process the florets a few at a time. Process them until they are just broken down to about the size of rice grains.
4. Empty into your Air Fryer basket and continue until all of the cauliflower has been processed.
5. Completely drain the water chestnut can and then chop them coarsely. Add them to the cauliflower in the Air Fryer basket.
6. Turn the Air Fryer on to 350 - degrees Fahrenheit and cook for 20 minutes. After the cauliflower has cooked for 20 minutes, drain the mushrooms and add them, as well as the peas, to the cauliflower.
7. Cook the mixture for an additional 15 minutes. In a frying pan; lightly spray it with high quality cooking spray. Then; make a solid omelet with the egg substitute or the beaten egg. Place the omelet on a cutting board and chop it up.
8. When the cauliflower concoction is done cooking for the additional 15 minutes, add the egg and cook it for a final 5 minutes. Serve immediately.

79. Potato Croquettes

Prep + Cook Time: 25 minutes   **Servings:** 10

Ingredients:

- 1/4 cup nutritional yeast
- 2 cups boiled potatoes; mashed
- 1 flax egg [1 tablespoon flaxseed meal + 3 tablespoon water]
- 2 tablespoon flour

- 2 tablespoon chives; chopped
- salt and pepper to taste
- 2 tablespoon vegetable oil
- 1/4 cup bread crumbs

Instructions:

1. Preheat the Air Fryer to 400 - degrees Fahrenheit.
2. Mix the nutritional yeast, potatoes, flax eggs, flour, and chives in a mixing bowl. Season with salt and pepper to taste.
3. In another bowl; combine the vegetable oil and bread crumbs until crumbly.
4. Form small balls of the potato mixture using your hands and dredge on the breadcrumb mixture. Place inside the Air Fryer and cook for 15 minutes or until the croquettes turn golden brown.

80. Sour and Sweet Sesame Tofu

Prep + Cook Time: 55 minutes   **Servings:** 2

Ingredients:

- 2 teaspoon apple cider vinegar
- 1 tablespoon coconut sugar
- 1 tablespoon soy sauce
- 3 teaspoon lime juice
- 1 teaspoon ground ginger
- 1 teaspoon garlic powder

- 1/2 block firm tofu; pressed to remove excess liquid and cut into cubes 1 teaspoon corn starch
- 2 green onions; chopped toasted sesame seeds for garnish

Instructions:

1. In a mixing bowl; mix together the first six ingredients. Mix until well combined.
2. Marinate the tofu in the sauce for at least 30 minutes.
3. Strain the marinated tofu and save the sauce.
4. Place the tofu in a preheated Air Fryer and cook at 400 - degrees Fahrenheit for 20 minutes or until crisp.

5. Meanwhile; pour the remaining sauce in a saucepan and add cornstarch. Turn on the flame and allow to thicken under medium low heat.
6. Toss the air fried tofu in the thickened sauce and add green onions and sesame seeds.
7. Serve with rice and enjoy!

81. Delicious Roasted Vegetable Salad

Prep + Cook Time: 20 minutes   **Servings:** 4

Ingredients:

- 6 plum tomatoes; halved
- 2 large red onions sliced
- 4 long red pepper; sliced
- 2 yellow pepper; sliced
- 6 cloves of garlic; crushed

- 1 tablespoon extra-virgin olive oil
- 1 teaspoon paprika
- 1/2 lemon; juiced
- salt and pepper to taste
- 1 tablespoon baby capers

Instructions:

1. Preheat the Air Fryer to 420 - degrees Fahrenheit.
2. Place the tomatoes, onions, peppers, and garlic in a mixing bowl. Add in the extra virgin olive oil, paprika, and lemon juice. Season with salt and pepper to taste.
3. Transfer into the Air Fryer lined with aluminum foil and cook for 10 minutes or until the edges of the vegetables have browned.
4. Place in a salad bowl and add the baby capers. Toss to combine all ingredients.

82. Fried Mediterranean Vegetables

Prep + Cook Time: 30 minutes   **Servings:** 4

Ingredients:

- 1 cup cherry tomatoes; halved
- 1 large zucchini; sliced
- 1 green pepper; sliced
- 1 parsnip; sliced
- 1 carrot; sliced

- 1 teaspoon mixed herbs
- 1 teaspoon mustard
- 2 teaspoon garlic puree
- 6 tablespoon olive oil
- salt and pepper to taste

Instructions:

1. Preheat the Air Fryer to 400 - degrees Fahrenheit.
2. Place all ingredients in a mixing bowl and toss until well combined. Dump all the seasoned vegetable inside the Air Fryer basket and cook for 6 minutes or until done.

83. Potato and Kale Nuggets

Prep + Cook Time: 35 minutes   **Servings:** 4

Ingredients:

- 1 teaspoon extra-virgin olive oil
- 1 clove of garlic; minced
- 4 cups kale; rinsed and chopped
- 2 cups boiled potatoes; finely chopped

- 1/8 cup almond milk
- 1/4 teaspoon salt
- 1/8 teaspoon black pepper
- cooking spray

Instructions:

1. Preheat the Air Fryer to 400 - degrees Fahrenheit.
2. Place a foil at the base of the Air Fryer basket and poke holes to allow air circulation. Heat oil in a large skillet and sauté the garlic for 2 minutes.

3. Add the kale until it wilts. Transfer to a large bowl. Add the potatoes and almond milk. Season with salt and pepper to taste.
4. Form balls and spray with cooking oil.
5. Place inside the Air Fryer and cook for 20 minutes or until golden brown.

84. Fried Zucchini Crisps

Prep + Cook Time: 25 minutes   **Servings:** 8

Ingredients:

- 1/4 bread crumbs
- 1/4 cup nutritional yeast
- 1/2 teaspoon garlic powder

- 2 green zucchinis; sliced into thin rounds
- 1 tablespoon olive oil

Instructions:

1. Place a foil at the base of the Air Fryer basket and poke holes. Preheat the Air Fryer to 400 - degrees Fahrenheit.
2. In a mixing bowl; combine the crumbs, nutritional yeast, and garlic powder.
3. In another bowl; toss the zucchini with the olive oil.
4. Dredge the zucchini slices with the crumb mixture and place inside the Air Fryer. Cook for 15 minutes or until crispy.

85. Baked Sweet Potatoes

Prep + Cook Time: 55 minutes   **Servings:** 4

Ingredients:

- 2 potatoes; peeled and cubed
- 4 carrots; cut into chunks
- 1 head broccoli; cut into florets
- 4 zucchinis; sliced thickly

- salt and pepper to taste
- 1/4 cup olive oil
- 1 tablespoon dry onion powder

Instructions:

1. Preheat the Air Fryer to 400 - degrees Fahrenheit. In a baking dish that can fit inside the Air Fryer; Mix all the ingredients and bake for 45 minutes or until the vegetables are tender and the sides have browned.

86. Tasty Chicken Escalope

Prep + Cook Time: 45 minutes   **Servings:** 4

Ingredients:

- 4 chicken breasts [skinless]
- 2 eggs [beaten]
- 1/2 cup flour [plain]
- 6 sage leaves

- 1/4 cup breadcrumbs [panko]
- 1/4 cup cheese [parmesan]
- oil for spray

Instructions:

1. Flatten the chicken breasts by cutting them into thin slices.
2. Mix sage, parmesan in a bowl.
3. Season the mixture with flour, salt and pepper. Dip chicken in the well beaten mixture of flour and eggs.
4. Cover the chicken with breadcrumbs.
5. Spray oil on the pan.
6. Preheat it to 390 – degrees Fahrenheit and cook the chicken in it for 20 minutes; until golden.
7. Serve with fried rice.

87. Crispy Fried Pickles

Prep + Cook Time: 30 minutes

Servings: 4

Ingredients:

- 14 dill pickles; sliced
- 1/4 cup all-purpose flour
- 1/8 teaspoon baking powder
- a pinch of salt
- 2 tablespoon cornstarch + 3 tablespoon water
- 6 tablespoon panko bread crumbs
- 1/2 teaspoon paprika
- oil for spraying

Instructions:

1. Dry the pickles using a paper towel then set aside.
2. In a bowl; mix together the all-purpose flour, baking powder and salt.
3. Add the cornstarch and water slurry. Whisk until well combined. Place the panko bread crumbs in a shallow bowl or plate and add paprika. Mix until combined.
4. Dredge the pickles in the flour batter first then on to the panko. Place on a plate and spray all pickles with oil.
5. Put inside a preheated Air Fryer and cook at 400 - degrees Fahrenheit for 15 minutes or until golden brown.

88. Glazed Cauliflower Bites

Prep + Cook Time: 30 minutes

Servings: 4

Ingredients:

- 1/3 cup oats flour
- 1/3 cup plain flour
- 1/3 cup desiccated coconut
- salt and pepper to taste
- 1 flax egg [1 tablespoon flaxseed meal + 3 tablespoon water]
- 1 small cauliflower; cut into florets
- 1 teaspoon mixed spice
- 1/2 teaspoon mustard powder
- 2 tablespoon maple syrup
- 1 clove of garlic; minced
- 2 tablespoon soy sauce

Instructions:

1. Preheat the Air Fryer to 400 – degrees Fahrenheit.
2. In a mixing bowl; mix together oats, flour, and desiccated coconut. Season with salt and pepper to taste. Set aside.
3. In another bowl; place the flax egg and add a pinch of salt to taste. Set aside. Season the cauliflower with mixed spice and mustard powder.
4. Dredge the florets in the flax egg first then in the flour mixture. Place inside the Air Fryer and cook for15 minutes.
5. Meanwhile; place the maple syrup, garlic, and soy sauce in a sauce pan and heat over medium flame.
6. Bring to a boil and adjust the heat to low until the sauce thickens.
7. After 15 minutes; take out the florets from the Air Fryer and place them in the saucepan. Toss to coat the florets and place inside the Air Fryer and cook for another 5 minutes.

89. Fried Chicken with Veggies

Prep + Cook Time: 30 minutes

Servings: 4

Ingredients:

- 8 chicken thighs
- 5 ounces. sliced mushrooms
- 1 red onion; diced
- Fresh black pepper; to taste
- 10 medium asparagus
- 1/2 cup carrots; diced

- 1/4 cup balsamic vinegar
- 2 red bell peppers; diced
- 1/2 teaspoon sugar
- 2 tablespoon extra-virgin olive oil
- 1 ½ tablespoon fresh rosemary
- 2 cloves garlic; chopped
- 1/2 tablespoon dried oregano
- 1 teaspoon kosher salt
- 2 fresh sage; chopped

Instructions:

1. Preheat the Air Fryer to 400 - degrees Fahrenheit.
2. Grease a baking tray using oil. Coat the chicken with salt and pepper. In a large bowl; add all the vegetables.
3. Add the sage, oregano, garlic, sugar, vinegar, and mushroom. Mix well and arrange onto your baking tray.
4. Add the chicken thighs as well. Roast in the Air Fryer for about 20 minutes. Serve hot.

90. Crispy Noodle Salad

Prep + Cook Time: 40 minutes   **Servings:** 2

Ingredients:

- 1 package wheat noodles
- 1 tablespoon cooking oil
- 1 tablespoon tamari
- 1 tablespoon. red chili sauce
- 1 tablespoon lime juice
- salt to taste
- 1 onion; sliced thinly
- 1 cup cabbage; sliced thinly
- 1 green bell pepper; sliced thinly
- 1 carrot; sliced thinly
- 1 tomato; chopped
- 1 sprig coriander; chopped

Instructions:

1. In a big pot; boil water and add a teaspoon of salt. Bring the water to a boil and add the noodles.
2. Boil the noodles until it is half-cooked. Drain.
3. In a mixing bowl; pour oil over the noodles and mix until the noodles are coated evenly.
4. Place a tin foil on the base of the Air Fryer basket and place the noodles inside. Cook in a preheated Air Fryer at 395 - degrees Fahrenheit for 15 to 20 minutes or until crisp.
5. Meanwhile; mix together the tamari, red chili sauce, and lime juice. Season with salt and pepper to taste. Once the noodles are cooked; assemble the salad by placing the air fried noodles in a bowl.
6. Add the vegetables and pour over sauce.

91. Fennel Potato Croquettes

Prep + Cook Time: 35 minutes   **Servings:** 4

Ingredients:

- 1/4 cup nutritional yeast
- 4 boiled potatoes; peeled and mashed
- 1 onion; chopped finely
- 1 teaspoon cumin powder
- 2 teaspoon fennel seeds
- 2 green chilies; chopped
- 1 sprig coriander leaves; chopped
- salt to taste
- 2 tablespoon all-purpose flour
- bread crumbs
- cooking spray for coating

Instructions:

1. Preheat the Air Fryer to 400 - degrees Fahrenheit. Place a foil at the base of the Air Fryer basket and poke holes.
2. Combine all the ingredients except for the bread crumbs and cooking spray.
3. Form small balls of the mixture and dredge the balls on the bread crumbs. Place inside the Air Fryer and coat with cooking spray. Cook for 15 to 20 minutes or until golden brown.

92. Easy Fried Falafel

Prep + Cook Time: 30 minutes   **Servings:** 8

Ingredients:

- 1 teaspoon cumin seeds
- 1/2 teaspoon coriander seeds
- 2 cups chickpeas from can; drained and rinsed
- 1/2 teaspoon red pepper flakes
- 3 cloves garlic
- 1/4 cup parsley; chopped
- 1/4 cup coriander; chopped
- 1/2 onion; diced
- 1 tablespoon juice from freshly squeezed lemon
- 3 tablespoon all-purpose flour
- 1/2 teaspoon salt
- cooking spray

Instructions:

1. In a skillet over medium heat, toast the cumin and coriander seeds until fragrant.
2. Place the toasted seeds in a mortar and grind the seeds.
3. In a food processor; place all ingredients except for the cooking spray.
4. Add the toasted cumin and coriander seeds. Pulse until fine.
5. Shape the mixture into falafels and spray cooking oil.
6. Place inside a preheated Air Fryer and make sure that they do not overlap.
7. Cook at 400 - degrees Fahrenheit for 15 minutes or until the surface becomes golden brown.

93. Easy Roasted Asparagus

Prep + Cook Time: 10 minutes   **Servings:** 4

Ingredients:

- 1-pound fresh asparagus spears; trimmed
- 1 tablespoon olive oil
- salt and pepper to taste

Instructions:

1. Preheat the Air Fryer to 375 - degrees Fahrenheit. Mix all ingredients and place the asparagus spears inside the Air Fryer. Cook for 5 minutes until tender.

94. Fried Cauliflower Steak

Prep + Cook Time: 30 minutes   **Servings:** 2

Ingredients:

- 1 cauliflower; sliced into two
- 1 tablespoon olive oil
- 2 tablespoon onion; chopped
- 1/4 teaspoon vegetable stock powder
- 1/4 cup almond milk
- salt and pepper to taste

Instructions:

1. Soak the cauliflower in salted water or brine for at least 2 hours.
2. Preheat the Air Fryer to 400 - degrees Fahrenheit. Rinse the cauliflower and place inside the Air Fryer and cook for 15 minutes.
3. Meanwhile; heat oil in a skillet over medium flame. Sauté the onions and stir until translucent. Add the vegetable stock powder and milk. Bring to boil and adjust the heat to low.
4. Allow the sauce to reduce and season with salt and pepper. Place cauliflower steak on a plate and pour over sauce.

95. Fried Figs, Rocket and Chickpeas Salad

Prep + Cook Time: 35 minutes   **Servings:** 4

Ingredients:

- 8 fresh figs; halved
- 1 ½ cups chickpeas; cooked
- 1 teaspoon cumin seeds; roasted then crushed
- 4 tablespoon balsamic vinegar
- 2 tablespoon extra-virgin olive oil
- salt and pepper to taste
- 3 cups arugula rocket; washed and dried

Instructions:

1. Preheat the Air Fryer to 375 - degrees Fahrenheit.
2. Line the Air Fryer basket with aluminum foil and brush with oil. Place the figs inside the Air Fryer and cook for 10 minutes.
3. In a mixing bowl; mix the chickpeas and cumin seeds.
4. Once the figs are cooked; take them out and place the chickpeas. Cook the chickpeas for 10 minutes. Allow to cool.
5. Meanwhile; mix the dressing by combining the balsamic vinegar, olive oil, salt and pepper. Place the arugula rocket in a salad bowl and place the cooled figs and chickpeas.
6. Pour over the sauce and toss to coat. Serve immediately.

96. Yummy Vegan Fried Ravioli

Prep + Cook Time: 15 minutes   **Servings:** 4

Ingredients:

- 1/2 cup panko bread crumbs
- 2 teaspoon nutritional yeast
- 1 teaspoon dried basil
- 1 teaspoon dried oregano
- 1 teaspoon garlic powder
- salt and pepper to taste
- 1/4 cup aquafaba
- 8-ounces vegan ravioli
- cooking spray

Instructions:

1. Line the Air Fryer basket with aluminum foil and brush with oil.
2. Preheat the Air Fryer to 400 - degrees Fahrenheit. Mix together the panko bread crumbs, nutritional yeast, basil, oregano, and garlic powder. Season with salt and pepper to taste.
3. In another bowl; place the aquafaba. Dip the ravioli in the aquafaba the dredge in the panko mixture. Spray with cooking oil and place in the Air Fryer.
4. Cook for 6 minutes making sure that you shake the Air Fryer basket halfway.

97. Fried Brussels Sprouts

Prep + Cook Time: 20 minutes   **Servings:** 6

Ingredients:

- 1 ½ pounds Brussels sprouts; cleaned and trimmed
- 3 tablespoon olive oil
- 1 teaspoon salt
- 1 teaspoon black pepper.

Instructions:

1. Preheat the Air Fryer to 375 - degrees Fahrenheit. Line the Air Fryer basket with aluminum foil and brush with oil.
2. In a mixing bowl; mix all ingredients and toss to coat.
3. Place in the Air Fryer basket and cook for 10 minutes. Make sure that you shake the Air Fryer basket to cook and brown evenly.

98. Roasted Garlic, Broccoli and Lemon

Prep + Cook Time: 25 minutes

Servings: 6

Ingredients:

- 2 heads broccoli; cut into florets
- 2 teaspoon extra virgin olive oil
- 1 teaspoon salt
- 1/2 teaspoon black pepper
- 1 clove of garlic; minced
- 1/2 teaspoon lemon juice

Instructions:

1. Line the Air Fryer basket with aluminum foil and brush with oil.
2. Preheat the Air Fryer to 375 - degrees Fahrenheit.
3. Combine all ingredients except the lemon juice in a mixing bowl and place inside the Air Fryer basket. Cook for 15 minutes. Serve with lemon juice.

99. Special Portabella Pepperoni Pizza

Prep + Cook Time: 15 minutes

Servings: 3

Ingredients:

- 3 portabella mushroom caps; cleaned and scooped
- 3 tablespoon olive oil
- 3 tablespoon tomato sauce
- 3 tablespoon mozzarella; shredded
- 12 slices pepperoni
- 1 pinch salt
- 1 pinch dried Italian seasonings

Instructions:

1. Preheat the Air Fryer to 330 - degrees Fahrenheit.
2. Drizzle olive oil on both sides of the portabella; then season the inside of the portabella with salt and the Italian seasonings.
3. Spread the tomato sauce evenly over the mushroom and then top with cheese.
4. Place the portabella into the cooking basket and slide into the Air Fryer.
5. After 1 minute; remove the cooking basket from the Air Fryer and place the pepperoni slices on top of the portabella pizza.
6. Cook for an additional 3 to 5 minutes. Finish with freshly grated parmesan cheese and crushed red pepper flakes.

100. Special Baby Corn Pakodas

Prep + Cook Time: 20 minutes

Servings: 5

Ingredients:

- 1 cup chickpea flour or besan
- 1/4 teaspoon baking soda
- 1/4 teaspoon salt
- 1/2 teaspoon curry powder
- 1/2 teaspoon red chili powder
- 1/4 teaspoon turmeric powder
- 1/4 cup water
- 10 pieces baby corn; blanched

Instructions:

1. Preheat the Air Fryer to 425 - degrees Fahrenheit.
2. Line the Air Fryer basket with aluminum foil and brush with oil.
3. In a mixing bowl; mix all ingredients except for the corn. Whisk until well combined.
4. Dip the corn in the batter and place inside the Air Fryer. Cook for 8 minutes until golden brown.

101. Mushroom Chicken Broccoli Casserole

Prep + Cook Time: 30 minutes

Servings: 4

Ingredients:

- 4 chicken breasts
- 1/2 cup shredded cheese
- salt to taste
- 1 cup coconut milk
- 1 cup mushrooms
- 1 broccoli; cut into florets
- 1 tablespoon curry powder

Instructions:

1. Preheat your Air Fryer to 350 - degrees Fahrenheit. Grease a casserole dish using cooking spray.
2. Cut the chicken breasts into small cubes. In a bowl combine the chicken with curry powder, coconut milk, and sprinkle in the salt.
3. Add the broccoli and mushroom and stir well.
4. Add the mixture into your greased dish. Sprinkle the cheese on top. Add to your Air Fryer and bake for about 20 minutes.
5. Serve warm and enjoy!

102. Delicious Pita Bread Pizza

Prep + Cook Time: 15 minutes

Servings: 1

Ingredients:

- 1 pita bread
- 1 tablespoon pizza sauce
- 6 pepperoni slices
- 1/4 cup grated mozzarella cheese
- 1 teaspoon olive oil
- 1/4 teaspoon garlic powder
- 1/4 teaspoon dried oregano

Instructions:

1. Preheat your Air Fryer to 350 - degrees Fahrenheit.
2. Spread the pizza sauce all over the pita bread. Arrange the pepperoni slices over it. Top with mozzarella cheese.
3. Sprinkle with garlic powder and oregano.
4. Place the pita pizza inside the Air Fryer and place a trivet on top. Cook for 6 minutes.

103. Fried Paprika Tofu

Prep + Cook Time: 25 minutes

Servings: 4

Ingredients:

- 1 block extra firm tofu; pressed to remove excess water and cut into cubes
- 1/4 cup cornstarch
- 1 tablespoon smoked paprika
- salt and pepper to taste

Instructions:

1. Line the Air Fryer basket with aluminum foil and brush with oil. Preheat the Air Fryer to 370 - degrees Fahrenheit.
2. Mix all ingredients in a bowl. Toss to combine. Place in the Air Fryer basket and cook for 12 minutes.

104. Amazing Mac and Cheese

Prep + Cook Time: 15 minutes

Servings: 2

Ingredients:

- 1 cup cooked macaroni
- 1/2 cup warm milk
- 1 tablespoon parmesan cheese
- 1 cup grated cheddar cheese
- salt and pepper; to taste

Instructions:

1. Preheat the Air Fryer to 350 - degrees Fahrenheit. Stir all of the ingredients; except Parmesan, in a baking dish.
2. Place the dish inside the Air Fryer and cook for 10 minutes. Top with the Parmesan cheese.

105. Delicious Pasta Salad

Prep + Cook Time: 2 hours 25 minutes	**Servings:** 8

Ingredients:

- 4 tomatoes; medium and cut in eighths
- 3 eggplants; small
- 3 zucchinis; medium sized
- 2 bell peppers; any color
- 4 cups large pasta; uncooked in any shape
- 1 cup cherry tomatoes; sliced
- 1/2 cup Italian dressing; fat-free
- 8 tablespoon parmesan; grated
- 2 tablespoon extra virgin olive oil
- 2 teaspoon pink Himalayan salt
- 1 teaspoon basil; dried
- high quality cooking spray

Instructions:

1. Wash eggplant; pat it dry and then slice off and discard the stem. Do not peel the eggplant. Slice it into 1/2-inch-thick rounds.
2. Toss the eggplant with 1 tablespoon of extra virgin olive oil, and put the rounds in the Air Fryer basket.
3. Cook eggplant for 40 minutes at 350 - degrees Fahrenheit. Once it is soft and has no raw taste remaining, set the eggplant aside.
4. Wash the zucchini; pat it dry and then slice off and discard the stem. Do not peel the zucchini. Slice the zucchini into 1/2 -inch rounds.
5. Toss together with extra virgin olive oil, and put it in the Air Fryer basket.
6. Cook zucchini for about 25 minutes at 350 - degrees Fahrenheit. Once it is soft with no raw taste remaining set the zucchini aside.
7. Wash the tomatoes and slice them into eighths. Arrange them in the Air Fryer basket and spray gently with high quality cooking spray. Roast the tomatoes for 30 minutes at 350 - degrees Fahrenheit. Once they have shrunk and are starting to brown, set them aside.
8. Cook the pasta according to the directions on the package, drain them through a colander, and run them under cold water. Set them aside so they will cool off.
9. Wash the bell peppers; cut them in half, take off the stem and remove the seeds. Rinse under water if you need to, and then pat them dry.
10. Wash the cherry tomatoes and cut them in half.
11. In a large bowl; combine bell peppers and cherry tomatoes. Then; add in the roasted vegetables, cooked pasta, pink Himalayan salt, dressing, chopped basil leaves, and grated parmesan. Mix thoroughly.
12. Set the salad in the fridge to chill and marinade. Serve the salad chilled or at room temperature.

106. Cheesy Prosciutto and Potato Salad

Prep + Cook Time: 15 minutes	**Servings:** 8

Ingredients:

- 4 pounds potatoes; boiled and cubed
- 15 slices prosciutto; diced
- 15 ounces. sour cream
- 2 cups shredded cheddar cheese
- 2 tablespoon mayonnaise
- 1 teaspoon salt
- 1 teaspoon black pepper
- 1 teaspoon dried basil

Instructions:

1. Preheat the Air Fryer to 350 - degrees Fahrenheit.
2. Combine potatoes, prosciutto, and cheddar in a baking dish. Place in the Air Fryer and cook for 7 minutes.

3. In another bowl; whisk together the sour cream, mayonnaise, salt, pepper, and basil.
4. Stir the dressing into the salad; making sure to coat the ingredients well.

107. Chicken Quesadillas

Prep + Cook Time: 20 minutes   **Servings:** 4

Ingredients:

- 2 soft taco shells
- 1-pound chicken breasts; boneless
- 1 large green pepper; sliced
- 1 medium-sized onion; sliced
- 1/2 cup Cheddar cheese; shredded
- 1/2 cup salsa sauce
- 2 tablespoon olive oil
- Salt and pepper; to taste

Instructions:

1. Preheat the Air Fryer to 370 - degrees Fahrenheit and sprinkle the basket with 1 tablespoon of olive oil.
2. Place 1 taco shell on the bottom of the fryer. Spread salsa sauce on the taco. Cut chicken breast into stripes and lay on taco shell.
3. Place onions and peppers on the top of the chicken.
4. Sprinkle with salt and pepper. Then; add shredded cheese and cover with second taco shell.
5. Sprinkle with 1 tablespoon of olive oil and put the rack over taco to hold it in place.
6. Cook for 4 – 6 minutes; until cooked and lightly brown. Cut and serve either hot or cold.

108. Mozzarella and Tomato Bruschetta

Prep + Cook Time: 10 minutes   **Servings:** 1

Ingredients:

- 6 small french loaf slices
- 1/2 cup finely chopped tomatoes
- 3 ounces grated mozzarella cheese
- 1 tablespoon. fresh basil; chopped
- 1 tablespoon olive oil

Instructions:

1. Preheat the Air Fryer to 350 - degrees Fahrenheit. Cook the bread for about 3 minutes.
2. Top with tomato, mozzarella, and prosciutto.
3. Drizzle the olive oil over this.
4. Place the bruschetta in the Air Fryer and cook for an additional minute. Serve and enjoy.

109. Cheesy Chicken Sausage Casserole

Prep + Cook Time: 30 minutes   **Servings:** 8

Ingredients:

- 2 cloves minced garlic
- ten eggs
- 1 cup chopped broccoli
- 1/2 tablespoon salt
- 1 cup divided shredded cheddar
- 1/4 tablespoon pepper
- 3/4 cup whipping cream
- 1 [12-oz] package of cooked chicken sausage

Instructions:

1. Preheat the Air Fryer to 400 - degrees Fahrenheit. Whisk the eggs in a large bowl. Add the whipping cream, and cheese and mix well.
2. In another bowl add in the garlic, broccoli, salt, pepper and cooked sausage.
3. Arrange the chicken sausage mix onto a casserole dish. Add the cheese mixture on top. Add to the Air Fryer and bake for nearly 20 minutes.

110. Cashew and Chicken Manchurian

Prep + Cook Time: 30 minutes   **Servings:** 6

Ingredients:

- 1 cup chicken boneless
- 1 spring onions [chopped]
- 1 onion [chopped]
- 3 green chili
- 6 cashew nuts
- 1 teaspoon ginger [chopped]
- 1/2 teaspoon garlic [chopped]
- One Egg
- 2 tablespoon flour
- 1 tablespoon cornstarch
- 1 teaspoon soy sauce
- 2 teaspoon chili paste
- 1 teaspoon pepper
- 1 pinch msg & sugar
- water as needed
- 1 tablespoon oil

Instructions:

1. Coat chicken with egg, salt and pepper. Mix cornstarch and flour, coat chicken and cook at preheated to 360 - degrees Fahrenheit Air Fryer for 10 minutes.
2. Cook nuts with oil in a pan.
3. Add onions and cook until translucent. Add the remaining ingredients and cook sauce.
4. Add chicken and garnish with spring onions.

111. Cheese and Bacon Rolls

Prep + Cook Time: 25 minutes   **Servings:** 4

Ingredients:

- 8 ounces. refrigerated crescent roll dough [usually 1 can]
- 6 ounces. very sharp cheddar cheese; grated
- 1-pound bacon; cooked and chopped

Instructions:

1. Unroll the crescent dough and, using a sharp knife, cut it into 1-inch by 1 1/2 - inch pieces.
2. In a medium bowl; combine the cheese and bacon. Spread about 1/4 cup of this mixture on each piece of dough.
3. Briefly preheat your Air Fryer to 330 – degrees Fahrenheit.
4. Place the rolls in the Fryer; either on the Air Fry tray or in the food basket.
5. Bake until golden brown; 6 – 8 minutes, and enjoy!

Note: The timing of this recipe can vary from one Fryer to the next; so watch carefully for the browning of the rolls.

112. Healthy Kidney Beans Oatmeal

Prep + Cook Time: 25 minutes   **Servings:** 3

Ingredients:

- 2 large bell peppers; halved lengthwise, deseeded
- 2 tablespoon cooked kidney beans
- 2 tablespoon cooked chick peas
- 2 cups oatmeal; cooked
- 1 teaspoon ground cumin
- 1/2 teaspoon paprika
- 1/2 teaspoon salt or to taste
- 1/4 teaspoon black pepper powder
- 1/4 cup yogurt

Instructions:

1. Place the bell peppers with its cut side down in the Air Fryer. Air fry in a preheated Air Fryer at 355 - degrees Fahrenheit for 2 – 3 minutes.
2. Remove from the Air Fryer and keep it aside.

3. Mix together rest of the ingredients in a bowl.
4. When the bell peppers are cool enough to handle, divide and stuff this mixture into the bell peppers.
5. Place it back in the Air Fryer and air fry at 355 – degrees Fahrenheit for 4 minutes. Serve hot and enjoy!.

113. Chicken Fillet with Brie and Turkey

Prep + Cook Time: 40 minutes | **Servings:** 4

Ingredients:

- 4 slices turkey [cured]
- 2 chicken fillets [large]
- 4 slices brie cheese
- 1 tablespoon chives [chopped]
- pepper and salt to taste

Instructions:

1. Preheat Air Fryer to 360 - degrees Fahrenheit. Cut chicken fillets into 4 pieces and season with salt and pepper.
2. Add chives and brie to it.
3. Add the ingredients onto the plain piece of turkey.
4. Close and wrap Turkey. Hold closed with toothpick. Air fry for 15 minutes, then roast until brown.

114. Cheese and Macaroni Balls

Prep + Cook Time: 25 minutes | **Servings:** 2

Ingredients:

- 2 cups leftover macaroni
- 1 cup cheddar cheese; shredded
- 3 large eggs
- 1 cup milk
- 1/2 cup flour
- 1 cup breadcrumbs
- 1/2 teaspoon salt
- 1/4 teaspoon black pepper

Instructions:

1. In a large bowl combine leftover macaroni and shredded cheese. Set aside.
2. In another bowl place flour; and in other - breadcrumbs. In medium bowl whisk eggs and milk.
3. Using ice-cream scoop, make balls from mac'n cheese mixture and roll them first in a flour, then in eggs mixture and then in breadcrumbs.
4. Preheat the Air Fryer to 365 - degrees Fahrenheit and cook mac'n cheese balls for about 10 minutes, stirring occasionally until cook and crispy. Serve with ketchup or another sauce.

115. Pita Bread Cheese Pizza

Prep + Cook Time: 15 minutes | **Servings:** 4

Ingredients:

- 1-piece Pita bread
- 1/2-pound Mozzarella cheese
- 1 tablespoon olive oil
- 2 tablespoon ketchup
- 1/3 cup sausage
- 1 teaspoon garlic powder

Instructions:

1. Using a tablespoon spread ketchup over Pita bread.
2. Then; add sausage and cheese. Sprinkle with garlic powder and with 1 tablespoon olive oil.
3. Preheat the Air Fryer to 340 - degrees Fahrenheit and carefully transfer your pizza to a fryer basket. Cook for 6 minutes and enjoy your quick & easy pizza.

116. Tasty Portabella Pizza

Prep + Cook Time: 15 minutes   **Servings:** 3

Ingredients:

- 3 tablespoon olive oil
- 3 portabella mushroom caps; cleaned and scooped
- 3 tablespoon mozzarella; shredded
- 3 tablespoon tomato sauce
- 1 pinch salt
- 12 slices pepperoni
- 1 pinch dried Italian seasonings

Instructions:

1. Preheat the Air Fryer to 330 - degrees Fahrenheit.
2. On both sides of the portabella; drizzle oil and then season the inside with Italian seasonings and salt. Spread tomato sauce evenly over the mushroom and top with cheese.
3. Place the portabella into the cooking basket of the Air Fryer. Place pepperoni slices on top of the portabella pizza after 1 minute of cooking. Cook for 3 to 5 minutes.

117. Amazing Hot Dogs

Prep + Cook Time: 20 minutes   **Servings:** 4

Ingredients:

- 3 brazilian sausages; cut into 3 equal pieces
- 9 bacon fillets; raw
- black pepper to taste
- salt to taste

Instructions:

1. Preheat the Air Fryer for 5 min on 355 - degrees Fahrenheit.
2. Wrap the bacon fillets around each piece of sausages then season them with some salt and pepper. Fry the wrapped sausages for 15 min then serve them and enjoy.

Tip: To make it tastier, sprinkle 1/2 teaspoon of Italian seasoning on the sausages pieces.

118. Roasted Potatoes with Garlic and Bacon

Prep + Cook Time: 40 minutes   **Servings:** 4

Ingredients:

- 4 potatoes; peeled and cut into bite-size chunks
- 6 cloves garlic; unpeeled
- 4 strips bacon; chopped
- 1 tablespoon fresh rosemary; finely chopped

Instructions:

1. In a large bowl; combine the potatoes, garlic, bacon, and rosemary and mix thoroughly. Transfer to a baking dish.
2. Briefly preheat your Air Fryer to 350 - degrees Fahrenheit. Cook the potatoes in the Fryer until golden brown; 25 – 30 minutes.

119. Homemade Mexican Pizza

Prep + Cook Time: 15 minutes   **Servings:** 4

Ingredients:

- 3/4 cup of refried beans
- 1 cup salsa
- 12 frozen beef meatballs; pre-cooked
- 2 jalapeno peppers; sliced
- 6 whole-wheat pita bread
- 1 cup pepper Jack cheese; shredded
- 1 cup Colby cheese; shredded

Instructions:

1. Take a bowl and combine salsa, meatball, jalapeno pepper and beans. Preheat the Air Fryer for 4 minutes at 370 - degrees Fahrenheit.
2. Top the pita with the mixture and sprinkle pepper jack and Colby cheese on top. Bake in Air Fryer for 10 minutes. Serve and enjoy.

120. Mozzarella Patties

Prep + Cook Time: 25 minutes   **Servings:** 6

Ingredients:

- 1-pound Mozzarella cheese
- 20 slices pepperoni
- 4 large eggs
- 1 tablespoon Italian seasoning
- 1 cup all-purpose flour
- 2 cups breadcrumbs
- Salt and black pepper; to taste

Instructions:

1. Slice Mozzarella cheese into 1/4-inch slices and cut each slice in half.
2. Create cheese sandwiches with Mozzarella halves and pepperoni inside. Press to seal.
3. In three different bowls place beaten eggs, breadcrumbs with Italian seasoning, and flour. Dip each cheese sandwich into flour; then into eggs and then into breadcrumb mixture.
4. Preheat the Air Fryer to 390 - degrees Fahrenheit and cook cheese patties for about 6 – 8 minutes, turning once while cooking. Serve with dipping sauce and enjoy.

121. Roasted Heirloom Tomato with Feta

Prep + Cook Time: 55 minutes   **Servings:** 4

Ingredients:

For the Tomato:

- 2 heirloom tomatoes
- 1 8-oz block of feta cheese
- 1/2 cup red onions; sliced paper thin
- 1 tablespoon olive oil
- 1 pinch salt

For the Basil Pesto:

- 1/2 cup parsley; roughly chopped
- 1/2 cup basil; rough chopped
- 1/2 cup parmesan cheese; grated
- 3 tablespoon pine nuts; toasted
- 1 garlic clove
- 1/2 cup olive oil
- 1 pinch salt

Instructions:

1. Make the pesto. In a food processor; add parsley, basil, parmesan, garlic, toasted pine nuts and salt.
2. Turn on the food processor and slowly add the olive oil.
3. Once all of the olive oil is incorporated into the pesto, store and refrigerate until ready to use.
4. Preheat the Air Fryer to 390 - degrees Fahrenheit.
5. Slice the tomato and the feta into 1/2 -inch thick circular slices. Pat tomato dry with a paper towel.
6. Spread 1 tablespoon of the pesto on top of each tomato slice and top with the feta.
7. Toss the red onions with 1 tablespoon of olive oil and place on top of the feta.
8. Place the tomatoes/feta into the cooking basket and cook for 12 – 14 minutes or until the feta starts to soften and brown.
9. Finish with a pinch of salt and an additional spoonful of basil pesto.

122. Easy Pesto Gnocchi

Prep + Cook Time: 30 minutes   **Servings:** 4

Ingredients:

- 1 package [16-ounce] shelf-stable gnocchi
- 1 medium-sized onion; chopped
- 3 garlic cloves; minced
- 1 jar [8 ounce] pesto
- 1/3 cup Parmesan cheese; grated
- 1 tablespoon extra virgin olive oil
- salt and black pepper; to taste

Instructions:

1. In the large mixing bowl combine onion, garlic, and gnocchi and sprinkle with the olive oil. Stir to combine.
2. Preheat the Air Fryer to 340 - degrees Fahrenheit. Cook for 15 – 20 minutes; stirring couple time while cooking, until gnocchi are lightly browned and crisp.
3. Stir in the pesto and Parmesan cheese.
4. Serve immediately.

123. Cheeseburger Sliders

Prep + Cook Time: 20 minutes   **Servings:** 3

Ingredients:

- 1-pound ground beef
- 6 slices cheddar cheese
- 6 dinner rolls
- salt to taste
- black pepper

Instructions:

1. Preheat the Air Fryer to 390 – degrees Fahrenheit. Form the ground beef into 6 2.5-ounce patties and season with salt and pepper.
2. Add the burgers to the cooking basket and cook for 10 minutes. Remove from the Air Fryer and place the cheese on top of the burgers and return to the Air Fryer to cook for one more minute.

124. Delicious Meatloaf with Black Peppercorns

Prep + Cook Time: 55 minutes   **Servings:** 4

Ingredients:

- 4 Pounds beef [minced]
- 1 onion [large; diced]
- 3 tablespoon tomato ketchup
- 1 teaspoon Worcester sauce
- 1 tablespoon oregano
- 1 tablespoon basil
- 1 tablespoon parsley
- 1 tablespoon mixed herbs
- salt according to taste
- pepper to taste
- 3 tablespoon breadcrumbs

Instructions:

1. Put beef mince in a bowl and mix it with onion, herbs, ketchup and Worcester sauce. Stir well.
2. Add breadcrumbs to the mixture.
3. Put the seasoned beef in a dish and put in Air Fryer. Cook for 25 minutes at 390 - degrees Fahrenheit.
4. Serve with rice or mashed potatoes.

125. Homemade Falafel Burger

Prep + Cook Time: 35 minutes   **Servings:** 2

Ingredients:

- 14 ounces. can chickpeas
- 1 small red onion
- 1 small lemon
- 5 ounces. gluten free oats
- 2 tablespoon cheese
- 2 tablespoon feta cheese
- 3 tablespoon greek yoghurt

- 4 tablespoon soft cheese
- 1 tablespoon garlic puree
- 1 tablespoon coriander
- 1 tablespoon oregano
- 1 tablespoon parsley
- salt & pepper to taste

Instructions:

1. Place in a food processor or blender all the seasonings, the garlic, the lemon rind, red onion and the drained chickpeas. Whiz until they are coarse but not smooth.
2. Mix them in bowl with 1/2 the soft cheese, the hard cheese and the feta.
3. Combine them into burger shapes.
4. Roll them in gluten free oats until you cannot see any of the chickpea mixture. Place them in the Air Fryer inside the Air Fryer baking pan and cook for 8 minutes at 360 - degrees Fahrenheit.
5. Make the burger sauce. In a mixing bowl add the rest of the soft cheese, the Greek Yoghurt and some extra salt and pepper.
6. Mix well until it is nice and fluffy. Add the juice of the lemon and mix one last time.
7. Place the falafel burger inside your homemade buns with garnish.
8. Load up with your burger sauce.

126. Simple Cheese Wraps

Prep + Cook Time: 35 minutes   **Servings:** 4

Ingredients:

- 1/2-pound cheese [provolone; diced]
- 1 steak [frozen; sliced]
- 1 pack egg roll wrapper

- 1 onion; chopped
- 1 bell pepper [green; chopped]
- salt and pepper to taste

Instructions:

1. Sauté onion and bell pepper for 5 minutes. Cook steak; then shred it.
2. Mix these with cheese. Fill the wrappers and roll them.
3. Air fry for 5 min at 350 - degrees Fahrenheit; then raise temp to 392 - degrees Fahrenheit and fry for 5 minutes.
4. The meal is ready to be served. Enjoy the taste.

127. Special Mac and Cheese

Prep + Cook Time: 25 minutes   **Servings:** 1

Ingredients:

- 1 cup elbow macaroni
- 1/2 cup broccoli or cauliflower; chopped
- 1/2 cup milk; warmed

- 1 ½ cups cheddar cheese; grated
- salt and pepper to taste
- 1 tablespoon parmesan; grated

Instructions:

1. Bring a medium pot of water to a boil and add the macaroni and vegetables.
2. Cook until just tender; 7 – 10 minutes and drain.

3. Toss the still-hot macaroni and vegetables with the milk and cheddar and transfer to a baking dish. Season with salt and pepper.
4. Briefly preheat your Air Fryer to 350 - degrees Fahrenheit.
5. Sprinkle the macaroni with the parmesan and bake until bubbling; about 15 minutes.
6. Let cool slightly before serving.

128. Fried Veggies with Golden Polenta Bites

Prep + Cook Time: 50 minutes   **Servings:** 6

Ingredients:

- 1 cup onions; chopped
- 2 cloves garlic; finely minced
- 1/2-pound zucchini; cut into bite-sized chunks
- 1/2-pound potatoes; peeled and cut into bite-sized chunks
- 1 tablespoon olive oil
- 1 teaspoon paprika

- 1/2 teaspoon salt
- 1/2 teaspoon freshly ground black pepper; or more to taste
- 1/2 teaspoon dried dill weed; or more to taste
- 14 ounces pre-cooked polenta tube; cut into slices
- 1/4 cup Cheddar cheese; shaved

Instructions:

1. Add the vegetables to an Air Fryer cooking basket.
2. Sprinkle them with olive oil, paprika, salt, pepper, and dill.
3. Now; set the machine to cook at 400 - degrees Fahrenheit. Cook for 6 minutes.
4. After that; pause the machine, shake the basket and set the timer for 6 minutes more. Set aside.
5. Next; spritz the polenta slices with non-stick cooking oil. Spritz the cooking basket too.
6. Set your Air Fryer to cook at 400 - degrees Fahrenheit Air-fry for 20 to 25 minutes.
7. Turn the polenta slices over and cook for another 10 minutes.
8. Top each polenta slice with air-fried vegetables and shaved cheese.

129. Hot Buttery Dinner Rolls

Prep + Cook Time: 3 hours 15 minutes   **Servings:** 6

Ingredients:

For the Rolls:

- 1 1/3 cups plain flour
- 1 ½ tablespoons white sugar
- 1 teaspoon of instant yeast
- A pinch of kosher salt

- 2 tablespoons melted butter
- One Egg yolk
- 1/3 cup milk
- A pinch of nutmeg

For the Topping:

- 2 tablespoons softened butter

- 2 tablespoons honey

Instructions:

1. Mix the flour, sugar, instant yeast, and salt using a stand mixer. Whisk on low speed for 1 minute or until smooth.
2. Now; stir in the butter. Continue to mix for 1 more minute as it all combines.
3. Lay the dough onto a lightly floured surface and knead several times.
4. Transfer the dough to a large bowl, cover and place it in a warm room to rise until doubled in size.
5. Now; whisk the egg yolk with milk and nutmeg. Coat the balls with the egg mixture.
6. Shape into balls; loosely cover and allow the balls to rise until doubled, it takes about 1 hour.
7. Then; bake them in the preheated Air Fryer at 320 - degrees Fahrenheit for 14 to 15 minutes.
8. In the meantime; make the topping by simply mixing the very soft butter with honey. Afterward, spread the topping onto each warm roll.
9. Cover the leftovers and keep in your fridge.

Side Dishes

130. Carrot Croquettes and Celery with Chive Mayo

Prep + Cook Time: 10 minutes   **Servings:** 4

Ingredients:

- 2 medium-sized carrots; trimmed and grated
- 2 medium-sized celery stalks; trimmed and grated
- 1/2 cup of leek; finely chopped
- 1 tablespoon garlic paste
- 1/4 teaspoon freshly cracked black pepper

- 1 teaspoon fine sea salt
- 1 tablespoon fresh dill; finely chopped
- One Egg; lightly whisked
- 1/4 cup all-purpose flour
- 1/4 teaspoon baking powder
- 1/2 cup breadcrumbs [seasoned or regular]
- Chive mayo; to serve

Instructions:

1. Place the carrots and celery on a paper towel and squeeze them to remove excess liquid.
2. Combine the vegetables with the other ingredients; except the breadcrumbs and chive mayo.
3. Shape the balls using 1 tablespoon of the vegetable mixture.
4. Then, gently flatten each ball with your palm or a wide spatula. Coat them with breadcrumbs, covering all sides. Spritz the croquettes with a non - stick cooking oil.
5. Air-fry the vegetable croquettes in a single layer for 6 minutes at 360 - degrees Fahrenheit.
6. Serve warm with chive mayo.

131. Peppers and Mushrooms in Puff Pastry

Prep + Cook Time: 25 minutes   **Servings:** 4

Ingredients:

- 1 ½ tablespoons sesame oil
- 1 cup sliced white mushrooms
- 2 cloves garlic; minced
- 1 bell pepper; seeded and chopped
- 1/4 teaspoon sea salt
- 1/4 teaspoon dried rosemary

- 1/2 teaspoon ground black pepper; or more to taste
- 11 ounces puff pastry sheets
- 1/2 cup crème fraiche
- One Egg; well whisked
- 1/2 cup Parmesan cheese, preferably freshly grated

Instructions:

1. Start by preheating your Air Fryer to 400 - degrees Fahrenheit.
2. Then; heat the sesame oil in a skillet that is placed over a moderate heat and cook the mushrooms, garlic, and pepper until tender and fragrant.
3. Season with salt, rosemary, and pepper.
4. Meanwhile; roll out the puff pastry and cut into 4-inch squares.
5. Evenly spread the crème fraiche on them.
6. Then; divide the vegetables among the puff pastry squares. Fold each square diagonally over the filling in order to form a triangle shape.
7. Pinch the edges and coat each triangle with whisked egg. Coat them with grated Parmesan.
8. Cook for 22 to 25 minutes.

132. Simple Sautéed Green Beans

Prep + Cook Time: 12 minutes   **Servings:** 4

Ingredients:

- 3/4-pound green beans; cleaned
- 1 tablespoon balsamic vinegar
- 1/4 teaspoon kosher salt
- 1/2 teaspoon mixed peppercorns; freshly cracked
- 1 tablespoon butter
- Sesame seeds; to serve

Instructions:

1. Set your Air Fryer to cook at 390 - degrees Fahrenheit. Mix the green beans with all of the above ingredients, apart from the sesame seeds. Set the timer for 10 minutes.
2. Meanwhile; toast the sesame seeds in a small-sized nonstick skillet and make sure to stir continuously.
3. Serve sautéed green beans on a nice serving platter sprinkled with toasted sesame seeds.

133. Horseradish Mayo with Gorgonzola Stuffed Mushrooms

Prep + Cook Time: 15 minutes   **Servings:** 5

Ingredients:

- 1/2 cup of breadcrumbs
- 2 cloves garlic; pressed
- 2 tablespoons fresh coriander; chopped
- 1/3 teaspoon kosher salt
- 1/2 teaspoon crushed red pepper flakes
- 1 ½ tablespoons olive oil
- 20 medium-sized mushrooms; cut off the stems
- 1/2 cup Gorgonzola cheese; grated
- 1/4 cup low-fat mayonnaise
- 1 teaspoon prepared horseradish; well-drained
- 1 tablespoon fresh parsley; finely chopped

Instructions:

1. Mix the breadcrumbs together with the garlic, coriander, salt, red pepper, and the olive oil, mix to combine well.
2. Stuff the mushroom caps with the breadcrumb filling. Top with grated Gorgonzola.
3. Place the mushrooms in the Air Fryer grill pan and slide them into the machine.
4. Grill them at 380 - degrees Fahrenheit for 8 to 12 minutes or until the stuffing is warmed through.
5. Meanwhile; prepare the horseradish mayo by mixing the mayonnaise, horseradish and parsley.
6. Serve with the warm fried mushrooms.

134. Scallion and Ricotta Stuffed Potatoes

Prep + Cook Time: 15 minutes   **Servings:** 4

Ingredients:

- 4 baking potatoes
- 2 tablespoons olive oil
- 1/2 cup Ricotta cheese; room temperature
- 2 tablespoons scallions; chopped
- 1 heaping tablespoon fresh parsley; roughly chopped
- 1 heaping tablespoon coriander; minced
- 2 ounces Cheddar cheese; preferably freshly grated
- 1 teaspoon celery seeds
- 1/2 teaspoon salt
- 1/2 teaspoon garlic pepper

Instructions:

1. First; prick your potatoes with a small paring knife.
2. Cook them in the Air Fryer cooking basket for approximately 13 minutes at 350 – degrees Fahrenheit.
3. Check for doneness and cook for 2 – 3 minutes longer if needed.

4. Meanwhile; make the stuffing by mixing the other items.
5. When your potatoes are thoroughly cooked, open them up.
6. Divide the stuffing among all potatoes and serve on individual plates.

135. Delicious Crumbed Beans

Prep + Cook Time: 10 minutes   **Servings:** 4

Ingredients:

- 1/2 cup all-purpose flour
- 1 teaspoon smoky chipotle powder
- 1/2 teaspoon ground black pepper
- 1 teaspoon sea salt flakes

- two eggs; beaten
- 1/2 cup crushed saltines
- 10 ounces wax beans

Instructions:

1. Mix the flour, chipotle powder, black pepper, and salt. Place the eggs in a second shallow bowl.
2. Add the crushed saltines to a third bowl. Rinse the beans under running water and remove any tough strings.
3. Dredge the beans into the flour mixture, then coat with the beaten egg. finally, roll them over the crushed saltines.
4. Spritz the beans with a non-stick cooking spray.
5. Air-fry at 360 - degrees Fahrenheit for 4 minutes.
6. Shake the cooking basket and continue to cook for 3 minutes.

136. Amazing Colby Potato Patties

Prep + Cook Time: 15 minutes   **Servings:** 8

Ingredients:

- 2 pounds white potatoes; peeled and grated
- 1/2 cup scallions; finely chopped
- 1/2 teaspoon freshly ground black pepper; or more to taste

- 1 tablespoon fine sea salt
- 1/2 teaspoon hot paprika
- 2 cups Colby cheese; shredded
- 1/4 cup canola oil
- 1 cup crushed crackers

Instructions:

1. First; boil the potatoes until fork tender. Drain, peel and mash your potatoes.
2. Thoroughly mix the mashed potatoes with scallions, pepper, salt, paprika, and cheese.
3. Then; shape the balls using your hands. Now, flatten the balls to make the patties.
4. In a shallow bowl; mix canola oil with crushed crackers. Roll the patties over the crumb mixture.
5. Next; cook your patties at 360 - degrees Fahrenheit approximately 10 minutes, working in batches.
6. Serve with tabasco mayo if desired.

137. Fried Potato Chips

Prep + Cook Time: 45 minutes   **Servings:** 2

Ingredients:

- 2 - 3 potatoes [russet/sweet]
- 1/2 teaspoon oil [olive/other]

- salt to taste

Instructions:

1. Wash and slice the potatoes thin, round and neat
2. Soak the sliced potatoes in chilled water for half an hour

3. Blot dry and spread the sliced potatoes over pan. Mix salt and oil and pour it over the sliced potatoes in pan
4. Put in Air Fryer for 20 – 25 minutes and the Temperature should be 390 – degrees Fahrenheit.
5. Shake and check the progress at halfway say after 15 minutes Serve the chips with ketchup or chili sauce.

138. Special Turkey Garlic Potatoes

Prep + Cook Time: 45 minutes **Servings:** 2

Ingredients:

- 3 turkey strips [unsmoked]
- 6 small potatoes
- 1 teaspoon garlic; minced
- 2 teaspoon olive oil
- salt to taste
- pepper to taste

Instructions:

1. Peel and chop potatoes into fine cubes. Add 1 teaspoon oil and cook in Air Fryer for 10 minutes at 350 – degrees Fahrenheit. Let it heat.
2. In a separate bowl cut Turkey into fine pieces and mix with garlic, oil, salt and pepper. Add potatoes into the bowl and mix well.
3. Put mixture on silver aluminum foil and cook for about 10 minutes. Serve with raita and enjoy the right combination.

139. Special Croutons

Prep + Cook Time: 25 minutes **Servings:** 4

Ingredients:

- 2 slices bread [whole meal]
- 1 tablespoon olive oil

Instructions:

1. Chop the bread slices into medium size chunks.
2. Add in oil to Air Fryer. Let it heat. Shallow fry the chunks in it. Cook for at least 8 minutes at 390 - degrees Fahrenheit.
3. Best to serve with soup and enjoy the right combination.

140. Healthy Garlic Stuffed Mushrooms

Prep + Cook Time: 25 minutes **Servings:** 4

Ingredients:

- 6 mushrooms [small]
- 1 ounce. onion [peeled; diced]
- 1 tablespoon breadcrumbs
- 1 tablespoon oil [olive]
- 1 teaspoon garlic [pureed]
- 1 teaspoon parsley
- salt to taste
- pepper to taste

Instructions:

1. Mix breadcrumbs, oil, onion, parsley, salt, pepper and garlic in a medium sized bowl. Remove middle stalks from mushrooms and fill them with crumb mixture.
2. Cook in Air Fryer for 10 minutes at 350 - degrees Fahrenheit. Serve with mayo dip and enjoy the right combination.

141. Zucchini and Peppers with Saucy Sweet Potatoes

Prep + Cook Time: 20 minutes

Servings: 4

Ingredients:

- 2 large-sized sweet potatoes; peeled and quartered
- 1 medium-sized zucchini; sliced
- 1 Serrano pepper; deveined and thinly sliced
- 1 bell pepper; deveined and thinly sliced
- 1 – 2 carrots; cut into matchsticks
- 1/4 cup olive oil

- 1 ½ tablespoon maple syrup
- 1/2 teaspoon porcini powder
- 1/4 teaspoon mustard powder
- 1/2 teaspoon fennel seeds
- 1 tablespoon garlic powder
- 1/2 teaspoon fine sea salt
- 1/4 teaspoon ground black pepper
- Tomato ketchup; to serve

Instructions:

1. Place the sweet potatoes, zucchini, peppers, and the carrot into the Air Fryer cooking basket.
2. Drizzle with olive oil and toss to coat, cook in the preheated machine at 350 - degrees Fahrenheit for 15 minutes.
3. While the vegetables are cooking; prepare the sauce by thoroughly whisking the other ingredients, without the tomato ketchup.
4. Lightly grease a baking dish that fits into your machine.
5. Transfer cooked vegetables to the prepared baking dish; add the sauce and toss to coat well.
6. Turn the machine to 390 - degrees Fahrenheit and cook the vegetables for 5 more minutes.
7. Serve warm with tomato ketchup on the side.

142. Amazing Cheese Lings

Prep + Cook Time: 25 minutes

Servings: 6

Ingredients:

- 1 cup flour [all-purpose]
- 3 small cubes cheese [grated]
- 1/4 teaspoon chili powder

- 1 teaspoon butter
- salt to taste
- 1 teaspoon baking powder

Instructions:

1. Make dough with all the ingredients mentioned above and add small amount water if needed.
2. Roll and cut the pieces into round shape.
3. Preheat Air Fryer to 360 - degrees Fahrenheit and air fry for 5 minutes. Stir halfway and periodically.

143. Special Potatoes Side Dish

Prep + Cook Time: 30 minutes

Servings: 2

Ingredients:

- 2 potatoes [medium]
- 1 teaspoon butter
- 3 tablespoon sour cream
- 1 teaspoon chives 1 teaspoon

- 1 ½ tablespoon cheese [grated]
- salt according to taste
- pepper according to taste

Instructions:

1. Stab potatoes with fork and put in Air Fryer having boiled water so they are cooked from the inside to the outside properly.
2. Cook for 15 minutes at 350 - degrees Fahrenheit.
3. In the meantime, mix sour cream, cheese and chives in a bowl. Cut open potatoes and spread butter and add toppings to them. Serve with raw salad.

144. Delicious Potatoes with Mediterranean Dipping Sauce

Prep + Cook Time: 55 minutes   **Servings:** 4

Ingredients:

- 2 pounds Russet potatoes; peeled and cubed
- 1 ½ tablespoons melted butter
- 1 teaspoon sea salt flakes
- 1 sprig rosemary; leaves only, crushed

- 2 sprigs thyme; leaves only, crushed
- 1/2 teaspoon freshly cracked black peppercorns

For Mediterranean Dipping Sauce:

- 1/2 cup mascarpone cheese
- 1/3 cup yogurt

- 1 tablespoon fresh dill; chopped
- 1 tablespoon olive oil

Instructions:

1. First; set your Air Fryer to cook at 350 - degrees Fahrenheit.
2. Now; add the potato cubes to the bowl with cold water and soak them approximately for 35 minutes.
3. After that; dry the potato cubes using a paper towel.
4. In a mixing dish; thoroughly whisk the melted butter with sea salt flakes, rosemary, thyme, and freshly cracked peppercorns.
5. Rub the potato cubes with this butter/spice mix.
6. Air-fry the potato cubes in the cooking basket for 18 to 20 minutes or until cooked through, make sure to shake the potatoes to cook them evenly.
7. Meanwhile; make the Mediterranean dipping sauce by mixing the remaining ingredients.
8. Serve warm potatoes with Mediterranean sauce for dipping and enjoy

145. Roasted Potatoes, Asparagus and Cheese

Prep + Cook Time: 55 minutes   **Servings:** 4

Ingredients:

- 4 potatoes [medium]
- 1 asparagus bunch
- 1/3 cup cheese [cottage]

- 1/3 cup crème fraiche [low fat]
- 1 tablespoon mustard [wholegrain]

Instructions:

1. Add oil and preheat Air Fryer to 390 - degrees Fahrenheit.
2. Cook potatoes in it for 20 minutes.
3. Boil asparagus in salted water for about 3 minutes.
4. Spoon out potatoes and make mash them with rest of ingredients mentioned above.
5. Refill the skins and season with salt and pepper. Serve with rice and enjoy!

146. Amazing Peppery Vegetable Omelet with Cheese

Prep + Cook Time: 15 minutes   **Servings:** 2

Ingredients:

- 3 tablespoons plain milk
- four eggs; whisked
- 1 teaspoon melted butter
- Kosher salt and freshly ground black pepper; to taste
- 1 red bell pepper; deveined and chopped

- 1 green bell pepper; deveined and chopped
- 1 white onion; finely chopped
- 1/2 cup baby spinach leaves; roughly chopped
- 1/2 cup Halloumi cheese; shaved

Instructions:

1. Start with spreading the canola cooking spray onto the Air Fryer baking pan.
2. Add all of the above ingredients to the baking pan, give them a good stir. Then; set your machine to cook at 350 degrees F; cook your omelet for 13 minutes.
3. Serve warm and enjoy!

147. Scrambled Eggs with Tomato and Spinach

Prep + Cook Time: 15 minutes   **Servings:** 2

Ingredients:

- 2 tablespoons olive oil; melted
- four eggs; whisked
- 5 ounces fresh spinach; chopped
- 1 medium-sized tomato; chopped

- 1 teaspoon fresh lemon juice
- 1/2 teaspoon coarse salt
- 1/2 teaspoon ground black pepper
- 1/2 cup of fresh basil; roughly chopped

Instructions:

1. Add the olive oil to an Air Fryer baking pan.
2. Make sure to tilt the pan to spread the oil evenly.
3. Simply combine the remaining ingredients; except for the basil leaves, whisk well until everything is well incorporated.
4. Cook in the preheated Air Fryer for 8 to 12 minutes at 280 - degrees Fahrenheit.
5. Garnish with fresh basil leaves.
6. Serve warm with a dollop of sour cream if desired.

148. Kernel and Sweet Corn Fritters

Prep + Cook Time: 20 minutes   **Servings:** 4

Ingredients:

- 1 medium-sized carrot; grated
- 1 yellow onion; finely chopped
- 4 ounces canned sweet corn kernels; drained
- 1 teaspoon sea salt flakes
- 1 heaping tablespoon fresh cilantro; chopped

- 1 medium-sized egg; whisked
- 2 tablespoons plain milk
- 1 cup of Parmesan cheese; grated
- 1/4 cup of self-rising flour
- 1/3 teaspoon baking powder
- 1/3 teaspoon brown sugar

Instructions:

1. Press down the grated carrot in the colander to remove excess liquid.
2. Then; spread the grated carrot between several sheets of kitchen towels and pat it dry.
3. Then; mix the carrots with the remaining ingredients in the order listed above.
4. Roll 1 tablespoon of the mixture into a ball; gently flatten it using the back of a spoon or your hand.
5. Now; repeat with the remaining ingredients.
6. Spitz the balls with a nonstick cooking oil. Cook in a single layer at 350 degrees for 8 to 11 minutes or until they're firm to touch in the center.
7. Serve warm and enjoy.

149. Amazing Onion Rings

Prep + Cook Time: 30 minutes   **Servings:** 8

Ingredients:

- 2 medium-sized yellow onions; cut into rings
- 2 cups white flour
- 1/2 teaspoon baking soda
- 1 teaspoon baking powder
- 1 ½ teaspoons sea salt flakes
- 2 medium-sized eggs

- 1 ½ cups plain milk
- 1 ¼ cups seasoned breadcrumbs
- 1/2 teaspoon green peppercorns; freshly cracked
- 1/2 teaspoon dried dill weed
- 1/4 teaspoon paprika

Instructions:

1. Begin by preheating your Air Fryer to 356 - degrees Fahrenheit.
2. Place the onion rings into the bowl with icy cold water and let them stay 15 to 20 minutes.
3. Drain the onion rings and dry them using a kitchen towel.
4. In a shallow bowl; mix the sifted flour together with baking soda, baking powder and sea salt flakes.
5. Then; coat each onion ring with the flour mixture.
6. In another shallow bowl; beat the eggs with milk, add the mixture to the remaining flour mixture and whisk well. Dredge the coated onion rings into this batter.
7. In a third bowl; mix the seasoned breadcrumbs, green peppercorns, dill, and paprika. Roll the onion rings over the breadcrumb mix, covering well. Air-fry them in the cooking basket for 8 to 11 minutes or until thoroughly cooked to golden.

150. Rosemary Cornbread

Prep + Cook Time: 1 hr.   **Servings:** 6

Ingredients:

- 1 cup cornmeal
- 1 ½ cups of flour
- 1/2 teaspoon baking soda
- 1/2 teaspoon baking powder
- 1/4 teaspoon kosher salt
- 1 teaspoon dried rosemary

- 1/4 teaspoon garlic powder
- 2 tablespoons caster sugar
- two eggs
- 1/4 cup melted butter
- 1 cup buttermilk
- 1/2 cup corn kernels

Instructions:

1. In a bowl; mix all dry Ingredients until well combined. In another bowl, combine all liquid Ingredients
2. Add the liquid mix to the dry mix. Fold in the corn kernels and stir to combine well.
3. Press the batter into the round loaf pan that is lightly greased with a non-stick cooking spray. Air-fry for 1 hour at 380 - degrees Fahrenheit.

151. Delicious Broccoli Bites with Hot Sauce

Prep + Cook Time: 20 minutes   **Servings:** 6

Ingredients:

For the Broccoli Bites:

- 1 medium-sized head broccoli; broken into florets
- 1/2 teaspoon lemon zest; freshly grated
- 1/3 teaspoon fine sea salt
- 1/2 teaspoon hot paprika

- 1 teaspoon shallot powder
- 1 teaspoon porcini powder
- 1/2 teaspoon granulated garlic
- 1/3 teaspoon celery seeds
- 1 ½ tablespoons olive oil

For the Hot Sauce:

- 1/2 cup tomato sauce
- 3 tablespoons brown sugar
- 1 tablespoon balsamic vinegar
- 1/2 teaspoon ground allspice

Instructions:

1. Toss all the ingredients for the broccoli bites in a mixing bowl; covering the broccoli florets on all sides.
2. Cook them in the preheated Air Fryer at 360 degrees for 13 to 15 minutes.
3. In the meantime; mix all ingredients for the hot sauce.
4. Pause your Air Fryer; mix the broccoli with the prepared sauce and cook for further 3 minutes.

152. Roasted Potatoes & Yoghurt

Prep + Cook Time: 55 minutes

Servings: 4

Ingredients:

- 1.8 Pounds potatoes [waxy]
- 1 tablespoon paprika [spicy]
- salt to taste
- black pepper [freshly ground] to taste
- 1 tablespoon olive oil
- 5.5 ounces. yoghurt [Greek]

Instructions:

1. Preheat Air Fryer at 350 – degrees Fahrenheit.
2. Peel and cut potatoes in small pieces of about 3 cm cubes, soak the pieces in cold water for 30 minutes.
3. After 30 minutes' drain and pat dry the potato pieces.
4. In a medium size bowl add 1 tablespoon. of oil, paprika and sprinkle pepper and stir well. Coat the cubes with the mixture.
5. Put in fryer and air fry for about 20 minutes. Serve them with dip or pari-pari sauce. Enjoy the delicious combination.

153. Easy Veggie Rolls

Prep + Cook Time: 30 minutes

Servings: 6

Ingredients:

- 2 potatoes [mashed]
- 1/4 cup peas
- 1/4 cup carrots [mashed]
- 1 cabbage [small; sliced]
- 1/4 beans
- 2 tablespoon sweet corn
- 1 onion [small; chopped]
- 1 teaspoon capsicum
- 1 teaspoon coriander
- 2 tablespoon butter
- ginger garlic to taste
- 1/2 teaspoon masala powder
- 1/2 teaspoon chili powder
- 1/2 cup breadcrumbs
- 1 packet roll sheets
- 1/2 cup cornstarch slurry

Instructions:

1. Boil all the vegetables in half cup of water on a low heat and let them dry.
2. Spread the roll sheet and place the filling onto it then make the fillings into rolls and coat the rolls with slurry and breadcrumbs.
3. Preheat Air Fryer to 390 - degrees Fahrenheit and cook it for 10 minutes. Serve with boiled rice and have a treat.

154. Special Grilled Cheese

Prep + Cook Time: 25 minutes   **Servings:** 2

Ingredients:

- 4 slices of brioche or white bread
- 1/2 cup sharp cheddar cheese
- 1/4 cup butter; melted

Instructions:

1. Preheat the Air Fryer to 360 - degrees Fahrenheit. Place cheese and butter in separate bowls. Brush the butter on each side of the 4 slices of bread.
2. Place the cheese on 2 of the 4 pieces of bread. Put the grilled cheese together and add to the cooking basket.
3. Cook for 5 – 7 minutes or until golden brown and the cheese has melted.

155. Different Potatoes Gratin

Prep + Cook Time: 55 minutes   **Servings:** 6

Ingredients:

- 1/2 cup milk
- 7 medium russet potatoes; peeled
- 1 teaspoon black pepper
- 1/2 cup cream
- 1/2 cup semi-mature cheese; grated
- 1/2 teaspoon nutmeg

Instructions:

1. Preheat the Air Fryer to 390 – degrees Fahrenheit.
2. Slice the potatoes wafer-thin. In a bowl; mix the milk and cream and season to taste with salt, pepper, and nutmeg.
3. Coat the potato slices with this mixture. Transfer the potato slices to an 8-inch heat-resistant baking dish. Pour the rest of the cream mixture on top of the potatoes.
4. In the cooking basket of the Air Fryer; place the baking dish and set the timer to 25 minutes.
5. Remove cooking basket and distribute the cheese evenly over the potatoes. Set the timer for 10 minutes and bake the gratin until it is nicely browned.

156. Yummy Potatoes Gratin

Prep + Cook Time: 55 minutes   **Servings:** 6

Ingredients:

- 7 medium russet potatoes; peeled
- 1/2 cup milk
- 1/2 cup cream
- 1 teaspoon black pepper
- 1/2 teaspoon nutmeg
- 1/2 cup Gruyère or semi-mature cheese; grated

Instructions:

1. Preheat the Air Fryer to 390 - degrees Fahrenheit.
2. Slice the potatoes wafer-thin. In a bowl; mix the milk and cream and season to taste with salt, pepper and nutmeg.
3. Coat the potato slices with the milk mixture.
4. Transfer the potato slices to 8-inch heat resistant baking dish and pour the rest of the cream mixture from the bowl on top of the potatoes.
5. Place the baking dish in the cooking basket into the Air Fryer.
6. Set the timer and cook for 25 minutes. Remove cooking basket and distribute the cheese evenly over the potatoes.
7. Set the timer for 10 minutes and bake the gratin until it is nicely browned.

Tips: Instead of milk you can substitute two eggs

157. Roasted Vegetables Dish

Prep + Cook Time: 30 minutes   **Servings:** 6

Ingredients:

- 1 1/3 cup parsnips [1 small]
- 1 1/3 cup celery [3 – 4 stalks]
- 2 red onions
- 1 1/3 cup butternut squash [1 small]
- 1 tablespoon fresh thyme needles
- 1 tablespoon olive oil
- pepper and salt to taste

Instructions:

1. Preheat the Air Fryer to 390 - degrees Fahrenheit.
2. Peel the parsnips and onions. Cut the parsnips and celery into 2 Cm cubes and the onions into wedges.
3. Halve the butternut squash; remove the seeds and cut into cubes. [There's no need to peel it.]
4. Mix the cut vegetables with the thyme and olive oil. Season to taste.
5. Place the vegetables into the basket and slide the basket into the Air Fryer.
6. Set the timer for 20 minutes and roast the vegetables until the timer rings and the vegetables are nicely brown and done.
7. Stir the vegetables once while roasting.

158. Easy Sweet Potato Curry Fries

Prep + Cook Time: 55 minutes   **Servings:** 4

Ingredients:

- 2.2 Pounds sweet potatoes
- 1 teaspoon curry powder
- 2 tablespoon olive oil
- salt to taste

Instructions:

1. Preheat Air Fryer to 390 - degrees Fahrenheit.
2. Wash and cut sweet potatoes into fine long fries. Add oil in the pan and bake the fried for 25 minutes.
3. Now season them with curry and salt. Serve with ketchup and enjoy.

159. Awesome Tartar Sauce Chips

Prep + Cook Time: 55 minutes   **Servings:** 4

Ingredients:

- 2 potatoes [large]
- 1 teaspoon rosemary
- 2 cloves garlic [crushed]
- 1 tablespoon oil [olive]

Sauce:

- 1 shallot [chopped]
- 3 tablespoon capers [drained; chopped]
- 1 squeeze lemon juice
- 2 tablespoon jalapenos [drained; chopped]
- 3 tablespoon parsley [fresh; chopped]
- 1 cup mayonnaise
- salt and pepper to taste

Instructions:

1. Cut potatoes into wedges and soak in salted water for about 20 minutes.
2. Preheat Air Fryer to 350 - degrees Fahrenheit.
3. Mix all the ingredients and coat it over the potatoes. Cook the coated potatoes for about 25 minutes.
4. Make a sauce and serve with it. Enjoy the delicious taste.

160. Rosemary Potato Chips

Prep + Cook Time: 1 hour 15 minutes

Servings: 4

Ingredients:

- 4 medium russet potatoes
- 1 tablespoon olive oil
- 2 teaspoon rosemary; chopped
- 2 pinches salt

Instructions:

1. Scrub the potatoes under running water to clean.
2. Cut the potatoes lengthwise and peel them into thin chips directly into a mixing bowl full of water.
3. Soak the potatoes for 30 minutes; changing the water several times. Drain thoroughly and pat completely dry with a paper towel.
4. Preheat the Air Fryer to 330 - degrees Fahrenheit. In a mixing bowl; toss the potatoes with olive oil. Place them into the cooking basket and cook for 30 minutes or until golden brown, shaking frequently to ensure the chips are cooked evenly.
5. When finished and still warm, toss in a large bowl with rosemary and salt.

161. Tasty Turkey Wrapped Prawns

Prep + Cook Time: 30 minutes

Servings: 6

Ingredients:

- 1 Pound. Turkey [sliced]
- 1 Pound. Prawns [tiger]

Instructions:

1. Preheat Air Fryer to 390 - degrees Fahrenheit.
2. Wrap prawns with Turkey and secure with toothpick. Refrigerate for 20 minutes.
3. Cook for 10 minutes in batches. Serve with tartar sauce and enjoy the yummy taste.

162. Yummy Cheesy Rice Balls

Prep + Cook Time: 40 minutes

Servings: 4

Ingredients:

- 1 cup rice [boiled]
- 1 cup paneer
- 1 tablespoon corn flour
- 1 green chili; chopped
- 1 cup cheese mozzarella; cubed
- 2 tablespoon carrot; chopped
- 2 tablespoon sweet corn
- 1 tablespoon corn flour slurry
- salt to taste
- garlic powder [optional] to taste
- 1/2 breadcrumbs
- 1 teaspoon oregano

Instructions:

1. Preheat Air Fryer to 390 - degrees Fahrenheit.
2. Mix all the above-mentioned ingredients and form into small ball shape.
3. Roll the mixture in slurry and breadcrumbs. Cook for 15 minutes.

163. Delicious French Fries

Prep + Cook Time: 25 minutes

Servings: 4

Ingredients:

- 6 medium russet potatoes; peeled
- 2 tablespoon olive oil

Instructions:

1. Peel the potatoes and cut them into 1/4 inch by 3-inch strips.
2. Soak the potatoes in water for at least 30 minutes; then drain thoroughly and pat dry with a paper towel.
3. Preheat the Air Fryer to 360 - degrees Fahrenheit.
4. Place the potatoes in a large bowl and mix in oil, coating the potatoes lightly. Add the potatoes to the cooking basket and cook for 30 minutes or until golden brown and crisp. Shake 2 – 3 times during cooking.

Tip: Thicker cut potatoes will take longer to cook; while thinner cut potatoes will cook faster.

164. Roasted Brussels Sprouts

Prep + Cook Time: 30 minutes   **Servings:** 4

Ingredients:

- 2 cups Brussels sprouts
- 1/4 cup pine nuts [toasted]
- 1 orange [juice and zest]
- 1/4 raisins [drained]
- 1 tablespoon oil [olive]

Instructions:

1. Preheat Air Fryer to 390 – degrees Fahrenheit.
2. Boil sprouts for about 4 minutes and then put them in cold water and drain the sprouts properly.
3. Meanwhile; soak raisins in orange juice for 15 minutes. Now roast the cooled sprouts with oil for 15 minutes. Serve with nuts, raisins and zest.

165. Cheese and Spinach Balls

Prep + Cook Time: 35 minutes   **Servings:** 6

Ingredients:

- 1 cup corn flour
- 1 cup bread crumbs
- 1 cup spinach [boiled]
- 2 onion [chopped]
- 1 tablespoon red chili flakes
- 1/2 cup mozzarella [grated]
- 1 teaspoon garlic [grated]
- 1 tablespoon salt
- 2 tablespoon olive oil

Instructions:

1. Mix all ingredients and form the mixture into small balls. Brush the pan with oil.
2. Air fry at 390 - degrees Fahrenheit for 15 minutes. Serve them with tartar sauce.

166. Special Walnut Stilton Circles

Prep + Cook Time: 45 minutes   **Servings:** 4

Ingredients:

- 1/4 cup flour [plain]
- 1/4 cup walnuts
- 1/4 cup butter
- 1/4 cup stilton

Instructions:

1. Make dough with the all the ingredients mentioned above by mixing them well till a thick texture appears. Cut dough into log shapes, approx. 3cm.
2. Wrap it in aluminum foil and let it freeze for about 30 minutes. Now cut the dough into circles.
3. Line Air Fryer with baking sheet and preheat to 350 - degrees Fahrenheit. Cook 20 minutes. And it is ready! Serve while its hot.

Fish & Seafood

167. Homemade Filipino Bistek

Prep + Cook Time: 10 minutes + marinating time   **Servings:** 4

Ingredients:

- A belly of 2 milkfish; deboned and sliced into 4 portions
- 3/4 teaspoon salt
- 1/4 teaspoon ground black pepper
- 1/4 teaspoon cumin powder
- 2 tablespoons calamansi juice
- 2 lemongrass; trimmed and cut crosswise into small pieces
- 1/2 cup tamari sauce
- 2 tablespoons fish sauce [Patis]
- 2 tablespoons brown sugar
- 1 teaspoon garlic powder
- 1/2 cup chicken broth
- 2 tablespoons olive oil

Instructions:

1. First; pat the fish dry using kitchen towels.
2. Put the fish into a large-sized mixing dish and add the remaining ingredients and marinate for 3 hours in the refrigerator.
3. Cook the fish steaks on an Air Fryer grill basket at 340 - degrees Fahrenheit for 5 minutes.
4. Pause the machine; flip the steaks over and set the timer for 4 more minutes.
5. Cook until the color turns medium brown. Serve over steamed white rice.

168. Amazingly Crunchy Saltine Fish Fillets

Prep + Cook Time: 15 minutes   **Servings:** 4

Ingredients:

- 1 cup crushed saltines
- 1/4 cup extra-virgin olive oil
- 1 teaspoon garlic powder
- 1/2 teaspoon shallot powder
- One Egg; well whisked
- 4 white fish fillets
- Salt and ground black pepper; to taste
- Fresh Italian parsley; to serve

Instructions:

1. Thoroughly combine the crushed saltines and olive oil in a shallow bowl.
2. In another bowl; combine the garlic powder, shallot powder, and the beaten egg.
3. Generously season the fish fillets with salt and pepper.
4. Dip each fillet into the beaten egg.
5. Then; roll the fillets over the crumb mixture. Set your Air Fryer to cook at 370 - degrees Fahrenheit. Air-fry for 10 to 12 minutes.
6. Serve garnished with fresh parsley and enjoy!

169. Fried Cod Nuggets

Prep + Cook Time: 25 minutes   **Servings:** 4

Ingredients:

- 1 Pound cod fillet; cut into chunks
- 1 tablespoon olive oil
- 1 cup cracker crumbs
- 1 tablespoon egg and water
- 1/2 cup plain flour
- pepper and salt to taste

Instructions:

1. Add crackers crumb and oil in food processor and process until it forms into crumbs. Season cod pieces with pepper and salt.
2. Coat seasoned cod pieces with flour then dip in egg and finally coated with cracker crumbs.
3. Preheat the Air Fryer to 350 - degrees Fahrenheit.
4. Place in Air Fryer basket and air fry to 350 - degrees Fahrenheit for 15 minutes or until lightly golden brown. Serve hot and enjoy.

170. Almond Sauce with Crispy Snapper Fillets

Prep + Cook Time: 20 minutes   **Servings:** 4

Ingredients:

- 4 skin-on snapper fillets
- Sea salt and ground pepper; to taste
- 1 cup breadcrumbs

- 2 tablespoons fresh cilantro; chopped
- 1 cup all-purpose flour
- 2 medium-sized eggs

For the Almond sauce:

- 1/4 cup almonds
- 2 garlic cloves; pressed
- 1 bread slice; chopped
- 1 cup tomato paste
- 1 teaspoon dried dill weed

- 1/2 teaspoon salt
- 1/4 teaspoon freshly ground mixed peppercorns
- 1/2 cup olive oil

Instructions:

1. Season fish fillets with sea salt and pepper.
2. In a shallow plate, thoroughly combine the breadcrumbs and fresh chopped cilantro.
3. In another shallow plate, whisk the eggs until frothy. Place the sifted flour into a third plate.
4. Dip the fish fillets in the flour, then in the egg, afterward, coat them with breadcrumbs.
5. Set the Air Fryer to cook at 390 degrees F; air fry for 14 to 16 minutes or until crisp.
6. To make the sauce; chop the almonds in a food processor. Add the remaining sauce ingredients, but not the olive oil.
7. Blitz for 30 seconds then; slowly and gradually pour in the oil and process until smooth and even.
8. Serve with the prepared snapper fillets.

171. Sweet Potatoes with Salmon Fillets

Prep + Cook Time: 45 minutes   **Servings:** 4

Ingredients:

For the Salmon Fillets:

- 4 [6-ounce] skin-on salmon fillets
- 1 tablespoon extra-virgin olive oil
- 1 teaspoon celery salt
- 1/4 teaspoon ground black pepper; or more to taste

- 2 tablespoons capers
- A pinch of dry mustard
- A pinch of ground mace
- 1 teaspoon smoked cayenne pepper

For the Potatoes:

- 4 sweet potatoes; peeled and cut into wedges

- 1 tablespoon sesame oil
- Kosher salt and pepper; to taste

Instructions:

1. First; brush the salmon filets with the oil on all sides. Add all seasonings for the fillets.
2. Air-fry at 360 - degrees Fahrenheit for 5 minutes; pause the Air Fryer and cook for 5 more minutes.

3. Toss the sweet potatoes with sesame oil, salt, and pepper and air-fry them at 380 - degrees Fahrenheit for 15 minutes. Now; pause the machine, flip the potatoes over and cook additional 15 to 20 minutes.
4. Serve with salmon fillets and enjoy!

172. Tasty Grilled Shrimp

Prep + Cook Time: 35 minutes   **Servings:** 4

Ingredients:

- 18 shrimps; shelled and deveined
- 2 tablespoons freshly squeezed lemon juice
- 1/2 teaspoon hot paprika
- 1/2 teaspoon salt
- 1 teaspoon lemon-pepper seasoning
- 2 tablespoons extra-virgin olive oil
- 2 garlic cloves; peeled and minced
- 1 teaspoon onion powder
- 1/4 teaspoon cumin powder
- 1/2 cup fresh parsley; coarsely chopped

Instructions:

1. Place all the ingredients in a mixing dish, gently stir, cover and let it marinate for 30 minutes in the refrigerator.
2. Air-fry in the preheated Air Fryer at 400 - degrees Fahrenheit for 5 minutes or until the shrimps turn pink. Serve over cooked pasta if desired.

173. Creamy Caper Sauce with Tilapia Filets

Prep + Cook Time: 15 minutes   **Servings:** 4

Ingredients:

- 4 tilapia fillets
- 1 tablespoon extra-virgin olive oil
- Celery salt; to taste
- Freshly cracked pink peppercorns; to taste

For the Creamy Caper Sauce:

- 1/2 cup crème fraiche
- 2 tablespoons mayonnaise
- 1/4 cup Cottage cheese; at room temperature
- 1 tablespoon capers; finely chopped

Instructions:

1. Toss the tilapia fillets with olive oil, celery salt, and cracked peppercorns until they are well coated.
2. Place the fillets in a single layer at the bottom of the Air Fryer cooking basket.
3. Air-fry at 360 - degrees Fahrenheit for about 12 minutes and turn them over once during cooking. Meanwhile; prepare the sauce by mixing the remaining items.
4. Lastly; garnish air-fried tilapia fillets with the sauce.

174. Homemade Italian Cod Fillets

Prep + Cook Time: 15 minutes   **Servings:** 4

Ingredients:

- 4 cod fillets
- 1/4 teaspoon fine sea salt
- 1/4 teaspoon ground black pepper; or more to taste
- 1 teaspoon cayenne pepper
- 1/2 cup non-dairy milk
- 1/2 cup fresh Italian parsley; coarsely chopped
- 1 teaspoon dried basil
- 1/2 teaspoon dried oregano
- 1 Italian pepper; chopped
- 4 garlic cloves; minced

Instructions:

1. Coat the inside of a baking dish with a thin layer of vegetable oil. Season the cod fillets with salt, pepper, and cayenne pepper.
2. Next; puree the remaining ingredients in your food processor. Toss the fish fillets with this mixture.
3. Set the Air Fryer to cook at 380 - degrees Fahrenheit. Cook for 10 to 12 minutes or until the cod flakes easily.

175. Christmas Sake Glazed Flounder

Prep + Cook Time: 15 minutes + marinating time

Servings: 4

Ingredients:

- 4 flounder fillets
- Sea salt and freshly cracked mixed peppercorns; to taste
- 1 ½ tablespoons dark sesame oil
- 2 tablespoons sake

- 1/4 cup soy sauce
- 1 tablespoon grated lemon rind
- 2 garlic cloves; minced
- 1 teaspoon brown sugar
- Fresh chopped chives; to serve

Instructions:

1. Place all the ingredients; without the chives, in a large-sized mixing dish.
2. Cover and allow it to marinate for about 2 hours in your fridge.
3. Remove the fish from the marinade and cook in the Air Fryer cooking basket at 360 - degrees Fahrenheit for 10 to 12 minutes and flip once during cooking.
4. Pour the remaining marinade into a pan that is preheated over a medium-low heat and let it simmer, stirring continuously, until it has thickened. Pour the prepared glaze over flounder and serve garnished with fresh chives.

176. Amazing Coconut Curried Prawns

Prep + Cook Time: 10 minutes

Servings: 4

Ingredients:

- 12 prawns; cleaned and deveined
- Salt and ground black pepper; to taste
- 1/2 teaspoon cumin powder
- 1 teaspoon fresh lemon juice
- 1 medium-sized egg; whisked
- 1/3 cup of beer

- 1/2 cup all-purpose flour
- 1 teaspoon baking powder
- 1 tablespoon curry powder
- 1/2 teaspoon grated fresh ginger
- 1 cup flaked coconut

Instructions:

1. Toss the prawns with salt, pepper, cumin powder, and lemon juice.
2. In a mixing dish; place the whisked egg, beer, 1/4 cup of flour, baking powder, curry, and the ginger and mix to combine well.
3. In another mixing dish, place the remaining 1/4 cup of flour, put the flaked coconut into a third bowl.
4. Now; dip the prawns in the flour holding them by the tails.
5. Then; dip them in the beer mix. afterwards, roll your prawns over flaked coconut.
6. Air-fry at 360 - degrees Fahrenheit for 5 minutes and turn them over, press the power button again and cook for additional 2 to 3 minutes.

177. Easy Cajun Shrimp

Prep + Cook Time: 25 minutes   **Servings:** 4

Ingredients:

- 1/4 teaspoon cayenne pepper
- 1/4 teaspoon paprika [smoked]
- 1/2 teaspoon old bay seasoning
- 1 tablespoon olive oil
- 1 pinch of salt
- 1 ¼ Pounds shrimp [tiger].

Instructions:

1. Preheat Air Fryer at 390 - degrees Fahrenheit.
2. Mix all the ingredients mentioned in the ingredients list in a large bowl. Coat the shrimps with the mixture and Cook for 5 minutes.
3. Serve them with boiled rice.

178. Healthy Catfish

Prep + Cook Time: 30 minutes   **Servings:** 4

Ingredients:

- 2 fish fillets [catfish]
- One Egg [medium; beaten]
- 1 cup breadcrumbs
- 1 ounce. cup tortilla chips
- 1 lemon [juice and rind]
- 1 teaspoon parsley
- salt to taste
- pepper to taste

Instructions:

1. Cut fish fillets into neat and nice pieces then season them with lemon juice. Do not overdo it.
2. In a separate bowl mix breadcrumbs with lemon rind, parsley, tortillas, salt and pepper in a food processor. Then lay the mixture in a tray spreading evenly.
3. After coating fish fillets with the mixture cook at 350 - degrees Fahrenheit for 15 minutes in Air Fryer. Serve it with Air Fryer chips and a cold drink.

179. Crispy Crust Fish Fillets

Prep + Cook Time: 25 minutes   **Servings:** 4

Ingredients:

- 4 fish fillets
- One Egg; beaten
- 1 cup breadcrumbs
- 4 tablespoon olive oil
- pepper and salt to taste

Instructions:

1. Preheat the Air Fryer to 350 - degrees Fahrenheit.
2. In a shallow dish; combine together breadcrumbs, oil, pepper, and salt. In another dish add beaten egg. Dip fish fillet in egg then coat with breadcrumbs and place in Air Fryer basket.
3. Cook fish fillets in preheated Air Fryer for 12 minutes.

180. Easy Bean Burritos

Prep + Cook Time: 15 minutes   **Servings:** 4

Ingredients:

- 4 tortillas
- 1 can beans
- 1 cup grated cheddar cheese
- 1/4 teaspoon paprika
- 1/4 teaspoon chili powder
- 1/4 teaspoon garlic powder
- salt and pepper; to taste

Instructions:

1. Preheat the Air Fryer to 350 – degrees Fahrenheit.
2. Combine the paprika, chili powder, and garlic powder with some salt and pepper in a small bowl.
3. Lay the tortillas on a flat surface and divide the beans between them.
4. Sprinkle with the spice mixture.
5. Top with the cheddar cheese. Line a baking dish with parchment paper. Roll the tortilla for making burritos.
6. Arrange on the baking dish. Place in the Air Fryer and cook the burritos for about 5 minutes. Serve and enjoy.

181. Tasty Fish Cakes

Prep + Cook Time: 35 minutes   **Servings:** 4

Ingredients:

- 2 cups white fish
- 1 cup potatoes; mashed
- 1 teaspoon mix herbs
- 1 teaspoon mix spice
- 1 teaspoon coriander
- 1 teaspoon Worcestershire sauce
- 2 teaspoon chili powder
- 1 teaspoon milk
- 1 teaspoon butter
- 1 small onion; diced
- 1/4 cup breadcrumbs
- pepper and salt to taste

Instructions:

1. Add all ingredients into the bowl and mix well to combine. Make small patties from mixture and place in refrigerator for 2 hours.
2. Place patties in Air Fryer basket and cook at 400 - degrees Fahrenheit for 15 minutes. Serve and enjoy.

182. Fried Salmon Croquettes

Prep + Cook Time: 20 minutes   **Servings:** 3

Ingredients:

- 1/2 Pound salmon fillet; chopped
- 2 eggs whites
- 2 tablespoon chives; chopped
- 2 tablespoon garlic; minced
- 1/2 cup onion; chopped
- 2/3 cup carrots; grated
- 2/3 cup potato; grated
- 1/2 cup breadcrumbs
- 1/4 cup plain flour
- Pepper and salt

Instructions:

1. Take three shallow dishes and in first dish add breadcrumbs with pepper and salt.
2. In second dish add flour and in third dish add egg whites.
3. Now in mixing bowl add all remaining ingredients and mix well.
4. Make small balls from mixture and roll in flour then dip in egg and finally coat with breadcrumbs. Place in Air Fryer basket and air fry at 320 - degrees Fahrenheit for 6 minutes.
5. Change temperature to 350 - degrees Fahrenheit and cook for 4 minutes.
6. Serve the dish hot

183. Easy Fried Fish Strips

Prep + Cook Time: 20 minutes   **Servings:** 4

Ingredients:

- 1 Pound catfish fillets; cut into strips
- 1/2 cup almond meal
- 1 teaspoon lemon pepper
- One Egg white beaten

Instructions:

1. Preheat the Air Fryer to 400 - degrees Fahrenheit.
2. In a shallow dish; combine together almond meal and lemon pepper.
3. In a small bowl add beaten egg white.
4. Dip fish strips in egg white then coat with almond meal and place in Air Fryer basket. Air fry in preheated Air Fryer for 12 minutes or until lightly golden brown.

184. Green Beans with Whitefish Cakes

Prep + Cook Time: 1 hr. 20 minutes   **Servings:** 4

Ingredients:

- 1 ½ cups whitefish fillets; minced
- 1 ½ cups green beans; finely chopped
- 1/2 cup scallions; chopped
- 1 chili pepper; deveined and minced
- 1 tablespoon red curry paste
- 1 teaspoon brown sugar
- 1 tablespoon fish sauce
- 2 tablespoons apple cider vinegar

- 1 teaspoon water
- Sea salt flakes; to taste
- 1/2 teaspoon cracked black peppercorns
- 1 ½ teaspoons butter; at room temperature
- Grated rind of 1 lemon
- Breadcrumbs

Instructions:

1. Add all ingredients in the order listed above to the mixing dish.
2. Mix to combine well using a spatula or your hands.
3. Form into small cakes and chill for 1 hour.
4. Place a piece of aluminum foil over the cooking basket. Place the cakes on foil.
5. Cook at 390 - degrees Fahrenheit for 10 minutes; then, pause the machine, flip each fish cake over and air-fry for additional 5 minutes.
6. Mound a cucumber relish onto the plates. add the fish cakes and serve warm.

185. Roasted Potatoes with Marinated Sardines

Prep + Cook Time: 1 hr. 15 minutes   **Servings:** 4

Ingredients:

- 3/4-pound sardines; cleaned and rinsed
- Salt and ground black pepper; to savor
- 1 teaspoon smoked cayenne pepper

- 1 tablespoon lemon juice
- 1 tablespoon soy sauce
- 2 tablespoons olive oil

For the Potatoes:

- 8 medium Russet potatoes; peeled and quartered
- 1/2 stick melted butter

- Salt and pepper; to savor
- 1 teaspoon granulated garlic

Instructions:

1. First; pat the sardines dry with a kitchen towel.
2. Add salt, black pepper, cayenne pepper, lemon juice, soy sauce, and olive oil and marinate them for 30 minutes.
3. Air-fry the sardines at 350 - degrees Fahrenheit for approximately 5 minutes.
4. Increase the temperature to 385 - degrees Fahrenheit and air-fry them for further 7 to 8 minutes. Then put the sardines in a nice serving platter.
5. Clean the Air Fryer cooking basket and add the potatoes, butter, salt, pepper, and garlic.
6. Roast at 390 - degrees Fahrenheit for 30 minutes. Serve with the prepared sardines.

186. Delicious Honey Glazed Halibut Steaks

Prep + Cook Time: 15 minutes

Servings: 4

Ingredients:

- 1-pound halibut steaks
- Salt and pepper; to taste
- 1 teaspoon dried basil
- 2 tablespoons honey
- 1/4 cup vegetable oil
- 2 ½ tablespoons Worcester sauce
- 1 tablespoon freshly squeezed lemon juice
- 2 tablespoons vermouth
- 1 tablespoon fresh parsley leaves; coarsely chopped

Instructions:

1. Place all the ingredients in a large-sized mixing dish.
2. Gently stir to coat the fish evenly.
3. Set your Air Fryer to cook at 390 degrees F; roast for 5 minutes.
4. Pause the machine and flip the fish over. Then; cook for another 5 minutes.
5. Check for doneness and cook for a few more minutes as needed.
6. Serve with a rich potato salad.

187. Cajun Salmon

Prep + Cook Time: 15 minutes

Servings: 2

Ingredients:

- 1/2 Pound salmon fillet
- 1/4 teaspoon thyme
- 1/2 teaspoon cayenne pepper
- 1 teaspoon garlic powder
- 1/2 teaspoon paprika
- 1/4 teaspoon sage
- 1/4 teaspoon oregano
- pepper and salt to taste

Instructions:

1. Rub seasoning all over the salmon.
2. Preheat the Air Fryer at 350 – degrees Fahrenheit. Place seasoned salmon fillet in Air Fryer basket and air fry for 8 minutes.

188. Fried Herb Fish Fingers

Prep + Cook Time: 40 minutes

Servings: 4

Ingredients:

- 3/4 Pound fish; cut into fingers
- 1 cup breadcrumbs
- 2 teaspoon mixed herbs
- 1/4 teaspoon baking soda
- two eggs; beaten
- 2 teaspoon corn flour
- 1 teaspoon rice flour
- 2 tablespoon Maida
- 1 teaspoon garlic ginger puree
- 1/2 teaspoon black pepper
- 2 teaspoon garlic powder
- 1/2 teaspoon red chili flakes
- 1/2 teaspoon turmeric powder
- 2 tablespoon lemon juice
- 1/2 teaspoon salt

Instructions:

1. Add fish, garlic ginger puree, garlic powder, red chili flakes, turmeric powder, lemon juice, and 1 teaspoon mixed herbs and salt in bowl and mixes well.
2. In a shallow dish; combine together corn flour, rice flour, Maida, and baking soda.
3. In a small bowl add beaten eggs. In another shallow dish combine together breadcrumbs, black pepper, and 1 teaspoon mixed herbs.
4. Preheat the Air Fryer to 350 - degrees Fahrenheit.

5. Roll fish fingers in flour then dip in egg and finally coat with breadcrumb mixture. Place coated fish fingers in Air Fryer basket and cook for 10 minutes or until crispy. Serve hot and enjoy!.

189. Crunchy Fish Taco Recipe

Prep + Cook Time: 30 minutes   **Servings:** 4

Ingredients:

- 12 ounces. cod filet
- 1 cup breadcrumbs
- 4 – 6 flour tortillas
- 1 cup tempura butter
- 1/2 cup salsa
- 1/2 cup guacamole
- 2 tablespoon freshly chopped cilantro
- 1/2 teaspoon salt
- 1/4 teaspoon black pepper
- lemon wedges for garnish

Instructions:

1. Cut cod filets lengthwise into 2-inch pieces and season with salt and pepper from all sides.
2. Place tempura butter to a bowl and dip each cod piece into it. Then dip filets into breadcrumbs.
3. Preheat the Air Fryer to 340 - degrees Fahrenheit and cook cod sticks for about 10 – 13 minutes, turning once while cooking. Meanwhile; spread guacamole on each tortilla.
4. Place cod stick to a tortilla and top with chopped cilantro and salsa. Squeeze lemon juice, fold and serve.

190. Yummy Crispy Fish Fillet

Prep + Cook Time: 15 minutes   **Servings:** 4

Ingredients:

- 2 fish fillets; cut each into 4 pieces
- 1 tablespoon lemon juice
- 1 teaspoon chili powder
- 4 tablespoon mayonnaise
- 3 tablespoon cornmeal
- 1/4 teaspoon black pepper
- 4 tablespoon plain flour
- 1/4 teaspoon salt

Instructions:

1. Preheat Air-fryer to 400 - degrees Fahrenheit.
2. Combine together flour, pepper, cornmeal, salt, and chili powder.
3. Mix lemon juice and mayonnaise in a shallow dish.
4. Now dip fillets into mayonnaise mixture, then coat with flour mixture. Place coated fish fillet into the Air-fryer basket and cook for 5 minutes or until crispy.
5. Serve and enjoy!

191. Fried Crispy Shrimp

Prep + Cook Time: 20 minutes   **Servings:** 8

Ingredients:

- 2 Pounds shrimp; peeled and deveined
- 4 egg whites
- 2 tablespoon olive oil
- 1 cup flour
- 1/2 teaspoon cayenne pepper
- 1 cup breadcrumbs
- Pepper to taste
- Salt to taste

Instructions:

1. In a shallow dish; combine together flour, pepper, and salt. In a small bowl add egg whites and whisk well.
2. In another shallow dish combine together breadcrumbs, cayenne pepper, and salt.
3. Preheat Air Fryer to 400 – degrees Fahrenheit. Coat shrimp with flour mixture then dip in egg white and finally coat with breadcrumbs.

4. Place coated shrimp in air fry basket and drizzle olive oil over them. Air fry shrimp in four batches.
5. Air fry shrimp at 400 – degrees Fahrenheit for 8 minutes. Serve and enjoy!

192. Tasty Fish Sticks

Prep + Cook Time: 20 minutes   **Servings:** 4

Ingredients:

- 1 Pound tilapia fillets; cut into strips
- 1 large egg; beaten
- 2 teaspoon old bay seasoning
- 1 tablespoon olive oil
- 1 cup breadcrumbs

Instructions:

1. Preheat the Air Fryer to 400 - degrees Fahrenheit. In a shallow dish combine together breadcrumbs, seasoning, and oil. In a small bowl add beaten egg.
2. Dip fish sticks in egg then coat with breadcrumbs and place in Air Fryer basket. Cook in preheated Air Fryer for 10 minutes or until lightly golden brown.
3. Serve hot and enjoy!

193. Fried Crab Herb Croquettes

Prep + Cook Time: 30 minutes   **Servings:** 6

Ingredients:

- 1 Pound crab meat
- 1 cup breadcrumbs
- 2 eggs whites
- 1/2 teaspoon parsley
- 1/4 teaspoon chives
- 1/4 teaspoon tarragon
- 2 tablespoon celery; chopped
- 1/4 cup red pepper; chopped
- 1 teaspoon olive oil
- 1/2 teaspoon lime juice
- 4 tablespoon sour cream
- 4 tablespoon mayonnaise
- 1/4 cup onion; chopped
- 1/4 teaspoon salt

Instructions:

1. Place breadcrumbs and salt in a bowl.
2. In a small bowl; add egg whites.
3. Add all remaining ingredients into the bowl and mix well to combine.
4. Make croquettes from the mixture and dip in egg white and coat with breadcrumbs. Place in Air Fryer basket and air fry for 18 minutes. Serve and enjoy.

194. Broiled Tilapia

Prep + Cook Time: 10 minutes   **Servings:** 4

Ingredients:

- 1 Pound tilapia fillets
- 1/2 teaspoon lemon pepper
- salt to taste

Instructions:

1. Spray Air Fryer basket with cooking spray.
2. Place tilapia fillets in Air Fryer basket and season with lemon pepper and salt.
3. Cook at 400 - degrees Fahrenheit for 7 minutes. Serve with veggies and enjoy.

195. Salmon Patties

Prep + Cook Time: 20 minutes   **Servings:** 4

Ingredients:

- One Egg
- 14 ounces. canned salmon; drained
- 4 tablespoon flour
- 4 tablespoon cup cornmeal
- 4 tablespoon onion; minced

- 1/2 teaspoon garlic powder
- 2 tablespoon mayonnaise
- pepper to taste
- salt to taste

Instructions:

1. Make salmon flake with fork. Place the salmon flake in a bowl and add garlic powder, mayonnaise, flour, cornmeal, egg, onion, pepper, and salt. Mix well to combine.
2. Make small patties from mixture and place in Air Fryer basket. Air fry patties at 350 – degrees Fahrenheit for 15 minutes. Serve and enjoy.

196. Air Fried Lemon Fish

Prep + Cook Time: 25 minutes   **Servings:** 2

Ingredients:

- 2 teaspoon green chilli sauce
- 2 teaspoon oil
- One Egg white salt to taste
- 1 teaspoon red chilli sauce
- 2 – 3 lettuce leaves

- 4 teaspoon cornflour slurry
- juice of 1 lemon
- 1/4 cup of sugar
- 4 pieces of fish fillets
- 1 lemon

Instructions:

1. Slice lemon and place in a bowl.
2. Boil 1/2 cup water in a non-stick pan, add sugar and stir continuously till sugar dissolves.
3. Put 1 cup refined flour, salt, green chili sauce, 2 teaspoon oil and egg white in a bowl and make sure it's mixed well. Add 3 tablespoon water and whisk well to create a thick and smooth mixture. Spread sufficient refined flour on a plate.
4. Dip the fish fillets in the batter and coat with refined flour. Heat an Air Fryer and brush the basket with oil.
5. Place the prepared fish fillets in it; fit the basket to the fryer and cook at 180 - degrees Fahrenheit for 10 – 15 minutes. Add salt to the pan with the syrup and mix well. Add corn flour slurry and mix again.
6. Add red chili sauce and mix well. Add lemon slices, lemon juice and mix well. Cook till the lemon sauce thickens.
7. Remove the fish from Air Fryer basket; brush with some oil and place in the air-fryer basket again. Continue to cook for 5 minutes more. Roughly tear lettuce leaves and make a bed on a serving platter.
8. Place fish over the lettuce, pour lemon sauce over them.

197. Chipotle Dijon Sauce with Jumbo Shrimp

Prep + Cook Time: 10 minutes   **Servings:** 4

Ingredients:

- 12 jumbo shrimps
- 1/2 teaspoon garlic salt

- 1/4 teaspoon freshly cracked mixed peppercorns

For the Sauce:

- 1 teaspoon Dijon mustard
- 4 tablespoons mayonnaise
- 1 teaspoon lemon rind; grated

- 1 teaspoon chipotle powder
- 1/2 teaspoon cumin powder

Instructions:

1. Season your shrimp with garlic salt and cracked peppercorns.
2. Now; air-fry them in the cooking basket at 395 - degrees Fahrenheit for 5 minutes.
3. After that; pause the machine. Flip them over and set the timer for 2 more minutes.
4. Meanwhile; mix all ingredients for the sauce and whisk to combine well.
5. Serve with the warm shrimps.

198. Fried Cod Sticks

Prep + Cook Time: 20 minutes   **Servings:** 5

Ingredients:

- 1 Pound cod
- 3 tablespoon milk
- 1 cup almond meal
- 2 cups breadcrumbs
- 2 large eggs; beaten
- 1/2 teaspoon pepper
- 1/4 teaspoon salt

Instructions:

1. In a small bowl; combine together milk and eggs.
2. In a shallow dish; combine together breadcrumbs, pepper, and salt. In another shallow dish, add almond meal.
3. Roll cod sticks into the almond meal then dip in egg and finally coat with breadcrumbs. Place coated cod sticks in Air Fryer basket. Air fry at 350 – degrees Fahrenheit for 12 minutes.
4. Shake basket half way through. Serve and enjoy.

199. Spicy Fried Cheese Tilapia

Prep + Cook Time: 20 minutes   **Servings:** 4

Ingredients:

- 1 Pound. tilapia fillets
- 3/4 cup parmesan cheese; grated
- 1 tablespoon parsley; chopped
- 2 teaspoon paprika
- 1 tablespoon olive oil
- pepper to taste
- salt to taste

Instructions:

1. Preheat the Air Fryer to 400 – degrees Fahrenheit.
2. In a shallow dish; combine together paprika, grated cheese, pepper, salt and parsley. Drizzle tilapia fillets with olive oil and coat with paprika and cheese mixture.
3. Place coated tilapia fillet on aluminum foil. Place foil into the Air Fryer basket and air fry for 10 minutes. Serve and enjoy.

200. Cheese Crust Salmon

Prep + Cook Time: 20 minutes   **Servings:** 5

Ingredients:

- 2 Pounds salmon fillet
- 2 garlic cloves; minced
- 1/4 cup fresh parsley; chopped
- 1/2 cup parmesan cheese; grated pepper
- salt to taste

Instructions:

1. Preheat the Air Fryer to 350 – degrees Fahrenheit. Place salmon skin side down on aluminum foil and cover with another foil.
2. Place salmon in Air Fryer basket and cook for 10 minutes.
3. Once 10 minutes finish then remove top foil and top with minced garlic, parmesan cheese, pepper, salt and parsley. Return salmon again in Air Fryer and cook for 1 minute.
4. Serve and enjoy!

201. Delicious Parmesan Crusted Tilapia

Prep + Cook Time: 15 minutes   **Servings:** 4

Ingredients:

- 3/4 cup grated parmesan cheese
- 4 tilapia fillets
- 1 tablespoon olive oil
- 1 tablespoon chopped parsley
- 2 teaspoon paprika
- pinch of garlic powder

Instructions:

1. Preheat your Air Fryer to 350 - degrees Fahrenheit. Brush the olive oil over the tilapia fillets.
2. Combine all of the remaining ingredients in a shallow bowl.
3. Coat the tilapia fillets with the parmesan mixture.
4. Line a baking dish with parchment paper and arrange the fillets on it. Place in the Air Fryer and cook for 5 minutes. Serve and enjoy!

202. Simple Salmon Croquettes

Prep + Cook Time: 15 minutes   **Servings:** 4

Ingredients:

- 1 Pound can red salmon; drained and mashed
- 1/3 cup olive oil
- two eggs; beaten
- 1 cup breadcrumbs
- 1/2 bunch parsley; chopped

Instructions:

1. Preheat the Air Fryer to 400 - degrees Fahrenheit.
2. In a bowl; add drained salmon, eggs, and parsley. Mix well to combine.
3. In a shallow dish; combine together breadcrumbs and oil.
4. Make croquettes from the salmon mixture and coat with breadcrumbs. Place in Air Fryer basket and air fry in preheated Air Fryer for 7 minutes. Serve and enjoy.

203. Yummy Salmon Patties

Prep + Cook Time: 35 minutes   **Servings:** 2

Ingredients:

- breadcrumbs
- olive oil spray
- A handful of parboiled frozen vegetables
- 3 large cooked russet potatoes
- 1 salmon portion
- chopped parsley
- 2 sprinkles of dill
- black pepper
- One Egg
- salt to taste

Instructions:

1. Peel, chop, and mash cooked potatoes. Put this mixture to the side for later.
2. Preheat for 5 minutes at 355 - degrees Fahrenheit; then grill salmon for five minutes. Air fry the salmon.
3. Perform an action called "flaking" which means to cut the salmon into smaller pieces with a fork. Set aside for later.
4. Remove your mashed potatoes from the refrigerator. Now add your vegetables, black pepper, chopped parsley, flaked salmon, and dill/salt.
5. Do a taste test since everything is already cooked, and adjust seasonings to your liking.
6. Add the egg and combine everything together. Shape the mixture into six to eight patties or smaller balls. Cover the balls with breadcrumbs.
7. Now make sure you spray oil onto the balls to keep them from sticking and breaking, and cook in Air Fryer at 355 – degrees Fahrenheit until golden brown.

204. Creamy Salmon

Prep + Cook Time: 20 minutes

Servings: 2

Ingredients:

- 3/4 Pound salmon; cut into 6 pieces
- 1/4 cup yogurt
- 1 tablespoon olive oil
- 1 tablespoon dill; chopped
- 3 tablespoon sour cream
- salt to taste

Instructions:

1. Season salmon with salt. Place salmon pieces in Air Fryer basket and drizzle with olive oil.
2. Air-fry salmon at 285 – degrees Fahrenheit for 10 minutes. Meanwhile; combine together cream, dill, yogurt, and salt.
3. Place salmon on serving dish and pour creamy sauce over salmon. Serve and enjoy!

205. Fried Cajun Shrimp

Prep + Cook Time: 10 minutes

Servings: 4

Ingredients:

- 1 ¼ Pounds shrimp; peeled and deveined
- 1/2 teaspoon old bay seasoning
- 1/4 teaspoon cayenne pepper
- 1 tablespoon olive oil
- 1/2 teaspoon paprika
- 1/4 teaspoon salt

Instructions:

1. Preheat the Air Fryer to 400 – degrees Fahrenheit. Add all ingredients into the mixing bowl and toss well.
2. Place seasoned shrimp in Air Fryer basket and air fry for 5 minutes. Serve and enjoy.

206. Cod with Kale, Grapes And Fennel

Prep + Cook Time: 30 minutes

Servings: 2

Ingredients:

- 1 small bulb fennel; sliced vi-inch thick
- 2 fillets of black cod [6 – 8 oz.] - may use sablefish alternatively
- 1 cup grapes; halved
- 1/2 cup pecans
- 2 teaspoon white balsamic vinegar or white wine vinegar
- 1+2+1 tablespoon extra virgin olive oil; separately
- 3 cups kale; minced
- sea salt to taste
- ground black pepper to taste

Instructions:

1. Prepare the air-fryer: preheat it to 400 – degrees Fahrenheit.
2. Take the fish fillets and season it with salt and pepper. Drizzle it with 1 tablespoon of olive oil.
3. Take the basket and place the fish inside; skin side down. Adjust the time to 10 minutes and fry.
4. After the end of cooking place it aside, covering it with foil loosely.
5. Combine in a bowl fennel, grapes, and pecans. Pour in 2 tablespoons of olive oil and season it with salt and pepper.
6. Then add them to the Air Fryer basket. Make sure the temperature is 400 – degrees Fahrenheit and cook it for 5 minutes; shaking the basket once during the process.
7. Take another bowl and combine minced kale and cooked grapes, fennel, and pecans. Cover the ingredients with balsamic vinegar and the remaining 1 tablespoon of olive oil. Season it with some more salt and pepper. Toss gently.
8. Serve the fish with the mixture from the previous step.

207. Yummy Salmon with Dill Sauce

Prep + Cook Time: 30 minutes   **Servings:** 4

Ingredients:

The Salmon:

- 1 ½ pounds of salmon
- 2 teaspoon olive oil

- pinch of salt

The Dill Sauce:

- 1/2 cup Greek yogurt - non-fat is fine
- 1/2 cup sour cream

- pinch of salt
- 2 tablespoon fresh dill; finely chopped

Instructions:

1. Cut the salmon into four 6- ounce portions and drizzle them with the olive oil
2. Briefly preheat your Air Fryer to 270 - degrees Fahrenheit.
3. Season the salmon with salt and place in the fryer, cooking until the fish flakes easily, 20 – 23 minutes.
4. While the salmon cooks, prepare the dill sauce in a small bowl, combine the yogurt, sour cream, dill, and a pinch of salt. Mix well; garnish with a sprig of dill, and serve alongside the salmon.
5. **Tips:** Follow the temperature and timing guidelines of this recipe particularly carefully to ensure that you end up with perfectly cooked fish.

208. Easy Grilled Salmon Fillets

Prep + Cook Time: 20 minutes   **Servings:** 2

Ingredients:

- 2 salmon fillets
- 1/3 cup of water
- 1/3 cup of light soy sauce
- 1/3 cup of brown sugar

- 2 tablespoon of olive oil
- black pepper to taste
- salt to taste

Instructions:

1. Season the salmon fillets with some salt and pepper.
2. Whisk the rest of the ingredients in a medium bowl and place in it the salmon fillet then let it marinate for 2 hours.
3. Preheat the Air Fryer on 355 - degrees Fahrenheit for 5 min. Drain the salmon fillets and air fry them for 8 min then serve them warm and enjoy.

Tips: To make it tastier, season the salmon with a pinch of garlic powder.

209. Fried Prawns

Prep + Cook Time: 30 minutes   **Servings:** 4

Ingredients:

- 1 Pound prawns; peeled

- 1 Pound bacon slices

Instructions:

1. Preheat the Air Fryer to 400 - degrees Fahrenheit. Wrap each prawn in bacon slices and place in Air Fryer basket.
2. Air fry in preheated Air Fryer for 5 minutes.
3. Serve and enjoy!

210. Salmon with Zucchini

Prep + Cook Time: 20 minutes

Servings: 2

Ingredients:

- The various components of this dish requires individual amounts of ingredients to be made properly

Salmon:

- 2 [5 – 6 ounces]. salmon fillets; skin on
- 1 teaspoon olive oil
- salt and pepper to taste

Courgette:

- 2 large zucchini; trimmed and spiralizer [or julienned with a julienne peeler]
- 1 avocado; peeled and roughly chopped
- 1/2 garlic clove; minced
- small handful parsley; roughly chopped
- small handful cherry tomatoes; halved
- small handful black olives; chopped
- 2 tablespoon pine nuts; toasted

Instructions:

1. Briefly preheat your Air Fryer to 350 – degrees Fahrenheit.
2. Brush the salmon with the olive oil and season with salt and pepper.
3. Place the salmon in the Fryer and cook until the skin is crisp; about 10 minutes.
4. While the salmon cooks; prepare the vegetables blend the avocado, garlic, and parsley in a food processor until smooth.
5. Toss in a large bowl with the zucchini, tomatoes, and olives.
6. Divide the vegetables between two plates, top each portion with a salmon fillet, sprinkle with pine nuts, and serve.

211. Celery Cakes and Chunky Fish

Prep + Cook Time: 10 minutes + chilling time

Servings: 4

Ingredients:

- 2 cans canned fish
- 2 celery stalks; trimmed and finely chopped
- One Egg; whisked
- 1 cup soft bread crumbs
- 1 teaspoon whole-grain mustard
- 1/2 teaspoon sea salt
- 1/4 teaspoon freshly cracked black peppercorns
- 1 teaspoon paprika

Instructions:

1. Mix all of the above ingredients in the order listed above, mix to combine well and shape into four cakes.
2. Chill for 50 minutes.
3. Place on an Air Fryer grill pan. Spritz each cake with a non-stick cooking spray, covering all sides.
4. Grill at 360 - degrees Fahrenheit for 5 minutes; then, pause the machine, flip the cakes over and set the timer for another 3 minutes.
5. Serve over mashed potatoes.

212. Spicy Glazed Halibut Steak

Prep + Cook Time: 70 minutes   **Servings:** 3

Ingredients:

- 1-pound halibut steak
- 2/3 cup soy sauce [low sodium]
- 1/2 cup mirin
- 2 tablespoon lime juice
- 1/4 cup sugar
- 1/4 teaspoon crushed red pepper flakes
- 1/4 cup orange juice
- 1 garlic clove [smashed]
- 1/4 teaspoon ginger ground

Instructions:

1. Prepare teriyaki glaze by combining all of the teriyaki glazes in a saucepan.
2. Bring mixture to a boil and then reduce by half. Set aside and allow to cool.
3. Once cooled pour half of the glaze into a re-sealable bag with the halibut and refrigerated for 30 minutes.
4. Preheat the Air Fryer to 390 - degrees Fahrenheit. Place marinated halibut into the Air Fryer and cook for 10 – 12 minutes.
5. When finished; brush a little of the remaining glaze over the halibut steak.
6. Serve over a bed of white rice or shredded vegetables.

213. Awesome Bread Crumbed Fish

Prep + Cook Time: 25 minutes   **Servings:** 2 – 4

Ingredients:

- 4 tablespoon vegetable oil
- 5 ounces. bread crumbs
- One Egg
- 4 fish fillets [medium thickness]

Instructions:

1. Preheat your Air Fryer to 350 – degrees Fahrenheit.
2. In a bowl; combine bread crumbs and oil. Stir it. Whisk the egg. Dip the fish first in the egg and then in crumbs mixture. Put in Air Fryer basket. Cook for 12 minutes

214. Cajun Lemon Salmon

Prep + Cook Time: 15 minutes   **Servings:** 1

Ingredients:

- 1 salmon fillet
- 1 teaspoon cajun seasoning
- juice of 1/2 lemon
- 1/4 teaspoon brown sugar
- 2 lemon wedges; for serving

Instructions:

1. Preheat the Air Fryer to 350 - degrees Fahrenheit.
2. Combine the lemon juice and sugar and coat the salmon with this mixture.
3. Sprinkle the Cajun seasoning all over the salmon. Place a piece of parchment paper in your Air Fryer.
4. Place the salmon on it and cook for 7 minutes.

215. Cheesy Breaded Salmon

Prep + Cook Time: 25 minutes   **Servings:** 4

Ingredients:

- 2 cups breadcrumbs
- 4 filets of salmon
- 1 cup Swiss cheese; shredded
- two eggs; beaten

Instructions:

1. Preheat your Air Fryer to 390 – degrees Fahrenheit. Dip each salmon filet into the egg mixture. Top with Swiss cheese.
2. Dip into the breadcrumbs and coat all sides of the fish. Place on an oven safe dish and cook for 20 minutes.

216. Homemade Asian Style Fish

Prep + Cook Time: 35 minutes   **Servings:** 2

Ingredients:

- 1 medium sea bass; halibut or fish cutlet [11 – 12 oz.]
- 1 tomato; cut into quarter
- 1 lime; cut thinly
- 1 stalk green onion; chopped
- 3 slices of ginger; julienned
- 2 garlic cloves; minced
- 1 chili; sliced
- 2 tablespoon cooking wine
- 1 tablespoon olive oil
- steamed rice; optional

Instructions:

1. Prepare the garlic ginger oil mixture: sauté ginger and garlic with oil till golden brown.
2. Preheat the Air Fryer to 360 - degrees Fahrenheit.
3. Prepare the fish: - clean, rinse and pat it. Cut it in half to fit in the Air Fryer.
4. Put the fish into the Air Fryer basket. Drizzle it with the cooking wine.
5. Layer the tomato and lime slices on top of the fish.
6. Cover it with the garlic ginger oil mixture. Top it with the green onion and slices of chili.
7. Cover ingredients with the aluminum foil. Put it into preheated Air Fryer and cook for 15 minutes.
8. After the end of cooking time check the fish. If it is not ready yet; continue cooking for another 5 minutes.
9. Serve hot with steamed rice or any other garnish.

217. Awesome Seafood Super Veggie Fritters

Prep + Cook Time: 50 minutes   **Servings:** 3

Ingredients:

- 2 cups clam meat
- 1 cup shredded carrot
- 1/2 cup shredded zucchini
- 1 cup chickpea flour; combined with
- 3/4 cup water to form batter
- 2 tablespoon olive oil
- 1/4 teaspoon pepper

Instructions:

1. Preheat your Air Fryer to 390 – degrees Fahrenheit.
2. Combine the clam meat, olive oil, shredded carrot and zucchini along with the pepper in a mixing bowl.
3. Form small balls using your hands. Coat the balls with the chickpea mixture.
4. Place in the Air Fryer and cook for 30 minutes or until nice and crispy.

218. Sweet Coconut Shrimp

Prep + Cook Time: 30 minutes   **Servings:** 2

Ingredients:

- 1/2 cup orange jam
- 8 large shrimp
- 8 ounces. coconut milk
- 1/2 cup shredded coconut
- 1/2 teaspoon cayenne pepper
- pinch of black pepper
- 1 teaspoon mustard
- 1/4 teaspoon salt
- 1/2 cup breadcrumbs
- 1/4 teaspoon hot sauce
- 1 tablespoon honey

Instructions:

1. Preheat your Air Fryer to 350 - degrees Fahrenheit.
2. Place breadcrumbs, salt, pepper, coconut, and cayenne pepper in a bowl. Mix to combine.
3. Dip the shrimp in the coconut milk first, then in the breadcrumb mixture.
4. Line a baking sheet and arrange the shrimp on it. Place in the Air Fryer and cook for 20 minutes.
5. Meanwhile; whisk together all of the remaining ingredients. Place the shrimp on a serving platter and drizzle the sauce over.

219. Honey and Sriracha Tossed Calamari

Prep + Cook Time: 25 minutes   **Servings:** 2

Ingredients:

- 1 cup club soda
- 1/2 Pound calamari tubes [or tentacles]; about 1/4 inch wide, rinsed and pat dry
- 1/2 cup honey
- 1 – 2 tablespoon sriracha

- 1 cup all-purpose flour
- sea salt to taste
- red pepper and black pepper to taste
- red pepper flakes to taste

Instructions:

1. Take a bowl; add calamari rings, cover it with club soda and stir well. Set aside for 10 minutes.
2. Take another bowl and mix flour, salt, red and black pepper.
3. Prepare the sauce tossing well in the separate small bowl the mixture of honey, pepper flakes, and Sriracha. Set aside.
4. Drain the calamari; gently pat dry and cover them with the flour mixture.
5. Set them on a plate until ready to fry.
6. Grease the basket with the cooking spray. Add the calamari, in one layer, leaving a little of space in between.
7. Adjust the temperature to 380 – degrees Fahrenheit and cook for 11 minutes. Shake the basket, at least twice during the process.
8. When the time is up; remove the calamari from the Air Fryer, cover with 1/2 of the sauce prepared in step 3 and place them again into the basket. Cook for another 2 minutes.
9. When ready; serve covered with the remaining sauce.

220. Delicious Salmon with Dill Sauce

Prep + Cook Time: 45 minutes   **Servings:** 4

Ingredients:

For the Salmon:
- 1 ½ pounds salmon [4 pieces; 6 oz. each]
- 2 teaspoon olive oil

For the Dill Sauce:
- 1/2 cup non-fat greek yogurt
- 1/2 cup sour cream

- 1 pinch salt

- 1 pinch salt 2 tablespoons dill; finely chopped

Instructions:

1. Preheat the Air Fryer to 270 - degrees Fahrenheit.
2. Cut the salmon into four 6-ounce portions and drizzle one teaspoon of olive oil over each piece. Season with a pinch of salt.
3. Place the salmon into the cooking basket and cook for 20 - 23 minutes.
4. Make the dill sauce. In a mixing bowl combine the yogurt, sour cream, chopped dill and salt.
5. Top the cooked salmon with the sauce and garnish with an additional pinch of chopped dill.

221. Tasty Coconut Shrimps

Prep + Cook Time: 25 minutes

Servings: 4

Ingredients:

- 2 pounds [12 – 15] raw shrimps
- 1 cup egg whites
- 1 cup dried coconut; unsweetened
- 1 cup breadcrumbs
- 1 cup all-purpose flour
- 1/2 teaspoon salt

Instructions:

1. Prepare shrimps and set aside
2. In the large mixing bowl combine breadcrumbs and coconut. Season with salt lightly.
3. In another bowl place flour and in the third bowl place egg whites.
4. Meanwhile; preheat the Air Fryer to 340 - degrees Fahrenheit. Dip each shrimp into the flour, then into egg whites and then into breadcrumbs mixture.
5. Transfer shrimps to a fryer and cook for about 8 – 10 minutes; shaking occasionally. Serve with dipping sauce you prefer.

222. Black Cod with Fennel, Kale and Pecans

Prep + Cook Time: 30 minutes

Servings: 2

Ingredients:

- 2 [6- to 8-ounce] fillets of black cod [or sablefish]
- salt and freshly ground black pepper
- olive oil
- 1 cup grapes; halved
- 1 small bulb fennel; sliced 1/4-inch thick
- 1/2 cup pecans
- 3 cups shredded kale
- 2 teaspoon white balsamic vinegar or white wine vinegar
- 2 tablespoon extra-virgin olive oil

Instructions:

1. Pre-heat the Air Fryer to 400 – degrees Fahrenheit.
2. Season the cod fillets with salt and pepper and drizzle, spread or spray a little olive oil on top.
3. Place the fish, presentation side up [skin side down], into the Air Fryer basket. Air-fry for 10 minutes. When the fish has finished cooking, remove the fillets to a side plate and loosely tent with foil to rest.
4. Toss the grapes, fennel and pecans in a bowl with a drizzle of olive oil and season with salt and pepper.
5. Add the grapes, fennel and pecans to the Air Fryer basket and air-fry for 5 minutes at 400 – degrees Fahrenheit; shaking the basket once during the cooking time. Transfer the grapes, fennel and pecans to a bowl with the kale.
6. Dress the kale with the balsamic vinegar and olive oil, season to taste with salt and pepper and serve alongside the cooked fish.

223. Tasty Fish Sticks

Prep + Cook Time: 30 minutes

Servings: 4

Ingredients:

- 1-pound cod
- three eggs
- 2 cups breadcrumbs
- 1/2 teaspoon black pepper
- 1 teaspoon salt
- 1 cup all-purpose flour
- 3 tablespoon skimmed milk
- cheese or tartar sauce for serving

Instructions:

1. In a large bowl whisk together, milk and eggs.

2. In another bowl place breadcrumbs and in the third bowl put all-purpose flour.
3. Cut cod fish into stripes and season with salt and pepper from both sides.
4. Dip each strip into flour; then into egg mixture, and then into breadcrumbs.
5. Preheat the Air Fryer to 340 - degrees Fahrenheit and cook cod strips for 10 – 13 minutes, turning once while cooking. Serve with dipping sauce.

224. Tilapia Fillets with Egg

Prep + Cook Time: 25 minutes   **Servings:** 3

Ingredients:

- 1 Pound. tilapia fillets [sliced]
- 4 wheat buns
- 2 eggs yolks
- 1 tablespoon fish sauce
- 2 tablespoon mayonnaise
- 3 sweet pickle relish
- 1 tablespoon hot sauce
- 1 tablespoon nectar

Instructions:

1. Mix egg yolks and fish sauce into a bowl. Mix well.
2. Add mayonnaise, sweet pickle relish, hot sauce and nectar.
3. Pour the mixture in a round baking tray.
4. Place it in Air Fryer with tilapia fillets on the sides. Let it cook for 15 minutes on 300 – degrees Fahrenheit.
5. When done; take it out and serve with buns.

225. Easy Salmon Mixed Eggs

Prep + Cook Time: 25 minutes   **Servings:** 2

Ingredients:

- 1 Pound. salmon [cooked]
- two eggs
- 1 onion [chopped]
- 1 cup celery [chopped]
- 1 tablespoon oil
- salt and pepper to taste

Instructions:

1. Whisk the eggs in a bowl.
2. Add celery, onion, salt and pepper.
3. Add oil in the round baking tray and pour the mixture. Place it in the Air Fryer on 300 - degrees Fahrenheit.
4. Let it cook for 10 minutes.
5. When done; serve and enjoy with cooked salmon.

226. Easy Cajun Salmon

Prep + Cook Time: 20 minutes   **Servings:** 1

Ingredients:

- 1 salmon fillet Cajun seasoning
- A light sprinkle of sugar
- Juice from a quarter of lemon; to serve

Instructions:

1. Preheat Air Fryer to 355 - degrees Fahrenheit.
2. In a plate; sprinkle Cajun seasoning all over and ensure all sides are coated. You don't need too much. If you prefer a tad of sweetness, add a light sprinkling of sugar.
3. For a salmon fillet; about 3/4 of an inch thick, air fry for 7 minutes, skin side up on the grill pan.
4. Serve immediately with a squeeze of lemon.

227. Yummy Salmon Croquettes

Prep + Cook Time: 25 minutes

Servings: 2

Ingredients:

- 7 ounces. salmon fillet; chopped
- 2/3 cup carrots; grated
- 2/3 cup potato; grated
- 1/2 cup onion; minced
- 2 tablespoon chives; chopped
- 3 cloves garlic; minced

- sea salt to taste
- black pepper to taste
- handful of breadcrumbs
- 1/2 cup all-purpose flour
- 2 eggs whites
- cooking spray

Instructions:

1. Preheat the Air Fryer to 320 - degrees Fahrenheit.
2. Take the cooking spray, egg whites, flour, bread crumbs and set them aside.
3. In a separate bowl toss well all the remaining ingredients and shape them into small balls. Cover the balls with the mixture from step 2. Drizzle them with the cooking spray.
4. Put the balls into the Air Fryer basket and set timer to 4 minutes. Cook.
5. Open the Air Fryer and turn the balls around. Cook for another 2 minutes. When the color of the balls is even, serve.

228. Garlic and Herb Fish Fingers

Prep + Cook Time: 40 minutes

Servings: 2

Ingredients:

- 2 Eggs
- 10 ounces. Fish; such as Mackerel, cut into fingers
- 1/2 teaspoon Turmeric Powder
- 1/2 Lemon; juiced
- 1 + 1 teaspoon Mixed Dried Herbs; separately
- 1 + 1 teaspoon Garlic Powder; separately
- 1/2 teaspoon Red Chili Flakes
- 1 cup Breadcrumbs

- 2 tablespoon Maida [All Purpose Flour]
- 2 teaspoon Com Flour
- 1 teaspoon Rice Flour
- 1/4 teaspoon Baking Soda
- 1 teaspoon Ginger Garlic Paste
- 1/2 teaspoon Black Pepper
- 1/2 teaspoon Sea Salt
- 1 – 2 tablespoon Olive Oil
- Ketchup or Tart are Sauce [optional]

Instructions:

1. Put the fish fingers to the bowl. Add in 1 teaspoon mixed herbs, 1 teaspoon garlic powder, salt, red chili flakes, turmeric powder, black pepper, ginger garlic paste, and lemon juice.
2. Stir all the ingredients and set aside for at least 10 minutes.
3. Take another bowl and combine Maida flour, rice flour, com flour, and baking soda. Break the eggs into this bowl.
4. Stir well and add marinated fish. Set aside again for at least 10 minutes.
5. Combine and toss well the bread crumbs and the remaining 1 teaspoon of mixed herbs and 1 teaspoon of garlic powder. Then cover the fish with breadcrumbs and herb mixture.
6. Prepare the Air Fryer by preheating it to 360 - degrees Fahrenheit.
7. Take the aluminum foil and lay it on the basket of the fryer. Then layer fish fingers and cover it with the olive oil.
8. Adjust the time to 10 minutes and cook until the fish is brown and crispy.
9. You may serve it with ketchup or tartar sauce.

229. Healthy Mediterranean Quinoa Salad

Prep + Cook Time: 15 minutes   **Servings:** 2

Ingredients:

- 1 cup cooked quinoa
- 1 red bell pepper; chopped
- 2 prosciutto slices; chopped
- 1/4 cup chopped kalamata olives
- 1/2 cup crumbled feta cheese
- 1 teaspoon olive oil
- 1 teaspoon dried oregano
- 6 cherry tomatoes; halved
- salt and pepper; to taste

Instructions:

1. Preheat your Air Fryer to 350 - degrees Fahrenheit.
2. Heat the olive oil and cook the red bell pepper for about 2 minutes. Add the prosciutto slices and cook for 3 more minutes.
3. Transfer to an oven-proof bowl and wipe the grease off your Air Fryer. Add the remaining ingredients; except the tomatoes, and stir to combine well.
4. Stir in the cherry tomato halves. Serve and enjoy!

230. Tuna with Roast Potatoes

Prep + Cook Time: 60 minutes   **Servings:** 3

Ingredients:

- 4 medium potatoes
- 1/2 a can of tuna in oil; drained
- 1 teaspoon olive oil
- 1 green onion; sliced
- 1/2 teaspoon chili powder
- 1 tablespoon greek yogurt
- 1/2 tablespoon capers
- freshly ground black pepper to taste
- salt to taste

Instructions:

1. Soak the potatoes in water for about 30 minutes and pat dry with a kitchen towel. Brush potatoes with olive oil.
2. Place the potatoes in the Air Fryer basket and air fry for 30 minutes in a preheated Air Fryer at 355 - degrees Fahrenheit. Place tuna in a bowl.
3. Add yogurt and chili powder. Mash well. Add half the green onions, salt and pepper to taste.
4. Slit the potatoes lengthwise a little. Slightly press the potatoes to open up a bit.
5. Stuff the tuna mixture into it. Place on a serving plate.
6. Sprinkle some chili powder and remaining green onions over the potatoes.
7. Serve with capers and a salad of your choice.

231. Mouthwatering Fish Cakes

Prep + Cook Time: 1 hour 15 minutes   **Servings:** 4

Ingredients:

- 2 ounces flour
- 10 ounces cooked salmon
- 1 handful capers
- 1 teaspoon olive oil
- 1 handful parsley; chopped
- 1 teaspoon lemon zest
- 14 ounces boiled and mashed potatoes

Instructions:

1. Place the potatoes, flaked salmon, lemon zest, capers, and parsley in a large bowl. Mix with your hands until fully incorporated.
2. Make 4 large or 8 smaller cakes out of the mixture. Dust the fish cakes with flour.
3. Refrigerate for about 1 hour.
4. Preheat your Air Fryer to 350 - degrees Fahrenheit.
5. Heat the olive oil. Add the salmon cakes and cook for 7 minutes. Serve and enjoy!

232. Simple Fish Nuggets

Prep + Cook Time: 25 minutes   **Servings:** 4

Ingredients:

- 1-pound fresh cod
- 3/4 cup panko [Japanese breadcrumbs]
- 2 tablespoon olive oil
- 1/2 cup all-purpose flour
- 2 large eggs; beaten.
- salt to taste

Instructions:

1. To prepare the breading; mix the panko, olive oil, and salt in a shallow dish.
2. Prepare two more shallow dishes, one with the flour and one with the eggs.
3. Cut the cod into 1-inch by 2-inch strips.
4. Briefly preheat your Air Fryer to 350 - degrees Fahrenheit.
5. Bread the fish: - dredge each strip in flour, then dip in egg, and finally coat with the breading. Arrange the fish in the Fryer and cook until golden brown.
6. About 8 – 10 min.

233. Easy Crispy Nacho Crusted Prawns

Prep + Cook Time: 35 minutes   **Servings:** 8

Ingredients:

- 18 large prawns; peeled and deveined
- One Egg; beaten
- 8 – 9 ounces. nacho-flavored chips; crushed

Instructions:

1. Prepare two shallow dishes, one with the egg and one with the crushed chips. Dip each prawn in the egg and then coat in nacho crumbs.
2. Briefly preheat your Air Fryer to 350 - degrees Fahrenheit. Arrange the prawns in the Air Fryer; cook for 8 min, and serve.

234. Tasty Calamari with Tomato Sauce

Prep + Cook Time: 25 minutes   **Servings:** 4

Ingredients:

- 3 pounds' calamari [squid]
- 1 tablespoon fresh oregano
- 1/3 cup olive oil
- 1 teaspoon lemon juice
- 1 tablespoon minced garlic
- 1/4 teaspoon chopped fresh lemon peel
- 1/4 cup vinegar
- 1/4 teaspoon crushed red pepper; or taste

Sauce ingredients:

- 1-pound fresh whole tomatoes
- 3 cloves garlic; minced
- 1 tablespoon olive oil
- 1 stalk celery; chopped
- 1/2 green bell pepper; chopped
- 1/2 cup chopped onion
- Salt and black pepper; to taste

Instructions:

1. To make the sauce; combine all the sauce ingredients and add to a blender.
2. Blend until the mixture is finely smooth. Set aside for now.
3. Clean the calamari and cut into pieces.
4. Coat the calamari into vinegar, red pepper, lemon peel, garlic, lemon juice and oregano.
5. Add the oil to the air fryer.
6. Add the calamari with its juice. Air fry for about 6 minutes.

7. Stir once and air fry for another 2 minutes.
8. Serve hot with sauce you made.

235. Cod Teriyaki with Vegetable

Prep + Cook Time: 20 minutes   **Servings:** 2

Ingredients:

- 1 napa cabbage leaf; sliced to 0.2-inch thickness
- 6 pieces mini king oyster mushrooms; sliced to 0.1-inch thickness
- codfish; 1-inch thickness
- 1 clove garlic; roughly chopped
- sea salt to taste

- 1 tablespoon olive oil
- 1 green onion; minced
- steam rice or veggies; optional
- teriyaki sauce ingredients:
- 1 tablespoon brown sugar
- 2 tablespoon mirin
- 2 tablespoon soy sauce

Instructions:

1. Prepare Teriyaki sauce by combining all sauce ingredients; stir and place it aside.
2. Take the Air Fryer basket and grease it with oil. Place the mushrooms, napa cabbage leaf, garlic, and salt inside. Then layer the fish on top.
3. Preheat the fryer to 360 - degrees Fahrenheit for about 3 minutes. When it's hot; put the basket into the fryer. Cook for 5 minutes. Stir the ingredients.
4. Pour Teriyaki sauce over the ingredients in the basket.
5. Cook for another 5 minutes at the same temperature.
6. Transfer the meal to the plate, sprinkle it with green onion and serve with steam rice or veggies.

236. Grilled Salmon with Dill And Capers

Prep + Cook Time: 25 minutes   **Servings:** 2

Main Ingredients:

- 10 – 11 ounce. salmon fillet
- 1 teaspoon capers; chopped
- 2 sprigs dill; chopped

- 1 tablespoon olive oil
- 1 lemon; zest
- sea salt to taste

Dressing Ingredients:

- 5 capers; chopped
- 1 pinch of lemon zest
- 2 tablespoon plain yogurt

- 1 sprig dill; chopped
- sea salt to taste
- black pepper to taste

to decorate:

- 3 – 4 slices of lemon; optional

Instructions:

1. Preheat the Air Fryer to 400 - degrees Fahrenheit.
2. Take a large bowl and combine the main ingredients such as lemon zest, dill, capers, olive oil, and salt.
3. Stir well and cover the salmon with this mixture.
4. When the Air Fryer is hot; adjust the time to 8 minutes. Put the salmon into the basket and cook.
5. In the meantime; make the dressing. Combine all the dressing ingredients and mix them in a separate bowl.
6. When the salmon is ready, transfer it to the plate, coat it with the dressing and serve hot.
7. You may add a few slices of lemon as a decoration.

Appetizers

237. Buffalo Cauliflower

Prep + Cook Time: 30 minutes   **Servings:** 4

Ingredients:

- 4 cups cauliflower florets [bite-sized]
- 1 cup panko breadcrumbs [mixed with 1teaspoon salt]
- 1/4 cup melted butter [vegan/other]
- 1/4 cup buffalo sauce [vegan/other]
- mayo [vegan/other] or creamy dressing for dipping

Instructions:

1. Take a bowl and mix butter and buffalo sauce in it. Stir it till it gives you a creamy paste.
2. Now dip each floret in the sauce using a stem until the floret is coated from everywhere. Make sure the florets are covered well.
3. After that cover the floret with the salt mixture that you have already prepared. Now fry the floret in the Air Fryer for approximately 15 minutes; at 350 - degrees Fahrenheit.
4. Check the progress half way and shake them periodically. Now serve them in a platter with any dip or sauce you like or with a raw vegetable salad.

238. Hot Air Fried Mushrooms

Prep + Cook Time: 40 minutes   **Servings:** 4

Ingredients:

- 2 pounds button mushrooms
- 3 tablespoons white or french vermouth [optional]

- 1 tablespoon coconut oil
- 2 teaspoon herbs of your choice
- 1/2 teaspoon garlic powder

Instructions:

1. Thoroughly wash your mushrooms and then dry them. Cut them into quarters and set them aside.
2. Heat your Air Fryer to 320 – degrees Fahrenheit and add the following ingredients to the basket: duck fat [or coconut oil], garlic powder, and herbs.
3. Warm the ingredients for 2 minutes; stir and then add the mushrooms.
4. Cook the mushrooms for 25 minutes; stirring periodically.
5. Add white vermouth; stir and cook for another 5 minutes.
6. Serve hot and enjoy!

239. Easy Cheesy Garlic Bread

Prep + Cook Time: 20 minutes   **Servings:** 2

Ingredients:

- 5 round bread slices
- 4 teaspoon melted butter
- 3 chopped garlic cloves

- 5 teaspoon sun dried tomato pesto
- 1 cup grated mozzarella cheese

Instructions:

1. As I'm using baguette bread for my preparation; I will first cut it into thick round slices.
2. Apply some melted butter [in which garlic cloves were added] on the bread slices.
3. Apply a teaspoon of sun dried tomato pesto to each of the slice.
4. Add a generous amount of grated cheese on the top of each slice.
5. Place these bread slices in Air Fryer and cook them at 180 - degrees Fahrenheit for 6 – 8 minutes.

6. Garnish with some more freshly chopped basil leaves, chilli flakes and oregano.
7. Enjoy tasty cheesy garlic bread with ketchup as snack or appetizer.

240. Tasty Garlic Stuffed Mushrooms

Prep + Cook Time: 25 minutes   **Servings:** 4

Ingredients:

- 6 small mushrooms
- 1 tablespoon onion; peeled/diced
- 1 tablespoon breadcrumbs
- 1 tablespoon olive oil
- 1 teaspoon garlic; pureed
- 1 teaspoon parsley
- salt to taste
- pepper to taste

Instructions:

1. Mix breadcrumbs, oil, onion, parsley, salt, pepper and garlic in a medium sized bowl.
2. Remove middle stalks from mushrooms and fill them with crumb mixture. Cook in Air Fryer for 10 minutes at 350 - degrees Fahrenheit.
3. Serve with mayo dip and enjoy the right combination

241. Herbed Grilled Tomatoes

Prep + Cook Time: 25 minutes   **Servings:** 2

Ingredients:

- 2 tomatoes; medium to large
- herbs of choice to taste
- pepper to taste
- high quality cooking spray

Instructions:

1. Thoroughly wash tomatoes, pat them dry, and halve them.
2. Turn them over so the skin is up, and lightly spray them with a quick spray of cooking oil.
3. Turn halves cut side up and spray again, lightly with one quick spray.
4. Sprinkle the halves with your choice of herbs and some black pepper. [Ideal herbs: oregano, basil, parsley, rosemary, thyme, sage, etc.] Place halves into the tray of your Air Fryer. Cook for 20 minutes at 320 - degrees Fahrenheit.
5. After 20 minutes; check to see if they are done.
6. If not; you can add an extra 5 minutes on the cook time until they are cooked to your desired doneness.
7. Larger tomatoes will need more cook time.

242. Roasted Carrots

Prep + Cook Time: 40 minutes   **Servings:** 4

Ingredients:

- 1-pound carrots
- 4 tablespoon orange juice; no pulp
- 2 teaspoon extra virgin olive oil
- 1 teaspoon herbes de provence; or herbs of choice

Instructions:

1. Thoroughly wash the carrots and cut them into 1-inch cubes. Do not peel them.
2. Preheat your Air Fryer to 320 - degrees Fahrenheit.
3. Put the carrot chunks into your Air Fryer basket; add the herbs and then coat with oil. [Always add oil after herbs so the herbs are wet and don't get blown around the Air Fryer.] Roast the mixture for 20 minutes.
4. After 20 minutes; add the orange juice and continue roasting for an additional 5 minutes.
5. Serve the carrots hot.

243. Carrots and Rhubarb

Prep + Cook Time: 35 minutes   **Servings:** 4

Ingredients:

- 1-pound heritage carrots
- 1-pound rhubarb
- 1 orange; medium
- 1/2 cup walnuts; halved
- 2 teaspoon walnut oil
- 1/2 teaspoon stevia [or a few drops of stevia extract]

Instructions:

1. Thoroughly wash carrots, and pat them dry.
2. Cut them into 1-inch pieces and place them in the Air Fryer basket with walnut oil.
3. Heat fryer to 320 - degrees Fahrenheit and cook the carrots for about 20 minutes.
4. In the meantime; thoroughly wash the rhubarb and cut it into 1/2-inch pieces. Set aside.
5. Roughly chop the walnuts; and set aside.
6. Thoroughly wash the orange, zest it and then set the zest aside. Peel and section the rest of the orange, and set the sections aside.
7. After cooking the carrots for 20 minutes; add the rhubarb, walnuts and stevia and cook it for another 5 minutes.
8. Stir in 2 tablespoons of orange zest, and add the peeled sections of the orange to the dish. Serve immediately.

244. Bacon Croquettes

Prep + Cook Time: 50 minutes   **Servings:** 6

Ingredients:

For the Filling

- 1-pound sharp cheddar cheese; block
- 1-pound bacon; thinly sliced, room temperature

For the Breading

- 4 tablespoon olive oil 1 cup all-purpose flour
- two eggs; beaten
- 1 cup seasoned breadcrumbs

Instructions:

1. Cut the cheddar cheese block into 6 equally sized portions, approximately 1-inch x 1 ¾ -inch each.
2. Take two pieces of bacon and wrap them around each piece of cheddar, fully enclosing the cheese. Trim any excess fat.
3. Place the cheddar bacon bites in the freezer for 5 minutes to firm. Do not freeze.
4. Preheat the Air Fryer to 390 - degrees Fahrenheit.
5. Mix the oil and breadcrumbs and stir until the mixture becomes loose and crumbly.
6. Place each cheddar block into the flour; then the eggs and then the breadcrumbs. Press coating to croquettes to ensure it adheres.
7. Place the croquettes in the cooking basket and cook for 7 – 8 minutes or until golden brown.

Tips: To ensure the cheese does not run out, double coat them by dipping them a second time into the egg and then into the bread crumbs.

245. Air Fried Broccoli

Prep + Cook Time: 30 minutes   **Servings:** 4

Ingredients:

- 1 head broccoli; large
- 1/2 lemon; juiced
- 3 cloves garlic; minced
- 1 tablespoon coconut oil
- 1 tablespoon sesame seeds; white
- 2 teaspoon maggi sauce; or other seasonings to taste

Instructions:

1. Thoroughly wash head of broccoli and then chop into bite-sized pieces.
2. Pat pieces dry and set them aside.
3. Peel garlic; mince and set aside in your Air Fryer basket, combine duck fat [or coconut oil] with lemon juice and Maggi sauce.
4. Heat the concoction for 2 minutes at 320 - degrees Fahrenheit and stir. Add garlic and broccoli, combine and cook for 13 minutes.
5. Sprinkle white sesame seeds over broccoli and cook for a final 5 minutes; just to toast the sesame seeds.

246. Yummy Maple Glazed Beets

Prep + Cook Time: 60 minutes   **Servings:** 8

Ingredients:

- 3.5 pounds beetroots
- 4 tablespoon maple syrup
- 1 tablespoon coconut oil

Instructions:

1. Gently but thoroughly wash the beets; then peel them. Chop them into 1-inch pieces and set them aside.
2. Put the duck fat or coconut oil in the Air Fryer and heat for 1 minute at 320 – degrees Fahrenheit until melted.
3. Add the beet cubes to the Air Fryer Basket Cook for 40 minutes. Cover the beetroots in half of the maple syrup and cook for an additional 10 minutes; or until the beets are fork tender.
4. When the beets are done to your desire, toss them with the remaining half of the maple syrup.
5. Serve immediately.

247. Endive Marinated in Curried Yogurt

Prep + Cook Time: 20 minutes   **Servings:** 6

Ingredients:

- 6 heads endive
- 1/2 cup yogurt; plain and fat-free
- 3 tablespoon lemon juice
- 1 teaspoon garlic powder [or 2 minced cloves of garlic]
- 1/2 teaspoon curry powder
- salt and ground black pepper to taste

Instructions:

1. Thoroughly wash endives; then halve them lengthwise through the root end. Set the endives aside.
2. In a bowl; combine yogurt, lemon juice, garlic powder [or mince], curry powder, salt and pepper.
3. If you need the marinated thinner, add more lemon juice.
4. Take the endive halves and either toss them in the marinade, or generously brush them with it. Cover the pieces and let them marinade for at least 30 minutes, or as long as a day.
5. Preheat Air Fryer to 320 – degrees Fahrenheit and cook the endives for 10 minutes Serve hot

248. Tasty Tofu

Prep + Cook Time: 35 minutes

Servings: 4

Ingredients:

- 1x 12 ounces. package tofu; low-fat and extra firm
- 2 tablespoon soy sauce; low-sodium
- 2 tablespoon fish sauce
- 1 tablespoon coriander paste
- 1 teaspoon sesame oil
- 1 teaspoon duck fat [or coconut oil]
- 1 teaspoon maggi sauce

Instructions:

1. Drain the package of tofu and then cut the contents into 1-inch cubes. Place them out on a paper towel lined plate evenly, and in a single layer.
2. Cover them with more paper towel, put another plate on top and place something on it to weigh it down.
3. This will thoroughly dry your tofu out. You can change the paper towel once or twice to get it extra dry.
4. Ideally you should dry tofu for at least 30 minutes before cooking with it; though you can go as long as overnight if you have the time.
5. In a medium bowl; mix together: sesame oil, Maggi sauce, coriander paste, fish sauce, and soy sauce. Blend thoroughly to make your marinade.
6. Place your dried tofu into the marinade bowl and mix thoroughly so they are evenly coated.
7. Let the cubes marinate for about 30 minutes; or longer if possible.
8. Toss the cubes a few times while marinating to keep them evenly coated and make sure they all get a strong dose of flavor.
9. If the marinade is too thick and isn't coating well, add an additional squirt of fish sauce or soy sauce to thin it out and help it spread easier.
10. Heat your Air Fryer to 350 – degrees Fahrenheit and let your duck fat or coconut oil melt for about 2 minutes. Add the tofu cubes to the basket and let them cook for about 20 minutes.
11. If you prefer them extra crispy; you can cook them for as long as 30 minutes. Turn the cubes or shake the basket every 10 minutes to keep them frying evenly and thoroughly.
12. Serve hot with your choice of dipping sauce.

249. Roasted Peppers

Prep + Cook Time: 40 minutes

Servings: 4

Ingredients:

- 12 bell peppers; medium
- 1 sweet onion; small
- 1 tablespoon maggi sauce
- 1 tablespoon extra virgin olive oil

Instructions:

1. Heat your Air Fryer to 320 – degrees Fahrenheit and warm the extra virgin olive oil and Maggi sauce together. Peel the onion, chop it into 1-inch slices, and put it in the warmed oil mixture in the Air Fryer.
2. Wash the peppers, destem them, cut them into 1-inch pieces, and clean out the seeds. If you need to, rinse away the tough seeds and pat the peppers dry.
3. Add them to the Air Fryer. Cook for about 25 minutes; give or take depending on what your preferred doneness is.

250. Roasted Parsnip

Prep + Cook Time: 55 minutes

Servings: 5

Ingredients:

- 2 pounds parsnips [about 6 large parsnips]
- 2 tablespoon maple syrup
- 1 tablespoon coconut oil
- 1 tablespoon parsley; dried flakes

Instructions:

1. Put the duck fat or coconut oil in your Air Fryer and heat for 2 minutes at 320 - degrees Fahrenheit until melted.
2. Thoroughly wash your parsnips and peel them; then cut into 1-inch cubes. Put the parsnip cubes into the melted duck fat [or coconut oil].
3. Cook the parsnip cubes for 40 minutes; tossing them periodically.
4. Test for fork tenderness and add a few minutes to the cook time if necessary. In the final five minutes of cooking, sprinkle the parsnips with parsley and maple syrup.
5. Serve immediately.

251. Zucchini Cheese Boats

Prep + Cook Time: 30 minutes   **Servings:** 2

Ingredients:

- 1 cup ground chicken
- 1 zucchini
- 1 ½ cups crushed tomatoes
- 1/2 teaspoon salt
- 1/4 teaspoon pepper

- 1/2 teaspoon garlic powder
- 2 tablespoon butter or olive oil
- 1/2 cup cheese; grated
- 1/4 teaspoon dried oregano

Instructions:

1. Peel the zucchini and cut them into half. Scoop out the flesh from inside.
2. Combine the ground chicken, tomato, garlic powder, butter, cheese, oregano, salt, pepper in a mixing bowl.
3. Mix well and add in the middle of the zucchinis.
4. Add them to the Air Fryer and bake for about 10 minutes with 400 - degrees Fahrenheit. Serve warm.

252. Cajun Spiced Snack

Prep + Cook Time: 30 minutes   **Servings:** 10

Ingredients:

- 1/2 cup butter; melted
- 2 tablespoon Cajun or Creole seasoning
- 2 cups mini wheat thin crackers

- 2 cups peanuts
- 2 cups mini pretzels
- 4 cups plain popcorn

Cajun Seasoning:

- 2 teaspoon salt
- 1 teaspoon cayenne pepper
- 1 teaspoon garlic
- 1 teaspoon paprika

- 1/2 teaspoon oregano
- 1/2 teaspoon thyme
- 1/2 teaspoon onion powder
- 1 teaspoon black pepper

Instructions:

1. Pre-heat Air Fryer to 370 - degrees Fahrenheit.
2. Combine the melted butter and Cajun spice in a small bowl.
3. In a large bowl; combine the crackers, peanuts, pretzels, and popcorn.
4. Pour the butter over the mixed snacks and toss evenly to coat the mixture.
5. Air-fry the snack mix two batches. Place half of the snack mix in the Air Fryer basket and air-fry for 8 to 10 minutes until lightly toasted.
6. Toss the basket several times throughout the process for even cooking.
7. Transfer the snack mix to a cookie sheet and cool completely.
8. Store in an airtight container for up to one week, or place in gift bags with tags and ribbons for gift giving.

253. Tasty Roasted Eggplant

Prep + Cook Time: 45 minutes   **Servings:** 6

Ingredients:

- 3 eggplants; medium
- 1/2 lemon; juiced
- 1 tablespoon duck fat; or coconut oil
- 1 tablespoon maggi sauce
- 3 teaspoon za'atar

- 1 teaspoon sumac
- 1 teaspoon garlic powder
- 1 teaspoon onion powder
- 1 teaspoon extra virgin olive oil
- 2 bay leaves

Instructions:

1. Thoroughly wash your eggplants and pat them dry. Destem the eggplants, then cut them into 1-inch cubes. Set the cubes aside.
2. In your Air Fryer basket; combine duck fat [or coconut oil], maggi sauce, za'atar, onion powder, garlic powder, sumac and bay leaves.
3. Cook the ingredients for 2 minutes at 320 - degrees Fahrenheit until melted. Stir together.
4. Add the eggplant into the Air Fryer basket. Cook the eggplant for 25 minutes.
5. In a large mixing bowl; combine the lemon juice and extra virgin olive oil. Stir in the cooked eggplant and toss until they are evenly coated.
6. Serve immediately with an optional garnish of grated parmesan or fresh chopped basil.

254. Sweet Potato Fries

Prep + Cook Time: 35 minutes   **Servings:** 5

Ingredients:

- 2 sweet potatoes; large

- 1 tablespoon extra-virgin olive oil

Instructions:

1. Wash and peel the sweet potatoes Chop into shoestring fries and place into a large bowl. Using clean hands, add the oil and then toss the fries thoroughly.
2. Make sure all of the fries are thoroughly coated so they don't stick to each other, and they cook evenly.
3. Set your Air Fryer to 320 - degrees Fahrenheit; place sweet potatoes in the Air Fryer basket and fry them for 15 minutes.
4. Toss them once about halfway through the cooking process.
5. After 15 minutes; give the fries a really thorough toss.
6. Raise the Air Fryer temperature to 350 - degrees Fahrenheit and cook sweet potato fries for another 5 minutes.
7. Thoroughly toss your sweet potato fries, and then let them fry for another 5 minutes. Serve your fries immediately, straight out of the Air Fryer.

255. Mushroom and Spinach Chicken Pizza

Prep + Cook Time: 25 minutes   **Servings:** 4

Ingredients:

- 10.5 ounces. minced chicken
- 1 teaspoon garlic powder
- 1 teaspoon black pepper

- 2 tablespoon tomato basil sauce
- 5 button mushrooms; sliced thinly
- A handful of spinach

Instructions:

1. Preheat Air Fryer 450 – degrees Fahrenheit.
2. Add parchment paper onto your baking tray.
3. In a large bowl add the chicken with the black pepper and garlic powder.
4. Add one spoonful of the chicken mix onto your baking tray.
5. Flatten them into 7-inch rounds.
6. Bake in the Air Fryer for about 10 minutes.
7. Take out off the Air Fryer and add the tomato basil sauce onto each round.
8. Add the mushroom on top. Bake again for 5 minutes.
9. Serve immediately.

256. Ground Turkey Sausage Patties

Prep + Cook Time: 20 minutes   **Servings:** 6

Ingredients:

- 1 Pound lean ground turkey
- 1 teaspoon olive oil
- 1 tablespoon chopped chives
- 1 small onion; diced
- 1 large garlic clove; chopped
- 3/4 teaspoon paprika
- Kosher salt and pepper to taste
- A pinch raw sugar
- 1 tablespoon vinegar
- 1 teaspoon fennel seed
- A pinch nutmeg

Instructions:

1. Preheat the Air Fryer to 375 - degrees Fahrenheit.
2. Add half the oil and the onion and garlic to the Air Fryer.
3. Air fry for 30 seconds and then add the fennel.
4. Transfer them to a plate. In a mixing bowl add in the ground turkey.
5. Add the sugar, paprika, nutmeg, vinegar, chives and the onion mixture. Mix well and form patties of your desired size.
6. Add the rest of the oil to the Air Fryer.
7. Add the patties and air fry for about 3 minutes.
8. Serve with lettuce leaves or buns.

257. Crispy Spring Rolls

Prep + Cook Time: 45 minutes   **Servings:** 4

Ingredients:

For the Filling:
- 4 ounces. cooked chicken breast; shredded
- 1 celery stalk; sliced thin
- 1 medium carrot; sliced thin
- 1/2 cup mushrooms; sliced thin
- 1/2 teaspoon ginger; finely chopped
- 1 teaspoon sugar
- 1 teaspoon chicken stock powder

For the Spring Roll Wrappers:
- One Egg; beaten
- 1 teaspoon cornstarch
- 8 spring roll wrappers
- 1/2 teaspoon vegetable oil

Instructions:

1. Make the filling. Place the shredded chicken into a bowl and mix with the celery, carrot and mushrooms.
2. Add the ginger, sugar and chicken stock powder and stir evenly.

3. Combine the egg with the cornstarch and mix to create a thick paste and set aside. Place some filling onto each spring roll wrapper and roll it up, sealing the ends with the egg mixture.
4. Preheat the Air Fryer to 390 - degrees Fahrenheit.
5. Lightly brush the spring rolls with oil prior to placing in the cooking basket.
6. Cook for 3 – 4 minutes or until golden brown.
7. Serve with sweet chili sauce or soy sauce.

258. Delicious Zucchini Wedges

Prep + Cook Time: 45 minutes   **Servings:** 4

Ingredients:

- 2 zucchinis; medium and fully ripe
- 1/2 cup panko bread crumbs; or anything else you have on hand
- 1/4 cup egg whites [approximately 2 eggs whites]
- 1/4 cup parmesan cheese; grated
- 1/4 teaspoon cayenne pepper
- 1/4 teaspoon basil
- 1/4 teaspoon oregano
- high quality cooking spray

Instructions:

1. In a medium bowl; combine panko bread crumbs, parmesan cheese, cayenne pepper, basil, and oregano.
2. Mix until well blended and then set aside. Thoroughly wash your zucchinis, and pat them dry. Don't peel them. Cut the zucchini in half crosswise and then cut it into wedges no more than 1/2 inch thick.
3. Spray the Air Fryer basket with a high-quality cooking spray. In a shallow bowl or dish, lightly beat egg whites.
4. Then; in another shallow dish, place a small portion of your breadcrumb mix. [Only work with a small portion at a time so it doesn't become drenched with egg whites and then unusable.]
5. With each wedge, dip the zucchini into the egg white and then thoroughly coat it with the bread crumbs, pressing them down so they stay in place.
6. Put your zucchini wedges into the Air Fryer pan. Do not overfill your Air Fryer pan; cook in a single layer in multiple batches if necessary. Once your basket is full, lightly spray the wedges with your high-quality cooking spray.
7. Heat the Air Fryer to 350 - degrees Fahrenheit and cook the wedges for about 7 minutes and then turn them over.
8. Cook them for an additional 7 minutes and then remove them from the Air Fryer. Place the finished wedges in a serving dish that can be kept warm while you complete additional batches.
9. Serve the wedges hot with your choice of dipping sauce.

259. Cheesy Bacon Fries

Prep + Cook Time: 60 minutes   **Servings:** 3

Ingredients:

- 2 large russet potatoes; peeled and cut into 1/2 inch sticks
- 5 slices of bacon; diced
- 2 tablespoon vegetable oil
- 2 ½ cups shredded Cheddar cheese
- 3 ounces. cream cheese; melted
- salt and freshly ground black pepper
- 1/4 cup chopped scallions
- Ranch dressing

Instructions:

1. Bring a large pot of salted water to a boil while you prepare the potatoes. Blanch the potatoes in the boiling water for 4 minutes.
2. Strain the potatoes in a colander and rinse them with cold water to wash off the starch. Dry them well with a clean kitchen towel.
3. Pre-heat the Air Fryer to 400 – degrees Fahrenheit.

4. Place the chopped bacon into the Air Fryer and air-fry for 4 minutes; shaking the basket halfway through the cooking process.
5. Drain the bacon on paper towels and discard the grease from the bottom of the Air Fryer drawer.
6. Toss the dried potato sticks with oil and place them in the Air Fryer basket. Air-fry at 360 - degrees Fahrenheit for 25 minutes, shaking the basket a few times throughout the cooking time to help them cook evenly.
7. Season the fries with salt and freshly ground black pepper midway through cooking.
8. Transfer the French fries from the basket to a 7- or 8-inch [whatever will fit your Air Fryer] baking pan or casserole dish.
9. Mix the 2 cups of the Cheddar cheese with the melted cream cheese.
10. Dollop the cheese mixture over the potatoes. Sprinkle the remaining Cheddar cheese over the potatoes and then top with the cooked bacon crumbles.
11. Lower the baking pan into the cooker using a sling made of aluminum foil [fold a piece of aluminum foil into a strip about 2-inches wide by 24-inches long].
12. Air-fry at 340 - degrees Fahrenheit for 5 minutes to melt the cheeses.
13. Sprinkle chopped scallions over the fries and serve in the baking dish with ranch dressing on the side.

260. Easy Toasted Pumpkin Seeds

Prep + Cook Time: 25 minutes   **Servings:** 4

Ingredients:

- 1 ½ cups pumpkin seeds [cut a whole pumpkin & scrape out the insides using a large spoon; separating the seeds from the flesh]
- 1 teaspoon smoked paprika
- 1 ½ teaspoon salt
- olive oil

Instructions:

1. Rinse the pumpkin seeds under cold running water.
2. Over moderate heat settings; bring two quarts of water, preferably well-salted, to a boil. Once boiling, add in the pumpkin seeds and let boil for 8 to 10 minutes.
3. Drain the seeds and then spread them on paper towels and let dry for a minimum of 20 minutes.
4. Pre-heat your Air Fryer to 350 - degrees Fahrenheit.
5. In a medium size bowl toss the pumpkin seeds with olive oil, smoked paprika and salt. Transfer them to the basket of your Air Fryer.
6. Air-fry for a minimum period of half an hour until slightly browned and crispy, during the cooking process, shake the basket couple of times.
7. Just before serving or storing the cooked seeds in an air-tight bag or container, let the seeds to cool at room temperature. Enjoy them as a topping for salads or as a snack.

261. Salmon Croquettes

Prep + Cook Time: 20 minutes   **Servings:** 4

Ingredients:

- two eggs [beaten; lightly]
- 1 large tin of red salmon [drained]
- 1 cup bread crumbs
- 1/3 cup vegetable oil
- 1/2 bunch of parsley; roughly chopped
- 1/8 teaspoon black pepper

Instructions:

1. Preheat Air Fryer to 390 - degrees Fahrenheit.
2. Mix together the salmon and mix with herbs, egg, and the seasoning.

3. Mix together the bread crumbs and oil in another bowl, until you get a loose mixture that can act as a glue for our croquettes.
4. Shape the salmon mix into 16 small croquettes, and coat them in the crumb mixture. In batches, put the croquettes in the basket and slide into the Air Fryer.
5. Wait until golden brown.
6. Serve and enjoy!

262. Stuffed Fried Banana Peppers

Prep + Cook Time: 20 minutes   **Servings:** 8

Ingredients:

- 1 cup full fat cream cheese cooking spray
- 16 avocado slices
- 16 salami pieces
- salt to taste
- 16 banana peppers
- pepper to taste

Instructions:

1. Preheat the Air Fryer to 400 - degrees Fahrenheit. Take a baking tray and grease it with cooking spray.
2. Use a knife to cut out the stem of banana peppers.
3. Cut a slit onto one side of each banana peppers and set aside for now.
4. Sprinkle the salt and pepper onto the cream cheese and mix well.
5. Add one spoonful of the cream cheese into each banana pepper. Add one slice of avocado in each banana pepper.
6. Wrap the banana peppers using salami pieces. Seal with a toothpick. Add your baking tray and add to the Air Fryer. Bake for about 8 to 10 minutes.

263. Spicy Molasses Barbecue Sauce With Wings

Prep + Cook Time: 20 minutes   **Servings:** 6

Ingredients:

For the Sauce:

- 1 tablespoon yellow mustard
- 1 tablespoon apple cider vinegar
- 1 tablespoon olive oil
- 1/4 cup unsulfured blackstrap molasses
- 1/4 cup ketchup
- 2 tablespoons brown sugar
- 1 garlic clove; minced
- Salt and ground black pepper; to taste
- 1/8 teaspoon ground allspice
- 1/4 cup water

For the Wings:

- 2 pounds chicken wings
- 1/4 teaspoon celery salt
- 1/4 cup habanero hot sauce
- Chopped fresh parsley; or garnish

Instructions:

1. In a sauté pan that is preheated over a medium-high flame, place all the ingredients for the sauce and bring it to a boil
2. Then; reduce the temperature and simmer until it has thickened.
3. Meanwhile; preheat your Air Fryer to 400 – degrees Fahrenheit cook the chicken wings for 6 minutes
4. flip them over and cook for additional 6 minutes. Season them with celery salt.
5. Serve with the prepared sauce and habanero hot sauce, garnished with fresh parsley leaves.

264. Tasty Coconut Shrimp

Prep + Cook Time: 20 minutes   **Servings:** 16

Ingredients:

- 1/2 teaspoon salt
- 1 Pound large shrimp [about 16 to 20 peeled/de-veined]
- 1/2 cup flour
- 2 eggs whites
- 1/2 cup fine breadcrumbs
- 1/2 cup shredded unsweetened coconut zest of one lime
- 1/4 teaspoon cayenne pepper spray can of vegetable or canola oil
- sweet chili sauce or duck sauce [for serving]

Instructions:

1. Whisk the eggs in a shallow dish.
2. Combine the breadcrumbs, coconut, lime zest, salt and cayenne pepper in another dish.
3. Pre-heat the Air Fryer to 400 – degrees Fahrenheit.
4. Dip each shrimp into the flour. Next; dip the shrimp into the egg mixture, and then into the breadcrumb coconut mixture to coat all sides.
5. Place the breaded shrimp on a plate and spray with oil. Air fry shrimp but don't overcrowd basket.
6. Cook the shrimp for 5 - 6 minutes or before it gets to the point that each shrimp is firm and cooked.

265. Tortilla Chips

Prep + Cook Time: 5 minutes   **Servings:** 2

Ingredients:

- 8 corn tortillas
- salt to taste
- 1 tablespoon olive oil

Instructions:

1. Set temperature to 390 - degrees Fahrenheit.
2. Cut corn tortillas into triangles. Brush with olive oil. Place tortilla pieces in wire basket in small batches and air fry for 3 minutes.
3. Repeat until all tortilla chips are cooked. Sprinkle with salt.

266. Chutney and Naan Bread Dippers

Prep + Cook Time: 50 minutes   **Servings:** 10

Ingredients:

- 4 loaves naan bread cut into 2-inch strips
- 3 tablespoon butter; melted
- 12 ounces light cream cheese; softened
- 1 cup plain yogurt
- 2 teaspoon curry powder
- 2 cups cooked chicken; shredded
- 4 scallions; minced
- 1/3 cup golden raisins
- 6 ounces Monterey Jack cheese; grated [about 2 cups]
- 1/4 cup chopped fresh cilantro
- salt and freshly ground black pepper
- 1/2 cup sliced almonds
- 1/2 cup Major Grey's Chutney

Instructions:

1. Pre-heat Air Fryer to 400 - degrees Fahrenheit. Cut the naan in thirds lengthwise and then cut crosswise into 2-inch strips. Place in large bowl and toss with melted butter.
2. In 2 batches, place naan strips into Air Fryer basket. Air-fry for 5 minutes until naan is toasted.
3. Shake and toss basket halfway through.
4. Using a hand mixer; stand mixer or food processor, beat the softened cream cheese and yogurt together.

5. Add the curry powder and mix until evenly combined.
6. Fold in the shredded chicken, scallions, golden raisins, Monterey Jack cheese and chopped cilantro.
7. Season to taste with salt and freshly ground black pepper.
8. Spread the mixture evenly into a 1-quart baking dish. Top with the sliced almonds. If making ahead, cover the dish with plastic wrap and refrigerate.
9. Remember to remove the dip one hour before ready to serve.
10. Air-fry at 300 - degrees Fahrenheit for 25 minutes.
11. Before serving; spoon the Major Grey's chutney in the center of the dip and garnish with scallions.
12. Serve hot with toasted naan dippers.

267. Salty and Sweet Snack Mix

Prep + Cook Time: 30 minutes　　　　　　　　**Servings:** 10

Ingredients:

- 1/2 cup honey
- 3 tablespoon butter; melted
- 1 teaspoon salt
- 2 cups sesame sticks
- 1 cup pepitas [pumpkin seeds]
- 2 cups granola
- 1 cup cashews
- 2 cups crispy corn puff cereal [Kix or Corn Pops]
- 2 cup mini pretzel crisps

Instructions:

1. Combine the honey, butter, and salt. Stir until combined.
2. In a large bowl; combine the sesame sticks, pepitas, granola, cashews, corn puff cereal, and pretzel crisps.
3. Pour the honey mixture over the top and toss to combine.
4. Preheat Air Fryer to 370 – degrees Fahrenheit.
5. Air fry the snack mix in two batches. Place half the mixture in the Air Fryer basket and air-fry for 10 to12 minutes; or until the snack mix is lightly toasted.
6. Toss the basket several times throughout the process so that it cooks evenly and doesn't get too dark on top.
7. Transfer the snack mix to a cookie sheet and let it cool completely.
8. Store in an airtight container for up to one week; or package in gift bags with tags and ribbons for holiday gift giving.

268. Veg Spring Rolls

Prep + Cook Time: 20 minutes　　　　　　　　**Servings:** 2

Ingredients:

Roll:
- 10 Spring roll sheets
- 2 tablespoon corn flour [you can substitute for maida if necessary]

Stuffing:
- 2 cups shredded cabbage
- 1 carrot
- 2 whole onions
- 1/2 teaspoon capsicum
- 1 whole ginger
- 1 whole garlic clove
- Pinch of sugar
- 1 tablespoon pepper powder
- 1 teaspoon soy sauce
- salt to taste
- 2 tablespoon cooking oil
- 2 spring onions [for garnish]

Instructions:

1. Defrost spring rolls until soft and room temperature.
2. Chop carrots, onions, ginger, garlic, and capsicum into thin slices.

3. Set Air Fryer temperature to 355 - degrees Fahrenheit.
4. Roll filling into the spring roll. Use a brush to lightly add oil to the spring rolls.
5. Place rolls in Air Fryer basket.
6. Bake the rolls in the Air Fryer for 10 minutes.
7. Remove the basket from the Air Fryer and flip each spring roll over to ensure that it is properly baked on both sides of the spring roll.
8. If rolls remain white; bake it for another 2 - 3 minutes.
9. serve hot and enjoy!

269. Yummy Feta Triangles

Prep + Cook Time: 55 minutes   **Servings:** 5

Ingredients:

- One Egg yolk
- 4 ounces. feta cheese
- 2 tablespoon flat-leafed parsley; finely chopped
- 1 scallion; finely chopped
- 2 sheets of frozen filo pastry; defrosted
- 2 tablespoon olive oil
- ground black pepper to taste

Instructions:

1. Beat the egg yolk in a bowl and mix in the feta, parsley and scallion.
2. Season with pepper to taste.
3. Cut each sheet of filo dough into three strips.
4. Scoop a full teaspoon of the feta mixture on the underside of a strip of pastry.
5. Fold the tip of the pastry over the filling to form a triangle, folding the strip in a zigzag manner until the filling is wrapped in a triangle. Repeat until all the filo and feta has been used.
6. Preheat the Air Fryer to 390 - degrees Fahrenheit. Brush the filo with a little oil and place six triangles in the cooking basket.
7. Slide the basket into the Air Fryer and cook for 3 minutes.
8. Change temperature to 360 - degrees Fahrenheit and then cook 2 minutes or until golden brown.
9. Serve & Enjoy!

270. Special Crab Rangoon Dip with Wonton Chips

Prep + Cook Time: 55 minutes   **Servings:** 6

Ingredients:

Wonton Chips:

- 1 [12-oz] package wonton wrappers
- vegetable oil
- sea salt

Crab Rangoon Dip:

- 8 ounces cream cheese; softened
- 3/4 cup sour cream
- 1 teaspoon Worcestershire sauce
- 1 ½ teaspoon soy sauce
- 1 teaspoon sesame oil
- 1/8 teaspoon cayenne pepper
- 1/4 teaspoon salt
- freshly ground black pepper
- 8 ounces. cooked crabmeat
- 1 cup grated white Cheddar cheese
- 1/3 cup chopped scallions
- paprika [for garnish]

Instructions:

1. Cut the wonton wrappers in half diagonally to form triangles. Working in batches, lay the wonton triangles on a flat surface and brush or spray both sides with vegetable oil.
2. Pre-heat the Air Fryer to 370 - degrees Fahrenheit.
3. Place about 10 to 12 wonton triangles in the air fry basket; letting them overlap slightly.

4. Air-fry for just 2 minutes; shaking the basket half way through the cooking time.
5. Transfer the wonton chips to large bowl and season immediately with sea salt. [You'll hear the chips start to spin around in the Air Fryer when they are almost done.]
6. Repeat with the rest of wontons [keeping those fishing hands at bay!].
7. To make the dip; combine the cream cheese, sour cream, Worcestershire sauce, soy sauce, sesame oil, cayenne pepper, salt, and freshly ground black pepper in a bowl.
8. Mix well and then fold in the crabmeat, Cheddar cheese, and scallions.
9. Transfer the dip to a 7-inch ceramic baking pan or shallow casserole dish.
10. Sprinkle paprika on top and cover the dish with aluminum foil.
11. Lower the dish into the Air Fryer basket using a sling made of aluminum foil [fold a piece of aluminum foil into a strip about 2-inches wide by 24-inches long]. Air-fry for 11 minutes.
12. Remove the aluminum foil and air-fry for another 5 minutes to finish cooking and brown the top.
13. Sprinkle with paprika and serve hot with the wonton chips.

271. Onion and Sage Stuffing Balls

Prep + Cook Time: 35 minutes　　　　　　　　　　**Servings:** 6

Ingredients:

- 2 Pounds. sausage meat
- 1/2 onion
- 1/2 teaspoon garlic puree
- 1 teaspoon sage

- 3 tablespoon breadcrumbs
- pinch of salt
- black pepper

Instructions:

1. Place all of your ingredients into a large bowl for mixing and make sure your ingredients are mixed well.
2. Form into medium sized balls and place them in the Air Fryer. Cook at 355 - degrees Fahrenheit for 15 minutes.

272. Fried Puppy Poppers

Prep + Cook Time: 25 minutes　　　　　　　　　**Servings:** 50 treats

Ingredients:

- 1/2 cup unsweetened applesauce
- 1 cup peanut butter
- 2 cup oats

- 1 cup four
- 1 teaspoon baking powder

Instructions:

1. Combine the applesauce and peanut butter in a bowl; stirring until smooth.
2. Add the oats, flour and baking powder, and mix together until a soft dough forms.
3. Roll the dough into balls about 1/2 teaspoon in size.
4. Pre-heat the Air Fryer to 350 – degrees Fahrenheit.
5. Spray or brush the bottom of the Air Fryer basket with oil.
6. Place 8 to12 balls into the Air Fryer basket. Air-fry for 8 minutes; turning the balls over halfway through the cooking time.
7. Repeat with the remaining poppers.
8. Allow the cooked poppers to cool completely and store in an airtight container for up to 2 weeks.

273. Masala Cashew

Prep + Cook Time: 20 minutes　　　　　　　　　**Servings:** 3

Ingredients:

- 1/2 Pound. cashew nuts

- 1/2 teaspoon garam masala powder

- 1 teaspoon coriander powder
- 1 teaspoon ghee
- 1 teaspoon red chili powder
- 1/2 teaspoon black pepper
- 2 teaspoon dry mango powder
- 1 teaspoon sea salt

Instructions:

1. Take a large bowl. Put in all the ingredients and toss well. Layer cashew nuts in the basket of a fryer.
2. Adjust the temperature to 250 - degrees Fahrenheit and set timer to 15 minutes.
3. Cook until the cashew nuts are brown and crispy.
4. After the end of cooking time set the nuts aside and let them cool.
5. Store for up to 2 weeks.

274. Amazing Bacon Wrapped Shrimp

Prep + Cook Time: 50 minutes   **Servings:** 4

Ingredients:

- 1 ¼ pounds tiger shrimp; peeled and deveined [16 pieces]
- 1-pound bacon; thinly sliced, room temperature [16 slices]

Instructions:

1. Take one slice of bacon and wrap it around the shrimp; star ting from the head and finishing at the tail.
2. Return the wrapped shrimp to the refrigerator for 20 minutes.
3. Preheat the Air Fryer to 390 - degrees Fahrenheit.
4. Remove the shrimp from the refrigerator and add them to the cooking basket, cooking for 5 – 7 minutes.
5. Drain on a paper towel prior to serving.

275. Tomato and Avocado Egg Rolls

Prep + Cook Time: 20 minutes   **Servings:** 5

Ingredients:

- 10 egg roll wrappers
- 3 avocados; peeled and pitted
- 1 tomato; diced
- salt and pepper; to taste

Instructions:

1. Preheat your Air Fryer to 350 - degrees Fahrenheit. Place the tomato and avocados in a bowl.
2. Season with some salt and pepper. Mash with a fork to make a smooth filling.
3. Divide the filling between the wrappers, and wrap them up securely.
4. Place them on a lined baking dish. Cook for 5 minutes.

276. Garlic Knots

Prep + Cook Time: 20 minutes   **Servings:** 4

Ingredients:

- 1-pound frozen pizza dough
- 4 garlic cloves; minced
- 1 teaspoon salt
- 1 tablespoon freshly chopped parsley
- 2 tablespoon Parmesan cheese; grated
- 4 tablespoon extra virgin olive oil
- Marinara sauce or ketchup for serving

Instructions:

1. Roll pizza dough out until 1 – 1/2 inch thick. Cut the dough lengthwise. Make knots rolling the dough between countertop and palm.

2. In the large mixing bowl combine olive oil, grated cheese, salt, minced garlic, chopped parsley. Stir to combine.
3. Preheat the Air Fryer to 360 - degrees Fahrenheit.
4. Dip each knot into the oil mixture and transfer to the Air Fryer.
5. Cook for 10 – 12 minutes; stirring occasionally, until ready and crispy.
6. Serve with ketchup or marinara sauce.

277. Yummy Grilled Cheese

Prep + Cook Time: 25 minutes   **Servings:** 2

Ingredients:

- 1/2 cup sharp cheddar cheese
- 1/4 cup butter; melted
- 4 slices of brioche or white bread

Instructions:

1. Preheat the Air Fryer to 360 - degrees Fahrenheit.
2. Place cheese and butter in separate bowls.
3. Brush butter on each side of the four slices of bread using a cooking brush.
4. Place the cheese on 2 of the four pieces of bread. Put the bread together and add to the cooking basket of the Air Fryer.
5. Cook for 5 to 7 minutes or until golden brown and the cheese has melted.

278. Asian Banana Chips

Prep + Cook Time: 40 minutes   **Servings:** 2

Ingredients:

- 4 bananas; sliced without skin
- 1 teaspoon olive oil
- 1/2 teaspoon turmeric powder
- 1/2 teaspoon chat masala [tangy spice mix]
- pinch of chili powder
- 1 teaspoon sea salt
- 1/2 cup water

Instructions:

1. Mix turmeric powder, chili powder, salt, and water.
2. Cover the slices of banana with this mixture. It will color the slices into yellow.
3. Set aside like this for 15 minutes.
4. Drain the chips and use paper towels to make them dry.
5. Preheat the Air Fryer to 355 - degrees Fahrenheit for 5 minutes and grease the basket with oil.
6. Cook bananas for 15 minutes tossing them halfway cooked.
7. After the end of cooking sprinkle bananas with chaat masala and more salt if desired.

279. Air Fried Meatballs in Tomato Sauce

Prep + Cook Time: 35 minutes   **Servings:** 4

Ingredients:

- 1 small onion
- 3/4 pounds [12 oz] ground beef
- 1 tablespoon chopped fresh parsley
- 1/2 tablespoon chopped fresh thyme leaves
- One Egg
- 3 tablespoon breadcrumbs
- pepper & salt to taste

Extra: 10 ounces. of your favorite tomato sauce

Instructions:

1. Finely chop the onion. Place all the ingredients into a bowl and mix well. Shape the mixture into 10 to 12 balls.
2. Preheat the Air Fryer to 390 - degrees Fahrenheit. Place the meatballs in the Air Fryer basket and slide the basket in the Air Fryer. Set the timer and cook for 8 minutes.
3. Transfer the meatballs to an oven dish, add the tomato sauce and place the dish into the basket of the Air Fryer. Slide the basket into the Air Fryer.
4. Set the temperature to 330 - degrees Fahrenheit and the timer for 5 minutes to warm everything through.

Tips: For a great snack, you can serve the meatballs without the tomato sauce.

280. Amazing Blooming Onion

Prep + Cook Time: 40 minutes   **Servings:** 4

Ingredients:

- 4 medium/small onions
- 1 tablespoon olive oil
- 4 dollops of butter

Instructions:

1. Peel the onion but keep it whole; then slice off the top and bottom so it sits easily on its end.
2. To get it to bloom; you need to cut slices into it as far down as possible but not all the way through, I found 4 cuts [makes 8 segments] works well.
3. Soak the onions for 4 hours in salt water; this helps take the harsh tang from them and starts to blooming process.
4. Preheat your Air Fryer to 355 – degrees Fahrenheit.
5. Place the Onions in the Air Fryer; drizzle with a little olive oil then add a dollop of butter to the top of each.
6. Cook in your Air Fryer for 30 minutes; the outside may get dark, but this layer can be removed to serve.

Tips: This recipe works really well also if you roast them.

281. Crab Croquettes Recipe

Prep + Cook Time: 5 minutes   **Servings:** 6

Ingredients:

For the Filling:

- 1-pound lump crab meat
- 2 eggs whites; beaten
- 1 tablespoon olive oil
- 1/4 cup red onion; finely chopped
- 1/4 red bell pepper; finely chopped
- 2 tablespoon celery; finely chopped
- 1/4 teaspoon tarragon; finely chopped
- 1/4 teaspoon chives; finely chopped
- 1/2 teaspoon parsley; finely chopped
- 1/2 teaspoon cayenne pepper
- 1/4 cup mayonnaise
- 1/4 cup sour cream

For the Breading:

- three eggs; beaten
- 1 cup all-purpose flour
- 1 cup panko breadcrumbs
- 1 teaspoon olive oil
- 1/2 teaspoon salt

Instructions:

1. In a small sauté pan over medium-high heat; add olive oil, onions, peppers, and celery.
2. Cook and sweat until translucent; about 4 – 5 minutes.

3. Remove from heat and set aside to cool.
4. In a food processor; blend the panko breadcrumbs, olive oil and salt to a fine crumb.
5. In three separate bowls; set aside panko mixture, eggs and flour.
6. Combine remaining ingredients: crabmeat, egg whites, mayonnaise, sour cream, spices and vegetables in a large mixing bowl.
7. Preheat Air Fryer to 390 - degrees Fahrenheit. Mold crab mixture to size of golf balls, roll each in flour, then in eggs and finally in panko. Press crumbs to croquettes to adhere.
8. Place croquettes in basket, being careful not to overcrowd.
9. Cook croquettes 8 – 10 minutes or until golden brown.

282. Tasty Crispy Fried Leek Rings

Prep + Cook Time: 15 minutes   **Servings:** 4

Ingredients:

- 1 large-sized leek; cut into 1/2-inch wide rings
- Salt and pepper; to taste
- 1/2 teaspoon mustard powder
- 1 cup milk
- One Egg
- 1 cup self-rising flour
- 3/4 teaspoon baking powder
- 1 cup crushed saltines
- 1 tablespoon olive oil

Instructions:

1. Toss your leeks with salt, pepper, and mustard powder.
2. Grab three mixing bowls to set up a breading station
3. In a mixing bowl; whisk the milk and egg until frothy and pale. Now, combine the flour and baking powder in another mixing bowl
4. In the third bowl; combine the crushed saltines with olive oil.
5. Coat the leek slices with the flour mixture.
6. Dredge the floured leek slices into the milk/egg mixture, coating well. Finally, roll them over the crumb mixture
7. Air-fry for approximately 10 minutes at 370 - degrees Fahrenheit.

283. Special Meatballs with Mint Yogurt

Prep + Cook Time: 60 minutes   **Servings:** 4

Ingredients:

For the Meatballs:

- 1-pound ground lamb
- 4 ounces ground turkey
- 1 ½ tablespoon parsley; finely chopped
- 1 tablespoon mint; finely chopped
- 1 teaspoon ground cumin
- 1 teaspoon ground coriander
-
- 1 teaspoon cayenne pepper
- 1 teaspoon red chili paste 2 garlic cloves; finely chopped
- 1/4 cup olive oil
- 1 teaspoon salt
- One Egg white

For the Mint Yogurt:

- 1/2 cup non-fat Greek yogurt
- 1/4 cup sour cream
- 2 tablespoon buttermilk
- 1/4 cup mint; finely chopped
- 1 garlic clove; finely chopped
- 2 pinches salt

Instructions:

1. Preheat the Air Fryer to 390 - degrees Fahrenheit. In a large mixing bowl combine all ingredients for the meatballs.

2. Roll the meatballs between your hands in a circular motion to smooth the meatball out to the size of a golf ball.
3. Place the meatballs into the cooking basket and cook for 6 – 8 minutes.
4. While the meatballs are cooking add all of the ingredients for the mint yogurt to a medium mixing bowl and combine well.
5. Serve with the meatballs and garnish with fresh mint and olives.

284. Fried Toasted Pumpkin Seeds

Prep + Cook Time: 55 minutes   **Servings:** 1 ½ cups

Ingredients:

- 1 ½ cups pumpkin seeds from a large whole pumpkin
- olive oil
- 1 ½ teaspoon salt
- 1 teaspoon smoked paprika

Instructions:

1. Cut the pumpkin open and scrape out the insides with a spoon.
2. Separate the flesh from the seeds and rinse the seeds with cold water.
3. Bring two quarts of well-salted water to a boil [the water should taste a little salty]. Add the pumpkin seeds to the boiling water and boil for 10 minutes.
4. Drain the seeds and spread them out on paper towels to dry for at least 20 minutes.
5. Pre-heat the Air Fryer to 350 - degrees Fahrenheit.
6. Toss the seeds with olive oil, salt and smoked paprika and transfer them to the Air Fryer basket.
7. Air-fry for 35 minutes; shaking the basket several times during the cooking process. Pumpkin seeds should be crispy and slightly browned.
8. Allow the seeds to cool before serving or storing in an air-tight container or bag.
9. Enjoy them as a snack or try using them as a topping for salads or yogurt

285. Basil and Harissa Corn

Prep + Cook Time: 15 minutes   **Servings:** 4

Ingredients:

- 4 ears corn; husked and cleaned
- 2 tablespoons harissa sauce
- 1 tablespoon melted ghee
- 1 teaspoon smoked cayenne pepper
- Juice of 2 small-sized lemons
- 1 tablespoon fresh basil leaves; coarsely chopped

Instructions:

1. Rub the corn with harissa sauce and melted ghee
2. Sprinkle with cayenne pepper. Arrange them on an Air Fryer grill pan.
3. Air-fry them at 390 - degrees Fahrenheit for 10 minutes
4. Pause the Air Fryer; turn the cobs over, and cook for additional 5 minutes
5. Drizzle warm corn with fresh lemon juice and garnish with fresh basil leaves

286. Delicious Cocktail Flanks

Prep + Cook Time: 45 minutes   **Servings:** 4

Ingredients:

- 1 12-oz package cocktail franks
- 1 8-oz can of crescent rolls

Instructions:

1. Remove the cocktail franks from the package and drain, then pat dry on paper towels.
2. Cut the dough into rectangular strips; approximately 1-inch x 1.5-inch.

3. Roll the strips around the franks, leaving the ends visible. Place in the freezer for 5 minutes to firm.
4. Preheat the Air Fryer to 330 - degrees Fahrenheit.
5. Remove the franks from the freezer and place them in the cooking basket. Cook for 6 – 8 minutes.
6. Change temperature to 390 - degrees Fahrenheit and cook for 3 minutes or until golden brown.

287. Hot Fried Cinnamon Banana Chips

Prep + Cook Time: 15 minutes | **Servings:** 4

Ingredients:

- 4 medium-sized bananas; peeled and cut into 1/4-inch slices
- Non-stick cooking spray
- 1/2 cup freshly squeezed lemon juice
- 1/2 teaspoon ground cinnamon
- A pinch of kosher salt

Instructions:

1. Lightly coat the bananas with olive oil and drizzle with the freshly squeezed lemon juice.
2. Air-fry at 185 - degrees Fahrenheit for 10 to 12 minutes
3. Take the banana slices out of the Air Fryer; sprinkle with cinnamon and salt.
4. Place in an airtight container for storage

288. Garlic Mushrooms Stuffed

Prep + Cook Time: 30 minutes | **Servings:** 4

Ingredients:

- 16 small button mushrooms

For the Stuffing:

- 1 ½ slices of white bread
- 1 garlic clove; crushed
- 1 tablespoon flat-leafed parsley; finely chopped
- Ground black pepper to taste
- 1 ½ tablespoon olive oil

Instructions:

1. Preheat the Air Fryer to 390 - degrees Fahrenheit.
2. In a food processor; grind the slices of bread into fine crumbs and mix in the garlic, parsley and pepper to taste.
3. When fully mixed; stir in the olive oil.
4. Cut off the mushroom stalks and fill the caps with the breadcrumbs.
5. Pat crumbs into caps to ensure loose crumbs do not get pulled up into fan.
6. Place the mushroom caps in the cooking basket and slide it into the Air Fryer. Cook the mushrooms for 7 – 8 minutes or until they are golden and crispy.

289. Tasty Crispy Eggplant Chips

Prep + Cook Time: 45 minutes | **Servings:** 4

Ingredients:

- 2 eggplants; peeled and thinly sliced
- Salt to taste
- 1/2 cup tapioca starch
- 1/4 cup canola oil
- 1/2 cup water
- 1 teaspoon garlic powder
- 1/2 teaspoon dried dill weed
- 1/2 teaspoon ground black pepper; to taste

Instructions:

1. Salt the eggplant slices and let them stay for about 30 minutes. Squeeze the eggplant slices and rinse them under cold running water
2. Toss the eggplant slices with the other ingredients
3. Cook at 390 - degrees Fahrenheit for 13 minutes; working in batches.
4. Serve with a sauce for dipping

290. Amazing Buttery Sage Potatoes

Prep + Cook Time: 45 minutes   **Servings:** 8

Ingredients:

- 1 ½ pounds fingerling potatoes; halved lengthwise
- 2 tablespoons melted butter
- 1/4 cup fresh sage leaves; finely chopped
- 2 sprigs thyme; chopped
- 1 teaspoon lemon zest; finely grated
- 1/4 teaspoon ground pepper
- 1 tablespoon sea salt flakes
- 1/2 teaspoon grated ginger

Instructions:

1. Soak the potatoes in cold water for about 30 minutes
2. Then; put them dry using a kitchen towel.
3. After that; roast at 400 - degrees Fahrenheit for 15 minutes
4. Serve in a nice serving bowl, accompanied by tomato ketchup and mayonnaise

291. Dijon and Quinoa Cocktail Meatballs

Prep + Cook Time: 20 minutes   **Servings:** 6

Ingredients:

- 1/2-pound ground pork
- 1/2-pound ground beef
- 1 cup quinoa; cooked
- 1 beaten egg
- 2 scallions; finely chopped
- 1/2 teaspoon onion powder
- 1 ½ tablespoons Dijon mustard
- 3/4 cup ketchup
- 1 teaspoon ancho chili powder
- 1 tablespoon sesame oil
- 2 tablespoons tamari sauce
- 1/4 cup balsamic vinegar
- 2 tablespoons sugar

Instructions:

1. Mix all the ingredients until everything is well incorporated. Roll into small meatballs
2. Cook at 370 - degrees Fahrenheit for 10 minutes. Now; shake the basket and cook for 5 minutes more

292. Yummy Ricotta Balls

Prep + Cook Time: 25 minutes   **Servings:** 3

Ingredients:

- 2 cups ricotta; grated
- two eggs; separated
- 2 tablespoon chives; finely chopped
- 2 tablespoon fresh basil; finely chopped
- 4 tablespoon whole wheat flour
- 1/4 teaspoon salt or to taste
- 1/4 teaspoon pepper powder or to taste
- 1 teaspoon orange zest; grated

For coating:

- 1/4 cup whole wheat breadcrumbs
- 1 tablespoon vegetable oil

Instructions:

1. Mix together in a bowl, yolks, flour, salt, pepper, chives and zest. Add ricotta and mix well with your hands.
2. Divide the mixture and shape into balls or desired shape.
3. Mix together oil and breadcrumbs until crumbly. Roll the balls in the breadcrumbs and place in the Air Fryer basket.
4. Place the basket in the Air Fryer. Air fry in a preheated Air Fryer at 390 – degrees Fahrenheit for 8 minutes or until golden brown.
5. Serve with ketchup or dip of your choice. Enjoy!

293. Spiced Nuts

Prep + Cook Time: 40 minutes   **Servings:** 3 cups

Ingredients:

- One Egg white; lightly beaten
- 1/4 cup sugar
- 1 teaspoon salt
- 1/2 teaspoon ground cinnamon
- 1/4 teaspoon ground cloves
- 1/4 teaspoon ground allspice
- pinch ground cayenne pepper
- 1 cup pecan halves
- 1 cup cashews
- 1 cup almonds

Instructions:

1. Combine the egg white with the sugar and spices in a bowl.
2. Pre-heat the Air Fryer to 300 - degrees Fahrenheit.
3. Spray or brush the Air Fryer basket with vegetable oil.
4. Toss the nuts together in the spiced egg white and transfer half of the nuts to the Air Fryer basket.
5. Air-fry for 25 minutes; stirring the nuts in the basket a few times during the cooking process.
6. Taste the nuts [carefully because they will be very hot] to see if they are crunchy and nicely toasted.
7. Air-fry for a few more minutes if necessary. Repeat with remaining nuts.
8. Serve warm or cool to room temperature and store in an airtight container for up to two weeks.

294. Yummy Shrimp Bites

Prep + Cook Time: 45 minutes   **Servings:** 10

Ingredients:

- 1 ¼ pounds shrimp; peeled and deveined
- 1 teaspoon paprika
- 1/2 teaspoon ground black pepper
- 1/2 teaspoon red pepper flakes; crushed
- 1 tablespoon salt
- 1 teaspoon chili powder
- 1 tablespoon shallot powder
- 1/4 teaspoon cumin powder
- 1 ¼ pounds thin bacon slices

Instructions:

1. Toss the shrimps with all the seasoning until they are coated well
2. Next; wrap a slice of bacon around the shrimps, securing with a toothpick, repeat with the remaining ingredients and chill for 30 minutes
3. Air-fry them at 360 – degrees Fahrenheit for 7 to 8 minutes; working in batches.
4. Serve with cocktail sticks if desired. Enjoy!

295. Cajun Spiced Snack

Prep + Cook Time: 30 minutes   **Servings:** 5

Ingredients:

- 2 tablespoon Cajun or Creole seasoning
- 1/2 cup butter; melted
- 2 cups peanut
- 2 cups mini wheat thin crackers
- 2 cups mini pretzels
- 2 teaspoon salt
- 1 teaspoon cayenne pepper
- 4 cups plain popcorn
- 1 teaspoon paprika
- 1 teaspoon garlic
- 1/2 teaspoon thyme
- 1/2 teaspoon oregano
- 1 teaspoon black pepper
- 1/2 teaspoon onion powder

Instructions:

1. Pre-heat Air Fryer to 370 - degrees Fahrenheit.
2. In a small bowl; combine the Cajun spice and melted butter.
3. Combine the peanuts, crackers, popcorn and pretzels in a large bowl. Pour butter over the mixed snacks and toss to coat the mixture evenly. Air-fry the snack mix in 2 batches.
4. Place half of the mix in the Air Fryer basket and air-fry for 8 to 10 minutes.
5. For even cooking, toss the basket several times throughout the process. Transfer the snack mix to a cookie sheet and allow to cool completely.
6. Store in an airtight container for up to one week.

296. Easy Cheesy Broccoli Balls

Prep + Cook Time: 20 minutes   **Servings:** 6

Ingredients:

- Two eggs; well whisked
- 2 cups Colby cheese; shredded
- 1 cup all-purpose flour
- Seasoned salt; to taste
- 1/4 teaspoon ground black pepper; or more to taste
- 1 head broccoli; chopped into florets
- 1 cup crushed saltines

Instructions:

1. Thoroughly combine the eggs, cheese, flour, salt, pepper, and broccoli to make the consistency of dough
2. Chill for 1 hour and shape into small balls, roll the patties over the crushed saltines. Spritz them with cooking oil on all sides.
3. Cook at 360 – degrees Fahrenheit for 10 minutes
4. Check for doneness and return to the Air Fryer for 8 to 10 more minutes.
5. Serve with a sauce for dipping

297. Classic Welsh Rarebit

Prep + Cook Time: 25 minutes   **Servings:** 2

Ingredients:

- 3 slices bread
- 2 large eggs [separated]
- 1 teaspoon mustard
- 1 teaspoon paprika
- 4.3 ounces. cheddar

Instructions:

1. Very lightly heat up the bread in the Air Fryer for 5 minutes at 350 – degrees Fahrenheit.
2. Whisk the egg whites in a bowl until soft peaks are formed.
3. Mix the cheese, mustard, egg yolks and paprika in a bowl.

4. Fold in the egg whites into this mixture.
5. Spoon mixture onto the toasted bread and cook in the Air Fryer for 10 minutes on 350 – degrees Fahrenheit.

298. Delicious Brussels Sprout Appetizer

Prep + Cook Time: 20 minutes   **Servings:** 4

Ingredients:

- 1-pound Brussels sprouts; trimmed and cut off the ends
- 1 teaspoon kosher salt
- 1 tablespoon lemon zest
- Non-stick cooking spray

Instructions:

1. Firstly; peel the Brussels sprouts using a small paring knife.
2. Toss the leaves with salt and lemon zest and spritz them with a cooking spray, coating all sides
3. Bake at 380 degrees for 8 minutes and shake the cooking basket halfway through the cooking time and cook for 7 more minutes
4. Make sure to work in batches so everything can cook evenly. Taste and adjust the seasonings.

299. Super Brussels Sprout Snack

Prep + Cook Time: 15 minutes   **Servings:** 4

Ingredients:

- 1-pound Brussels sprouts; ends and yellow leaves removed and halved lengthwise
- Salt and black pepper; to taste
- 1 tablespoon toasted sesame oil
- 1 teaspoon fennel seeds
- Chopped fresh parsley; for garnish

Instructions:

1. Place the Brussels sprouts, salt, pepper, sesame oil, and fennel seeds in a resealable plastic bag.
2. Seal the bag and shake to coat
3. Air-fry at 380 - degrees Fahrenheit for 15 minutes or until tender. Make sure to flip them over halfway through the cooking time
4. Serve sprinkled with fresh parsley.

300. Amazing Roasted Squash Bites

Prep + Cook Time: 20 minutes   **Servings:** 6

Ingredients:

- 1 ½ pounds winter squash; peeled and cut into 1/2-inch chunks
- 1/4 cup dark brown sugar
- 2 tablespoons melted coconut oil
- A pinch of coarse salt
- A pinch of pepper
- 2 tablespoons sage; finely chopped
- Zest of 1 small-sized lemon
- 1/8 teaspoon ground allspice

Instructions:

1. Toss the squash chunks with the other items
2. Roast in the Air Fryer's cooking basket at 350 - degrees Fahrenheit for 10 minutes
3. Pause the machine; and turn the temperature to 400 degrees Fahrenheit and stir and roast for additional 8 minutes

301. Thai Style Pecorino Broccoli Melts

Prep + Cook Time: 20 minutes   **Servings:** 6

Ingredients:

- 1 large-sized head of broccoli; broken into small florets
- 1/2 teaspoon sea salt
- 1/4 teaspoon ground black pepper; or more to taste
- 1 tablespoon Shoyu sauce
- 1 teaspoon groundnut oil
- 2 tablespoons Pecorino Toscano; freshly grated
- Paprika; to taste

Instructions:

1. Add the broccoli florets to boiling water and boil approximately 4 minutes and drain well. Season with salt and pepper, drizzle with Shoyu sauce and groundnut oil
2. Air-fry at 390 – degrees Fahrenheit for 10 minutes and shake the Air Fryer basket, push the power button again, and continue to cook for 5 minutes more. Toss the fried broccoli with the cheese and paprika

Poultry Recipes

302. Tasty Chicken Sausage with Mustard-Honey Sauce

Prep + Cook Time: 20 minutes   **Servings:** 4

Ingredients:

- 4 chicken sausages
- 2 tablespoons honey
- 1/4 cup mayonnaise
- 2 tablespoons Dijon mustard
- 1 tablespoon balsamic vinegar
- 1/2 teaspoon dried rosemary

Instructions:

1. Arrange the sausages on the grill pan and transfer it to the preheated Air Fryer.
2. Grill the sausages at 350 - degrees Fahrenheit for approximately 13 minutes.
3. Turn them halfway through cooking.
4. Meanwhile; prepare the sauce by mixing the remaining ingredients with a wire whisk.
5. Serve the warm sausages with chilled mustard-honey sauce.

303. Chicken Sausage Meatballs with Penne

Prep + Cook Time: 20 minutes   **Servings:** 4

Ingredients:

- 1 cup chicken meat; ground
- 1 sweet red pepper; minced
- 1/4 cup green onions; chopped
- 1 green garlic; minced
- 4 tablespoons seasoned breadcrumbs
- 1/2 teaspoon cumin powder
- 1 tablespoon fresh coriander; minced
- 1/2 teaspoon sea salt
- 1/4 teaspoon mixed peppercorns; ground
- 1 package penne pasta; cooked

Instructions:

1. Place the chicken, red pepper, green onions, and garlic into a mixing bowl and mix to combine well.
2. Now; add seasoned breadcrumbs, followed by all seasonings, mix again until everything is well incorporated.
3. Next; shape into small balls [e.g. the size of a golf ball] and cook them in the preheated Air Fryer at 350 - degrees Fahrenheit for 15 minutes
4. Shaking once or twice to ensure evenness of cooking.
5. Serve over cooked penne pasta.

304. Spicy Tarragon Chicken

Prep + Cook Time: 40 minutes   **Servings:** 4

Ingredients:

- 2 cups of roasted vegetable broth
- 2 chicken breasts; cut into halves
- 3/4 teaspoon fine sea salt
- 1/4 teaspoon mixed peppercorns; freshly cracked
- 1 teaspoon cumin powder
- 1 ½ teaspoons sesame oil
- 1 ½ tablespoons Worcester sauce
- 1/2 cup of spring onions; chopped
- 1 Serrano pepper; deveined and chopped
- 1 bell pepper; deveined and chopped
- 1 tablespoon tamari sauce
- 1/2 chopped fresh tarragon

Instructions:

1. Place the vegetable broth and chicken breasts in a deep saucepan and cook for 10 minutes.
2. Reduce the temperature and let it simmer for additional 10 minutes.

3. After that; allow the chicken to cool slightly, shred the chicken using a stand mixer or two forks.
4. Toss the shredded chicken with the salt, cracked peppercorns, cumin, sesame oil and the Worcester sauce, air-fry them at 380 - degrees Fahrenheit for 18 minutes, check for doneness.
5. Meanwhile; in a non-stick skillet, cook the remaining ingredients over a moderate flame.
6. Cook until the onions and peppers are tender and fragrant.
7. Remove the skillet from the heat, add the shredded chicken and toss to combine.
8. Serve the dish right away.

305. Tasty Pizza Stuffed Chicken

Prep + Cook Time: 20 minutes   **Servings:** 4

Ingredients:

- 4 small-sized chicken breasts; boneless and skinless
- 1/4 cup pizza sauce
- 1/2 cup Colby cheese; shredded

- 16 slices pepperoni
- Salt and pepper; to savor
- 1 ½ tablespoons olive oil
- 1 ½ tablespoons dried oregano

Instructions:

1. Carefully flatten out the chicken breast using a rolling pin.
2. Divide the ingredients among four chicken fillets.
3. Roll the chicken fillets with the stuffing and seal them using a small skewer or two toothpicks.
4. Roast in the preheated Air Fryer grill pan for 13 to 15 minutes at 370 – degrees Fahrenheit.

306. Special Maple-Glazed Chicken

Prep + Cook Time: 20 minutes   **Servings:** 4

Ingredients:

- 2 ½ tablespoons maple syrup
- 1 tablespoon tamari soy sauce
- 1 tablespoon oyster sauce
- 1 teaspoon fresh lemon juice
- 1 teaspoon minced fresh ginger

- 1 teaspoon garlic puree
- Seasoned salt and freshly ground pepper; to taste
- 2 chicken breasts; boneless and skinless

Instructions:

1. To prepare the marinade, in a mixing dish, combine maple syrup, tamari sauce, oyster sauce, lemon juice, fresh ginger and garlic puree.
2. Now; season the chicken breasts with salt and pepper. Put the chicken breast into the bowl with the marinade and make sure to coat them well.
3. Cover with foil and place in the refrigerator for 3 hours or overnight.
4. Discard the marinade. Air-fry marinated chicken breast for 15 minutes at 365 – degrees Fahrenheit and turn them once or twice.
5. Meanwhile; add the remaining marinade to a pan that is preheated over a moderate flame, let it simmer until reduced by half, it will take 3 to 5 minutes.
6. Serve the chicken with the sauce.

307. Quinoa Skewers and Crowd-Pleasing Turkey

Prep + Cook Time: 15 minutes   **Servings:** 8

Ingredients:

- 1 cup red quinoa; cooked
- 1 ½ cups of water
- 14 ounces ground turkey

- 2 small eggs; beaten
- 1 teaspoon ground ginger
- 2 ½ tablespoons vegetable oil

- 1 cup chopped fresh parsley
- 2 tablespoons seasoned breadcrumbs
- 3/4 teaspoon salt
- 1 heaping teaspoon fresh rosemary; finely chopped
- 1/2 teaspoon ground allspice

Instructions:

1. Mix all of the above ingredients in a bowl.
2. Knead the mixture with your hands.
3. Then; take small portions and gently roll them into balls.
4. Now; preheat your Air Fryer to 380 - degrees Fahrenheit. Air fry for 8 to 10 minutes in the Air Fryer basket.
5. Serve on a serving platter with skewers and eat with your favorite dipping sauce.

308. Cabbage-Potato Cakes with Cajun Chicken Wings

Prep + Cook Time: 40 minutes   **Servings:** 4

Ingredients:

- 4 large-sized chicken wings
- 1 teaspoon Cajun seasoning
- 1 teaspoon maple syrup
- 3/4 teaspoon sea salt flakes
- 1/4 teaspoon red pepper flakes; crushed
- 1 teaspoon onion powder
- 1 teaspoon porcini powder
- 1/2 teaspoon celery seeds
- 1 small-seized head of cabbage; shredded
- 1 cup mashed potatoes
- 1 small-sized brown onion; coarsely grated
- 1 teaspoon garlic puree
- 1 medium-sized whole egg; well whisked
- 1/2 teaspoon table salt
- 1/2 teaspoon ground black pepper
- 1 ½ tablespoons all-purpose flour
- 3/4 teaspoon baking powder
- 1 heaping tablespoon cilantro
- 1 tablespoon sesame oil

Instructions:

1. Start by preheating your Air Fryer to 390 - degrees Fahrenheit.
2. Dry the chicken wings. Now; prepare the rub by mixing Cajun seasoning, maple syrup, sea salt flakes, red pepper, onion powder, porcini powder, and celery seeds.
3. Cook for 25 to 30 minutes or until the wings are no longer pink in the middle.
4. Then; mix the shredded cabbage, potato, onion, garlic puree, egg, table salt, black pepper, flour, baking powder and cilantro in a mixing bowl.
5. Divide the cabbage mixture into 4 portions and create four cabbage/potato cakes.
6. Sprinkle each cake with the sesame oil.
7. Bake cabbage/potato cakes for 10 minutes; flipping them once and working in batches.
8. Finally; serve with the chicken wings and enjoy!

309. Tasty Fried Chicken Tenders

Prep + Cook Time: 1 hr. 15 minutes   **Servings:** 4

Ingredients:

- 3/4 cup of buttermilk
- 1-pound chicken tenders
- 1 ½ cups all-purpose flour
- Salt; to taste
- 1/2 teaspoon pink peppercorns; freshly cracked
- 1 teaspoon shallot powder
- 1/2 teaspoon cumin powder
- 1 ½ teaspoon smoked cayenne pepper
- 1 tablespoon sesame oil

Instructions:

1. Place the buttermilk and chicken tenders in the mixing dish and gently stir to coat and let it soak for 1 hour.
2. Then; mix the flour with all seasonings. Coat the soaked chicken tenders with the flour mixture.
3. Now; dip them into the buttermilk. Finally; dredge them in the flour.
4. Brush the prepared chicken tenders with sesame oil and lower them onto the bottom of a cooking basket.
5. Air-fry for 15 minutes at 365 - degrees Fahrenheit and make sure to shake them once or twice.

310. Bacon with Saucy Provençal Chicken

Prep + Cook Time: 25 minutes   **Servings:** 4

Ingredients:

- 4 medium-sized skin-on chicken drumsticks
- 1 ½ teaspoons herbs de Provence
- Salt and pepper; to taste
- 1 tablespoon rice vinegar
- 2 tablespoons olive oil
- 2 garlic cloves; crushed
- 12 ounces crushed canned tomatoes
- 1 small-size leek; thinly sliced
- 2 slices smoked bacon; chopped

Instructions:

1. Sprinkle the chicken drumsticks with herbs de Provence, salt and pepper. then, drizzle them with rice vinegar and olive oil.
2. Cook in the baking pan at 360 - degrees Fahrenheit for 8 to 10 minutes.
3. Pause the Air Fryer; stir in the remaining ingredients and continue to cook for 15 minutes longer, make sure to check them periodically.
4. Serve over rice garnished with lemon wedges.

311. Amazing Gourmet Chicken Omelet

Prep + Cook Time: 15 minutes   **Servings:** 2

Ingredients:

- four eggs; whisked
- 4 ounces ground chicken
- 1/2 cup scallions; finely chopped
- 2 cloves garlic; finely minced
- 1/2 teaspoon salt
- 1/2 teaspoon ground black pepper
- 1/2 teaspoon paprika
- 1 teaspoon dried thyme
- A dash of hot sauce

Instructions:

1. Thoroughly combine all the ingredients in a mixing dish.
2. Now; scrape the egg mixture into two oven safe ramekins that are previously greased with a thin layer of the vegetable oil.
3. Set your machine to cook at 350 degrees F; air-fry for 13 minutes or until thoroughly cooked.
4. Serve immediately.

312. Tasty Peppery Turkey Sandwiches

Prep + Cook Time: 25 minutes   **Servings:** 4

Ingredients:

- 1 cup leftover turkey; cut into bite-sized chunks
- 2 bell peppers; deveined and chopped
- 1 Serrano pepper; deveined and chopped
- 1 leek; sliced
- 1/2 cup sour cream

- 1 teaspoon hot paprika
- 3/4 teaspoon kosher salt
- 1/2 teaspoon ground black pepper

- 1 heaping tablespoon fresh cilantro; chopped
- A few dashes of Tabasco sauce
- 4 hamburger buns

Instructions:

1. Toss all ingredients; without the hamburger buns, in an Air Fryer baking pan, toss until everything is well coated.
2. Now; roast it for 20 minutes at 385 - degrees Fahrenheit.
3. Serve on hamburger buns; add some extra sour cream and Dijon mustard if desired.

313. Delicious Chicken Wings with Piri Piri Sauce

Prep + Cook Time: 1 hr. 30 minutes   **Servings:** 6

Ingredients:

- 12 chicken wings
- 1 ½ ounces butter; melted
- 1 teaspoon onion powder

- 1/2 teaspoon cumin powder
- 1 teaspoon garlic paste

For the Sauce:

- 2 ounces piri piri peppers; stemmed and chopped
- 1 tablespoon pimiento; deveined and minced
- 1 garlic clove; chopped

- 2 tablespoons fresh lemon juice
- 1/3 teaspoon sea salt
- 1/2 teaspoon tarragon
- 3/4 teaspoon brown sugar

Instructions:

1. Steam the chicken wings using a steamer basket that is placed over a saucepan with boiling water, reduce the heat.
2. Now; steam the wings for 10 minutes over a moderate heat.
3. Toss the wings with butter, onion powder, cumin powder, and garlic paste.
4. Let the chicken wings cool to room temperature. Then; refrigerate them for 45 to 50 minutes.
5. Roast in the preheated Air Fryer at 330 - degrees Fahrenheit for 25 to 30 minutes. Make sure to flip them halfway through.
6. While the chicken wings are cooking, prepare the sauce by mixing all of the sauce ingredients in a food processor.
7. Toss the wings with prepared PiriPiri Sauce and serve.

314. Tasty Turkey Meatballs

Prep + Cook Time: 15 minutes   **Servings:** 6

Ingredients:

- 1-pound ground turkey
- 1 tablespoon fresh mint leaves; finely chopped
- 1 teaspoon onion powder
- 1 ½ teaspoons garlic paste

- 1 teaspoon crushed red pepper flakes
- 1/4 cup melted butter
- 3/4 teaspoon fine sea salt
- 1/4 cup grated Pecorino Romano

Instructions:

1. Simply place all of the above ingredients into the mixing dish, mix until everything is well incorporated. Use an ice cream scoop to shape the meat into golf ball sized meatballs.

2. Air fry the meatballs at 380 - degrees Fahrenheit for approximately 7 minutes, work in batches, shaking them to ensure evenness of cooking. Serve with simple tomato sauce garnished with fresh basil leaves.

315. Turmeric and Mustard Chicken Thighs

Prep + Cook Time: 20 minutes   **Servings:** 6

Ingredients:

- 1 large-sized egg; well whisked
- 2 tablespoons whole-grain Dijon mustard
- 1/4 cup of mayonnaise
- 1/4 cup of chili sauce
- 1/2 teaspoon brown sugar
- 1 teaspoon fine sea salt
- 1/2 teaspoon ground black pepper; or more to taste
- 1/2 teaspoon turmeric powder
- 10 chicken thighs
- 2 cups crushed saltines

Instructions:

1. Firstly; in a large-sized mixing bowl, thoroughly combine the egg, mustard, mayonnaise, chili sauce, brown sugar, salt, pepper, and turmeric.
2. Add the chicken thighs to the mixing bowl and cover with foil and let them marinate for at least 5 hours or overnight in your fridge.
3. After that; set your Air Fryer to cook at 360 - degrees Fahrenheit.
4. Remove the chicken from the marinade.
5. Put the crushed saltines into a shallow dish. Roll the marinated chicken over the crumbs.
6. Set the timer for 15 minutes and cook until the thighs are cooked through.
7. Serve with remaining marinade.

316. Vegetables with Roasted Turkey Thighs

Prep + Cook Time: 1 hr. 15 minutes   **Servings:** 4

Ingredients:

- 1 red onion; cut into wedges
- 1 carrot; trimmed and sliced
- 1 celery stalk; trimmed and sliced
- 1 cup Brussel sprouts; trimmed and halved
- 1 cup roasted vegetable broth
- 1 tablespoon apple cider vinegar
- 1 teaspoon maple syrup
- 2 turkey thighs
- 1/2 teaspoon mixed peppercorns; freshly cracked
- 1 teaspoon fine sea salt
- 1 teaspoon cayenne pepper
- 1 teaspoon onion powder
- 1/2 teaspoon garlic powder
- 1/3 teaspoon mustard seeds

Instructions:

1. Take a baking dish that easily fits into your device, place the vegetables on the bottom of the baking dish and pour in roasted vegetable broth.
2. In a large-sized mixing dish; place the remaining ingredients, let them marinate for about 30 minutes.
3. Lay them on the top of the vegetables.
4. Roast at 330 - degrees Fahrenheit for 40 to 45 minutes.
5. Serve the dish and enjoy!

317. Vegetables with Stylish Sweet Italian Turkey Sausage

Prep + Cook Time: 40 minutes   **Servings:** 4

Ingredients:

- 1 onion; cut into wedges
- 2 carrots; trimmed and sliced
- 1 parsnip; trimmed and sliced
- 2 potatoes; peeled and diced
- 1 teaspoon dried thyme
- 1/2 teaspoon dried marjoram
- 1 teaspoon dried basil
- 1/2 teaspoon celery seeds
- Sea salt and ground black pepper; to taste
- 1 tablespoon melted butter
- 3/4-pound sweet Italian turkey sausage

Instructions:

1. Mix the vegetables with all seasonings and melted butter.
2. Arrange the vegetables on the bottom of the Air Fryer cooking basket.
3. Lower the sausage onto the top of the vegetables.
4. Roast at 360 - degrees Fahrenheit for 33 to 37 minutes or until the sausages are no longer pink.
5. Work in batches as needed, shaking halfway through the roasting time.

318. Ricotta Wraps and Spring Chicken

Prep + Cook Time: 20 minutes   **Servings:** 12

Ingredients:

- 2 large-sized chicken breasts; cooked and shredded
- 1/3 teaspoon sea salt
- 1/4 teaspoon ground black pepper; or more to taste
- 2 spring onions; chopped
- 1/4 cup soy sauce
- 1 tablespoon molasses
- 1 tablespoon rice vinegar
- 10 ounces Ricotta cheese
- 1 teaspoon grated fresh ginger
- 50 wonton wrappers

Instructions:

1. Combine all of the above ingredients; except the wonton wrappers, in a mixing dish.
2. Lay out the wrappers on a clean surface. Brush them with a nonstick cooking spray.
3. Spread the wonton wrappers with the prepared filling.
4. Fold the outside corners to the center over the filling and roll up every wonton wrapper tightly. You can moisten the edges with a little water.
5. Set the Air Fryer to cook at 375 – degrees Fahrenheit. Air-fry the rolls for 5 minutes; working in batches.
6. Serve with a dipping sauce of your choice.

319. Mustard Turkey Fingers and Cajun

Prep + Cook Time: 20 minutes   **Servings:** 4

Ingredients:

- 1/2 cup cornmeal mix
- 1/2 cup all-purpose flour
- 1 ½ tablespoons Cajun seasoning
- 1 ½ tablespoons whole-grain mustard
- 1 ½ cups buttermilk
- 1 teaspoon soy sauce
- 3/4-pound turkey tenderloins; cut into finger-sized strips
- Salt and ground black pepper; to taste

Instructions:

1. Grab three bowls. Combine the cornmeal, flour, and Cajun seasoning in the first bowl.
2. Mix the whole-grain mustard, buttermilk and soy sauce in the second one.

3. Season the turkey fingers with the salt and black pepper.
4. Now; dip each strip into the buttermilk mix. after that; cover them with the cornmeal mixture on all sides.
5. Transfer the prepared turkey fingers to the Air Fryer baking pan and cook for 15 minutes at 360 - degrees Fahrenheit.
6. Serve hot with tomato ketchup.

320. Delicious Honey Glazed Turkey Breast

Prep + Cook Time: 55 minutes   **Servings:** 6

Ingredients:

- 2 teaspoons butter; softened
- 1 teaspoon dried sage
- 2 sprigs rosemary; chopped
- 1 teaspoon salt
- 1/4 teaspoon freshly ground black pepper; or more to taste

- 1 whole turkey breast
- 2 tablespoons turkey broth
- 1/4 cup honey
- 2 tablespoons whole-grain mustard
- 1 tablespoon butter

Instructions:

1. Start by preheating your Air Fryer to 360 – degrees Fahrenheit.
2. To make the rub; combine 2 tablespoons of butter, sage, rosemary, salt, and pepper.
3. Mix well to combine and spread it evenly over the surface of the turkey breast.
4. Roast for 20 minutes in an Air Fryer cooking basket. Flip the turkey breast over and cook for a further 15 to 16 minutes.
5. Now; flip it back over and roast for 12 minutes more.
6. While the turkey is roasting, whisk the other ingredients in a saucepan.
7. After that; spread the glaze all over the turkey breast.
8. Return to the Air Fryer for another 5 minutes. let the turkey rest for a few minutes before carving.

321. Easy Chicken Curry

Prep + Cook Time: 60 minutes   **Servings:** 2

Ingredients:

- 2 chicken thighs
- 1 zucchini [small]
- 2 garlic cloves
- 6 apricots [dried]
- 3.5 ounces. turnip [long]
- 6 basil leaves

- 1 tablespoon pistachios [whole]
- 1 tablespoon raisin soup
- 1 tablespoon oil [olive]
- 1 large pinch salt
- 1 pinch pepper
- 1 teaspoon curry powder

Instructions:

1. Preheat Air Fryer at 320 - degrees Fahrenheit.
2. Cut the chicken into 2 fine pieces and Cut vegetables into bite sizes.
3. Add all ingredients in a dish and mix well.
4. Cook for at least 30 minutes. Sprinkle basin at top for decoration.
5. Best to serve with rice or roti and enjoy the right combination.

322. Mouthwatering Marjoram Chicken

Prep + Cook Time: 1 hr.   **Servings:** 2

Ingredients:

- 2 small-sized chicken breasts; skinless and boneless
- 2 tablespoons butter
- 1 teaspoon sea salt
- 1/2 teaspoon red pepper flakes; crushed
- 2 teaspoons marjoram
- 1/4 teaspoon lemon pepper

Instructions:

1. Add all of the above ingredients to a mixing dish and let it marinate for 30 minutes to 1 hour.
2. Then; set your Air Fryer to cook at 390 degrees.
3. Cook for 20 minutes; turning halfway through cooking time.
4. Check for doneness using an instant-read thermometer. Serve over jasmine rice.

323. Amazing Hoisin Glazed Turkey Drumsticks

Prep + Cook Time: 40 minutes + marinating time   **Servings:** 4

Ingredients:

- 2 turkey drumsticks
- 2 tablespoons balsamic vinegar
- 2 tablespoons dry white wine
- 1 tablespoon extra-virgin olive oil
- 1 sprig rosemary; chopped
- Salt and ground black pepper; to taste
- 2 ½ tablespoons butter; melted

For the Hoisin Glaze:

- 2 tablespoons hoisin sauce
- 1 tablespoon honey
- 1 tablespoon honey mustard

Instructions:

1. Add the turkey drumsticks to a mixing dish and add the vinegar, wine, olive oil, and rosemary.
2. Let them marinate for 3 hours.
3. Then; preheat the Air Fryer to 350 – degrees Fahrenheit.
4. Season the turkey drumsticks with salt and black pepper. spread the melted butter over the surface of drumsticks.
5. Cook turkey drumsticks at 350 – degrees Fahrenheit for 30 to 35 minutes; working in batches.
6. Turn the drumsticks over a few times during the cooking.
7. While the turkey drumsticks are roasting, prepare the Hoisin glaze by mixing all the glaze ingredients.
8. After that; drizzle the turkey with the glaze mixture, roast for a further 5 minutes.
9. Let it rest about 10 minutes before carving and serving.

324. Amazing Turkey Sliders with Chive Mayonnaise

Prep + Cook Time: 20 minutes   **Servings:** 6

Ingredients:

For the Turkey Sliders:

- 3/4-pound turkey mince
- 1/4 cup pickled jalapeno; chopped
- 1 tablespoon oyster sauce
- 1 – 2 cloves garlic; minced
- 1 tablespoon chopped fresh cilantro
- 2 tablespoons chopped scallions
- Sea salt and ground black pepper; to savor

For the Chive Mayo:

- 1 cup mayonnaise
- 1 tablespoon chives
- 1 teaspoon salt
- Zest of 1 lime

Instructions:

1. In a mixing bowl; thoroughly combine all ingredients for the turkey sliders. Mold the mixture into 6 even-sized slider patties.
2. Air-fry them at 365 – degrees Fahrenheit for 15 minutes. Meanwhile; make the Chive Mayo by mixing the rest of the above ingredients.
3. Assemble the sandwiches with burger buns and serve warm.

325. Delicious Thai Sticky Turkey Wings

Prep + Cook Time: 40 minutes   **Servings:** 4

Ingredients:

- 3/4-pound turkey wings; cut into pieces
- 1 teaspoon ginger powder
- 1 teaspoon garlic powder
- 3/4 teaspoon paprika
- 2 tablespoons soy sauce
- 1 handful minced lemongrass
- Sea salt flakes and ground black pepper; to savor
- 2 tablespoons rice wine vinegar
- 1/4 cup peanut butter
- 1 tablespoon sesame oil
- 1/2 cup Thai sweet chili sauce

Instructions:

1. In a saucepan with boiling water, cook the turkey wings for 20 minutes.
2. Transfer the turkey wings to a large-sized mixing dish, toss with the remaining ingredients, without Thai sweet chili sauce.
3. Air-fry them for 20 minutes at 350 - degrees Fahrenheit or until they are thoroughly cooked. make sure to flip them over during the cooking time.
4. Serve the turkey wings with Thai sweet chili sauce and lemon wedges.

326. Ground Turkey Stuffed Peppers and Quinoa

Prep + Cook Time: 30 minutes   **Servings:** 4

Ingredients:

- 1/4 cup canola oil
- 7 ounces ground turkey
- 1/2 cup onion; finely chopped
- 2 cloves garlic; peeled and finely minced
- 1/2 cup quinoa; cooked
- 1 tablespoon fresh cilantro; chopped
- 1 tablespoon fresh parsley; chopped
- 1 ½ cups chopped tomatoes
- 1 teaspoon dried basil
- Salt and black pepper; to taste
- 4 bell peppers; slice off the tops; deveined
- 1/2 cup fat-free chicken broth
- 1 tablespoon cider vinegar
- 1/3 cup shredded three-cheese blend

Instructions:

1. Preheat the oil in a saucepan over a moderate heat.
2. Now; sauté the turkey, onion and garlic for 4 to 5 minutes or until they have softened.
3. Add cooked quinoa, cilantro, parsley, 1 cup of tomatoes, basil, salt, and black pepper.
4. Stuff the peppers with the prepared meat filling. Transfer them to a baking dish.
5. After that; thoroughly combine the remaining tomatoes with chicken broth and cider vinegar. Add the sauce to the baking dish.
6. Cook covered at 360 – degrees Fahrenheit for 18 minutes.
7. Uncover; top with cheese and cook for 5 minutes more or until cheese is bubbling.
8. Serve right away.

327. Tasty Scallion Stuffed Turkey Roulade

Prep + Cook Time: 50 minutes

Servings: 4

Ingredients:

- 1 turkey fillet
- Salt and garlic pepper; to taste
- 1/3 teaspoon onion powder
- 1/2 teaspoon dried basil
- 1/3 teaspoon ground red chipotle pepper
- 1 ½ teaspoons mustard seeds

- 1/2 teaspoon fennel seeds
- 2 tablespoons melted butter
- 3 tablespoons coriander; finely chopped
- 1/2 cup scallions; finely chopped
- 2 clove garlic; finely minced

Instructions:

1. Place the turkey fillets on a clean and dry surface. Then; flatten the fillets to a thickness of about 1/2-inch using a meat mallet.
2. Sprinkle them with salt, garlic pepper, and onion powder.
3. Then; mix the basil, chipotle pepper, mustard seeds, fennel seeds and butter in a small-sized bowl.
4. Spread this mixture over the fillets, leaving an inch border.
5. Top with coriander, scallions and garlic. Roll the fillets towards the border.
6. Lastly; secure the rolls with a cooking twine and transfer them to the Air Fryer cooking basket.
7. Roast at 350 – degrees Fahrenheit for about 50 minutes; turn it halfway through the roasting time.
8. Check for doneness and serve warm.

328. Delicious Chicken Nuggets

Prep + Cook Time: 40 minutes

Servings: 4

Ingredients:

- 2 slices whole meal breadcrumbs
- 9 ounces. chicken breast [chopped]
- 1 teaspoon garlic [minced]
- 1 teaspoon tomato ketchup
- 2 eggs [medium]

- 1 tablespoon oil [olive]
- 1 teaspoon paprika
- 1 teaspoon parsley
- salt and pepper to taste

Instructions:

1. Make a batter using breadcrumbs, paprika, salt, pepper and oil. Mix the ingredients well to make a thick paste.
2. In chopped chicken add parsley, one egg and ketchup.
3. Make the chicken mixture into a nugget shape and dip it in other egg, then add in crumbs for coating. Cook at 390 - degrees Fahrenheit for 10 minutes in Air Fryer. Serve it with mayo dip to enjoy the combined flavor.

329. Sunday Colby Turkey Meatloaf

Prep + Cook Time: 50 minutes

Servings: 6

Ingredients:

- 1-pound turkey mince
- 1/2 cup scallions; finely chopped
- 2 garlic cloves; finely minced
- 1 teaspoon dried thyme
- 1/2 teaspoon dried basil
- 3/4 cup Colby cheese; shredded
- 3/4 cup crushed saltines

- 1 tablespoon tamari sauce
- Salt and black pepper; to taste
- 1/4 cup roasted red pepper tomato sauce
- 1 teaspoon brown sugar
- 3/4 tablespoons olive oil
- 1 medium-sized egg; well beaten

Instructions:

1. In a nonstick skillet; that is preheated over a moderate heat, sauté the turkey mince, scallions, garlic, thyme, and basil until just tender and fragrant.
2. Then set your Air Fryer to cook at 360 degrees.
3. Combine sautéed mixture with the cheese, saltines and tamari sauce.
4. Then form the mixture into a loaf shape.
5. Mix the remaining items and pour them over the meatloaf.
6. Cook in the Air Fryer baking pan for 45 to 47 minutes. serve warm.

330. Special Chicken Tenders

Prep + Cook Time: 35 minutes   **Servings:** 4

Ingredients:

- two eggs [beaten]
- 1/2 cup flour [all purpose]
- 1/2 teaspoon salt [or to taste]
- 1/2 cup breadcrumbs [seasoned]
- 2 tablespoon oil [olive]
- 3/4 Pounds chicken tenders

Instructions:

1. Preheat Air Fryer at 330 - degrees Fahrenheit
2. Put breadcrumbs in one bowl and eggs and flour in separate bowls.
3. Mix eggs and flour well.
4. Mix salt and pepper with breadcrumbs and add oil.
5. Coat the tenders with flour, then eggs followed by crumbs. Cook in Air Fryer for 10 minutes.
6. After 10 minutes raise temperature to 390 - degrees Fahrenheit and cook for another 5 minutes. Serve the tenders with chili sauce.

331. Chicken Drumsticks

Prep + Cook Time: 35 minutes   **Servings:** 4

Ingredients:

- 8 chicken drumsticks
- 1 teaspoon cayenne pepper
- 2 tablespoon mustard powder
- 2 tablespoon oregano
- 2 tablespoon thyme
- 3 tablespoon coconut milk
- 1 large egg; lightly beaten
- 1/3 cup cauliflower
- 1/3 cup oats
- pepper and salt to taste

Instructions:

1. Preheat the Air Fryer to 350 - degrees Fahrenheit.
2. Season chicken drumsticks with pepper and salt. Rub coconut milk all over chicken drumsticks.
3. Add all ingredients except egg into the food processor and process until it looks like breadcrumbs.
4. Add food processor mixture into the bowl. In a small bowl; add beaten egg. Dip each chicken drumstick in breadcrumb mixture then dip in egg and again dip in breadcrumbs.
5. Place coated chicken drumsticks in Air Fryer basket and cook for 20 minutes.
6. Serve the drumsticks hot.

332. Bacon Wrapped Chicken

Prep + Cook Time: 20 minutes   **Servings:** 6

Ingredients:

- 1 chicken breast; cut into 6 pieces
- 6 rashers back bacon
- 1 tablespoon soft cheese

Instructions:
1. Place bacon rashers on dish and spread soft cheese over them.
2. Place chicken pieces on each bacon rashers and roll up them and secure with wooden stick. Place them in Air Fryer basket. Air fry at 350 – degrees Fahrenheit for 15 minutes.
3. Serve the dish and enjoy.

333. Chicken Wings Recipe

Prep + Cook Time: 20 minutes   **Servings:** 6

Ingredients:

- 6 chicken wings
- 1 tablespoon honey
- 2 garlic cloves; chopped

- 1 teaspoon red chili flakes
- 2 tablespoon Worcestershire sauce
- pepper and salt to taste

Instructions:
1. Add all ingredients except chicken wings in bowl and mix well.
2. Now add chicken wings and mix well and place in refrigerator for 1 hour.
3. Place marinated chicken wings into the Air Fryer basket and spray with cooking spray.
4. Air-fry chicken wings at 320 - degrees Fahrenheit for 8 minutes. After 8 minutes turn heat to 350 - degrees Fahrenheit and air fry for another 4 minutes.
5. Serve hot and enjoy.

334. Chicken Sandwich

Prep + Cook Time: 30 minutes   **Servings:** 2

Ingredients:

- 2 chicken breasts; boneless and skinless
- 2 large eggs
- 1/2 cup skimmed milk
- 6 tablespoon soy sauce
- 1 cup all-purpose flour
- 1 teaspoon smoked paprika

- 1 teaspoon salt
- 1/4 teaspoon black pepper
- 1/2 teaspoon garlic powder
- 1 tablespoon olive oil
- 4 Hamburger buns

Instructions:
1. Cut chicken breast into 2 – 3 pieces; depending on its size.
2. Transfer to a large bowl and sprinkle with soy sauce. Season with smoked paprika, black pepper, salt, and garlic powder and stir to combine.
3. Set aside for 30 – 40 minutes.
4. Meanwhile; combine eggs with milk in a mixing bowl. In another bowl place all-purpose flour.
5. Dip marinated chicken into egg mixture and then into flour. Make sure pieces are coated with all ingredients.
6. Preheat the Air Fryer to 380 - degrees Fahrenheit.
7. Sprinkle with olive oil and place chicken pieces into the fryer.
8. Cook for 10 – 12 minutes; turning once, until ready.
9. Toast Hamburger buns and assemble sandwiches.
10. You may also use ketchup; BBQ sauce or any other for your preference.

335. Lemon Garlic Chicken

Prep + Cook Time: 25 minutes   **Servings:** 1

Ingredients:

- 1 chicken breast
- 1 teaspoon garlic; minced

- 1 tablespoon chicken seasoning
- 1 lemon juice

- handful black peppercorns
- pepper and salt to taste

Instructions:
1. Preheat the Air Fryer to 350 - degrees Fahrenheit.
2. Season chicken with pepper and salt. Rub chicken seasoning all over chicken breast and place seasoned chicken on aluminum foil sheet.
3. Add garlic, lemon juice, and black peppercorns over chicken and seal foil tightly.
4. Place chicken in Air Fryer basket and cook for 15 minutes. Open foil and serve.

336. Cajun Seasoned Chicken

Prep + Cook Time: 15 minutes   **Servings:** 2

Ingredients:
- 2 chicken breasts; boneless
- 3 tablespoon cajun spice

Instructions:
1. Season chicken breasts with Cajun spice from both the sides. Place seasoned chicken in Air Fryer basket.
2. Air fry at 350 - degrees Fahrenheit for 10 minutes or until cooked. Cut into slices and serve.

337. Delicious Chicken Fillets

Prep + Cook Time: 30 minutes   **Servings:** 3

Ingredients:
- 8 pieces of chicken fillet [approximately 3 x 1 x 1-inch dimensions]
- One Egg
- 1 ounce. salted butter; melted
- 1 cup panko bread crumbs
- 1 teaspoon garlic powder
- 1/2 cup parmesan cheese
- 1 teaspoon Italian herbs

Instructions:
1. Marinate the pieces of the chicken fillet in the mixture consisting of the whisked egg, melted butter, garlic powder, and Italian herbs.
2. Then mix the Panko bread crumbs and parmesan and cover the fillet.
3. Make sure bread crumbs are moistened and set the chicken aside for 10 minutes.
4. Place the aluminum foil in your Air Fryer basket.
5. Preheat the fryer to 390 – degrees Fahrenheit for about 3 minutes.
6. Layer 4 pieces of the chicken on the foil in the basket. Cook it for 6 minutes without flipping. The chicken is ready when golden brown.
7. Repeat the procedure for the remaining 4 chicken pieces.
8. Serve the chicken fillets hot.

338. Different Chicken Nuggets

Prep + Cook Time: 30 minutes   **Servings:** 4

Ingredients:
- 1/2 Pound chicken breast; cut into pieces
- 1 teaspoon parsley
- 1 teaspoon paprika
- 1 tablespoon olive oil
- Two eggs; beaten
- 1 teaspoon tomato ketchup
- 1 teaspoon garlic; minced
- 1/2 cup breadcrumbs
- pepper and salt to taste

Instructions:
1. In a shallow dish; combine together breadcrumbs, olive oil, paprika, pepper, and salt.

2. Add chicken, ketchup, One Egg, garlic, and parsley in food processor and make puree. Add remaining one egg in bowl.
3. Make chicken nugget from chicken puree and dip in egg then coat with breadcrumb mixture.
4. Place coated chicken nugget in Air Fryer basket and air fry at 390 – degrees Fahrenheit for 10 minutes. Serve the nuggets hot.

339. Crispy Chicken Tenders

Prep + Cook Time: 30 minutes   **Servings:** 4

Ingredients:

- 2 pounds chicken tenders; skinless and boneless
- 3 large eggs
- 6 tablespoon skimmed milk
- 1/2 cup all-purpose flour
- 1 cup breadcrumbs
- 1/4 teaspoon black pepper
- 1 teaspoon salt
- 2 tablespoon olive oil

Instructions:

1. In the large mixing bowl combine breadcrumbs and olive oil. Stir to combine and set aside.
2. In another bowl whisk together eggs and milk. Add salt and black pepper and also set aside.
3. In the third bowl add flour.
4. Cut chicken tenders into 1-inch strips. Dip each strip into flour; then into egg mixture and then into breadcrumbs.
5. Preheat the Air Fryer to 380 - degrees Fahrenheit and cook coated chicken tenders for about 13 – 15 minutes; shaking couple times until crispy and ready. Serve with mashed potatoes and dipping sauce on your preference.

340. Roasted Chicken with Herbs

Prep + Cook Time: 55 minutes   **Servings:** 4

Ingredients:

- 5 – 7 pounds whole chicken with skin
- 1 teaspoon garlic powder
- 1 teaspoon onion powder
- 1/2 teaspoon dried thyme
- 1/2 teaspoon dried basil
- 1/2 teaspoon dried rosemary
- 1/2 teaspoon black pepper
- 2 teaspoon salt
- 2 tablespoon extra virgin olive oil

Instructions:

1. Rub the chicken with salt, pepper, herbs, and olive oil. Set aside for at least 20 – 30 minutes.
2. Meanwhile, preheat the Air Fryer to 340 F.
3. Cook chicken for 18 – 20 minutes; and then carefully turn for another side.
4. Cook for another 20 minutes, until ready.
5. When cooked; let the chicken rest for 10 minutes, then slice and serve.

341. Herbed Chicken Wings

Prep + Cook Time: 40 minutes   **Servings:** 6

Ingredients:

- 4 Pound chicken wings
- 6 tablespoon red wine vinegar
- 6 tablespoon lime juice
- 1 teaspoon fresh ginger; minced
- 1 tablespoon brown sugar
- 1 teaspoon thyme; chopped
- 1/2 teaspoon white pepper
- 1/4 teaspoon ground cinnamon
- 1 habanero pepper; chopped
- 6 garlic cloves; chopped
- 2 tablespoon soy sauce
- 2 ½ tablespoon olive oil
- 1/4 teaspoon salt

Instructions:

1. Add all ingredients into the mixing bowl and mix well.
2. Place marinated chicken in refrigerator for 1 hour.
3. Preheat the Air Fryer to 390 – degrees Fahrenheit. Add half marinated chicken in Air Fryer basket and cook for 15 minutes. Shake basket once.
4. Cook remaining chicken using same temperature and time. Serve hot.

342. Rosemary Lemon Chicken

Prep + Cook Time: 30 minutes   **Servings:** 2

Ingredients:

- 3/4 Pound chicken
- 1/2 tablespoon olive oil
- 1 tablespoon soy sauce
- 1 teaspoon fresh ginger; minced
- 1 tablespoon oyster sauce
- 3 tablespoon brown sugar
- 1 tablespoon fresh rosemary; chopped
- 1/2 fresh lemon; cut into wedges

Instructions:

1. Add chicken, oil, soy sauce, and ginger in bowl and mix well.
2. Place marinated chicken in refrigerator for 30 minutes.
3. Preheat the Air Fryer to 390 - degrees Fahrenheit for 3 minutes.
4. Add marinated chicken into the baking pan and place in Air Fryer and cook for 6 minutes
5. Meanwhile; in a small bowl combine together rosemary, sugar, and oyster sauce.
6. Pour rosemary mixture over chicken then place lemon wedges over chicken. Continue cook chicken in Air Fryer at 390 - degrees Fahrenheit for 13 minutes.
7. Flip chicken pieces halfway. Serve hot and enjoy.

343. Yummy Chicken Strips

Prep + Cook Time: 25 minutes   **Servings:** 2

Ingredients:

- 1 chicken breast; cut into strips
- One Egg; beaten
- 1/4 cup plain flour
- 3/4 cup breadcrumbs
- 1 teaspoon mix spice
- 1 tablespoon plain oats
- 1 tablespoon desiccated coconut
- pepper and salt to taste

Instructions:

1. In a bowl; combine together breadcrumbs, mix spice, oats, coconut, pepper, and salt.
2. Place beaten egg in another bowl. Place flour in shallow dish.
3. Coat chicken strips with flour then dip in egg and finally roll in breadcrumb mixture. Place coated chicken strips in Air Fryer basket and air fry at 350 - degrees Fahrenheit for 8 minutes.
4. After 8 minutes turn temperature at 320 - degrees Fahrenheit and cook for 4 minutes.
5. Serve the dish hot.

344. Special Grandma's Chicken Recipe

Prep + Cook Time: 20 minutes   **Servings:** 4

Ingredients:

- 12 ounces. chicken breast; diced
- 6 ounces. genral tso sauce
- 1/2 teaspoon white pepper
- 1/4 cup milk
- 1 cup cornstarch

Instructions:

1. Add chicken and milk in mixing bowl and set aside for 2 minutes.
2. Drain milk from chicken and toss chicken with cornstarch.

3. Place chicken in Air Fryer basket and air fry at 350 - degrees Fahrenheit for 12 minutes.
4. Place chicken on serving dish and sprinkle with white pepper.
5. Drizzle tso sauce over chicken and serve.

345. Orange Chicken Wings

Prep + Cook Time: 40 minutes   **Servings:** 6

Ingredients:

- 6 chicken wings
- 1 ½ tablespoon Worcestershire sauce
- 1 tablespoon sugar
- 1 orange juice and zest
- 1/2 teaspoon thyme; dried
- 1/2 teaspoon sage

- 1 teaspoon mint
- 1 teaspoon basil
- 1/2 teaspoon oregano
- 1 teaspoon parsley
- 1 teaspoon rosemary
- salt and pepper to taste

Instructions:

1. Add chicken and all remaining ingredients into the mixing bowl and mix well.
2. Place marinated chicken into the refrigerator for 30 minutes. Preheat the Air Fryer to 350 - degrees Fahrenheit.
3. Wrap marinated chicken in aluminum foil with juices. Place wrapped chicken in Air Fryer basket and air fry at 350 – degrees Fahrenheit for 20 minutes.
4. Open foil wrap chicken and discard orange zest and air fry chicken wings at 350 – degrees Fahrenheit for another 15 minutes. Serve the dish hot.

346. Lime Honey Chicken Wings

Prep + Cook Time: 7 hour   **Servings:** 2

Ingredients:

- 16 winglets
- 1/2 teaspoon sea salt
- 2 tablespoon light soya sauce
- 1/4 teaspoon white pepper powder

- 1/2 crush black pepper
- 2 tablespoon honey
- 2 tablespoon lime juice

Instructions:

1. Pour all ingredients [except winglets] into a glass dish, add in mid wings, mix well and let it marinate for at least 6 hours if you don't have time.
2. Cover with lip and refrigerate them.
3. Bring out to rest in room temperature for 30 minutes.
4. Air fry the wings with 355 - degrees Fahrenheit for 6 minutes, flip over for another 6 minutes.
5. Let it cool for 5 minutes. Serve with a wedge of lemon.

347. Asian Chicken Kebabs

Prep + Cook Time: 30 minutes   **Servings:** 3

Ingredients:

- 1-pound chicken breasts; diced
- 5 tablespoon honey
- 1/2 cup soy sauce
- 6 large mushrooms; cut in halves
- 3 medium-sized bell peppers; cut

- 1 small zucchini; cut into rings
- 2 medium tomatoes; cut into rings
- Salt and pepper; to taste
- 1/4 cup sesame seeds
- 1 tablespoon olive oil

Instructions:

1. Cut chicken breasts into cubes and transfer to a large bowl.
2. Add some salt and pepper. Add one tablespoon of olive oil and stir to combine.
3. Add honey and soy sauce, and sprinkle with some sesame seeds. Set aside for 15 – 30 minutes.
4. Cut mushrooms, tomatoes, bell peppers, and zucchini. Take wooden skewers and start putting chicken and vegetables, mixing each other.
5. Preheat the Air Fryer to 340 – degrees Fahrenheit and place chicken kebabs into the fryer basket.
6. Cook for about 15 minutes; turning once during cooking, until crispy and brown.

348. Tasty Chicken Tenderloins

Prep + Cook Time: 25 minutes   **Servings:** 4

Ingredients:

- 8 chicken tenderloins
- One Egg; beaten
- 2 tablespoon olive oil
- 1 cup breadcrumbs
- pepper and salt to taste

Instructions:

1. Preheat the Air Fryer to 350 – degrees Fahrenheit.
2. In a shallow dish; combine together breadcrumbs, olive oil, pepper, and salt.
3. Add beaten egg in another dish.
4. Dip chicken into the egg then coat with breadcrumb mixture and place in Air Fryer basket. Air fry chicken in preheated Air Fryer for 12 minutes.

349. Special Buffalo Wings

Prep + Cook Time: 35 min. + [2 - 12 hours marinate]   **Servings:** 4

Ingredients:

- 2 Pounds. chicken wings; without the wing tips
- 1/4 cup + 1/4 cup hot sauce; separately
- 3 + 3 tablespoon. melted butter; separately
- sea salt to taste
- blue cheese; optional
- celery sticks; optional

Instructions:

1. Prepare the chicken wings: divide the drumettes from the wingettes. Place them into the bowl.
2. In another bowl mix together 3 tablespoons of melted butter and 1/4 cup of hot sauce stirring them well.
3. Cover the chicken pieces with this mixture and marinate it for 2 hours or even overnight.
4. Preheat the Air Fryer to 400 - degrees Fahrenheit for about 3 minutes. Split the wings into 2 batches.
5. Place the first batch into the Air Fryer and cook for about 12 minutes; shaking halfway.
6. Repeat the same with the second batch.
7. When the cooking process ends for both batches of wings, combine them and put all of them into the Air Fryer again for 2 minutes.
8. Prepare the sauce: mix the remaining 3 table-spoons of butter and the remaining 1/4 cup of hot sauce.
9. Dip the cooked wings in this sauce and serve.
10. It tastes great with the blue cheese and celery sticks.

350. Crispy Chicken Popcorn

Prep + Cook Time: 25 minutes   **Servings:** 12

Ingredients:

- 1 chicken breast; boneless
- 1/4 cup plain flour
- One Egg; beaten
- 1 cup breadcrumbs
- 2 teaspoon mix spice
- pepper and salt to taste

Instructions:

1. Add chicken into the food processor and process until it forms into minced chicken.
2. In a small bowl; add beaten egg. In a shallow dish add plain flour.
3. In another shallow dish combine together breadcrumbs, mix spice, pepper, and salt.
4. Make small chicken balls from minced chicken. Roll chicken balls in flour then dip in egg and finally coat with breadcrumb mixture.
5. Place coated chicken balls in Air Fryer and air fry at 350 – degrees Fahrenheit for 10 minutes or until cooked. Serve the dish hot.

351. Homemade Moroccan Chicken

Prep + Cook Time: 25 minutes   **Servings:** 2

Ingredients:

- 1/2-pound shredded chicken
- 1 cup broth
- 1 carrot
- 1 broccoli; chopped
- A pinch of cinnamon
- A pinch of cumin
- A pinch of red pepper
- A pinch of sea salt

Instructions:

1. In a mixing bowl combine the shredded chicken with cumin, red pepper, sea salt and cinnamon.
2. Cut the carrots into small pieces. Add the carrot and broccoli to the chicken mixture.
3. Pour in the broth and mix well. Let it stand for 30 minutes.
4. Add the mixture to the Air Fryer. Cook for about 15 minutes. Serve hot.

352. Homemade Chinese Chicken Wings

Prep + Cook Time: 45 minutes   **Servings:** 4

Ingredients:

- 8 chicken wings
- 2 tablespoons five spice
- 2 tablespoon soy sauce
- 1 tablespoon mixed spices
- salt and pepper to taste

Instructions:

1. Mix all the ingredients into a bowl.
2. Line fryer with an aluminum foil and preheat the fryer to 360 – degrees Fahrenheit. Cook the mixture in oil for 15 minutes.
3. Raise temperature to 390 – degrees Fahrenheit; flip and cook for 5 minutes. Serve them with mayo dip and enjoy the taste.

353. Roasted Chicken And Potatoes

Prep + Cook Time: 45 minutes   **Servings:** 6

Ingredients:

- 1 Pound potatoes
- 2 Pound chicken
- 2 tablespoon olive oil
- Pepper and Salt to taste

Instructions:

1. Preheat the Air Fryer to 350 – degrees Fahrenheit. Add chicken in Air Fryer basket then add potatoes. Season with pepper and salt.
2. Drizzle with olive oil all over chicken and potatoes. Cook chicken and potatoes in preheated Air Fryer for 40 minutes.

354. Yummy Chicken Tenders

Prep + Cook Time: 30 minutes   **Servings:** 4

Ingredients:

- 1 Pound chicken tenders
- 1 teaspoon ginger; minced
- 4 garlic cloves; minced
- 2 tablespoon sesame oil
- 6 tablespoon pineapple juice
- 2 tablespoon soy sauce
- 1/2 teaspoon pepper

Instructions:

1. Add all ingredients except chicken in bowl and mix well.
2. Skewer chicken and place in bowl and marinate for 2 hours.
3. Preheat the Air Fryer to 350 - degrees Fahrenheit. Place marinated chicken in Air Fryer basket and cook for 18 minutes. Serve the dish hot.

355. Lime Dijon Chicken

Prep + Cook Time: 20 minutes   **Servings:** 6

Ingredients:

- 8 chicken drumsticks
- 1 lime juice
- 1 lime zest
- kosher salt to taste
- 1 tablespoon light mayonnaise
- 3/4 teaspoon black pepper
- 1 clove garlic; crushed
- 3 tablespoon dijon mustard
- 1 teaspoon dried parsley

Instructions:

1. Preheat the Air Fryer to 375 - degrees Fahrenheit.
2. Get rid of the skin of the chicken. Season the chicken with salt. In a bowl add the Dijon mustard with lime juice.
3. Add in the lime zest, pepper, parsley and garlic and mix well. Coat the chicken into the lime mixture. Let it marinate for about 10 to 15 minutes.
4. Add some oil into the Air Fryer. Add the chicken drumstick and set the timer to 5 minutes.
5. Toss the chicken drumsticks and fry for another 5 minutes. Serve hot with the mayo.

356. Fried Chicken Thighs

Prep + Cook Time: 35 minutes   **Servings:** 4

Ingredients:

- 4 chicken thighs
- 1 ½ tablespoon Cajun seasoning
- One Egg; beaten
- 1/2 cup plain flour
- 1 teaspoon seasoning salt

Instructions:

1. Preheat the Air Fryer to 350 – degrees Fahrenheit.
2. In a shallow dish combine together flour, Cajun seasoning, and seasoning salt.
3. Coat chicken with flour then dip in egg and again coat with flour mixture. Place chicken in preheated Air Fryer and cook for 25 minutes. Serve hot and enjoy.

357. Delicious Fried Chicken Recipe

Prep + Cook Time: 30 minutes

Servings: 4

Ingredients:

- 4 chicken legs [bone-in and skin-on]; cut into drumsticks and thighs [about 3 ½ pounds]
- pickle juice from a 24-ounce jar of kosher dill pickles
- 1/2 cup flour
- salt and freshly ground black pepper
- Two eggs

- 2 tablespoon vegetable or canola oil
- 1 cup fine breadcrumbs
- 1 teaspoon salt
- 1 teaspoon freshly ground black pepper
- 1/2 teaspoon ground paprika
- 1/8 teaspoon cayenne pepper
- vegetable or canola oil in a spray bottle

Instructions:

1. Place the chicken in a shallow dish and pour the pickle juice over the top.
2. Cover and transfer the chicken to the refrigerator to brine in the pickle juice for 3 to 8 hours.
3. When you are ready to cook; remove the chicken from the refrigerator to let it come to room temperature while you set up a dredging station.
4. Place the flour in a shallow dish and season well with salt and freshly ground black pepper.
5. Whisk the eggs and vegetable oil together in a second shallow dish.
6. In a third shallow dish; combine the breadcrumbs, salt, pepper, paprika and cayenne pepper.
7. Pre-heat the Air Fryer to 370 - degrees Fahrenheit.
8. Remove the chicken from pickle brine and gently dry it with a clean kitchen towel. Dredge each piece of chicken in the flour, then dip it into the egg mixture, and finally press it into the breadcrumb mixture to coat all sides of the chicken.
9. Place the breaded chicken on a plate or baking sheet and spray each piece all over with vegetable oil.
10. Air-fry the chicken in two batches. Place two chicken thighs and two drumsticks into the Air Fryer basket. Air-fry for 10 minutes.
11. Then; gently turn the chicken pieces over and air fry for another 10 minutes.
12. Remove the chicken pieces and let them rest on plate, do not cover.
13. Repeat with the second batch of chicken, air frying for 20 minutes, turning the chicken over halfway through.
14. Lower the temperature of the Air Fryer to 340 – degrees Fahrenheit.
15. Place the first batch of chicken on top of the second batch already in the basket and air fry for an additional 7 minutes.
16. Serve the dish warm.

358. Hot Fried Wings

Prep + Cook Time: 35 minutes

Servings: 6

Ingredients:

- 4 Pound chicken wings
- 1 tablespoon brown sugar
- 1 tablespoon Worcestershire sauce

- 1/2 cup butter; melted
- 1/2 cup hot sauce
- 1/2 teaspoon salt

Instructions:

1. Add brown sugar, Worcestershire sauce, butter, salt, and hot sauce in bowl and mix well and set aside.
2. Add chicken wings into the Air Fryer basket and air fry to 380 – degrees Fahrenheit for 25 minutes. Shake basket halfway through.
3. After 25 minutes change temperature to 400 – degrees Fahrenheit for 5 minutes.
4. Add air fried chicken wings into the bowl mixture and toss well. Serve the dish hot.

359. Teriyaki Chicken

| **Prep + Cook Time:** 30 minutes | **Servings:** 2 |

Ingredients:

- 2 chicken drumsticks; boneless
- 1 teaspoon ginger; grated
- 1 tablespoon cooking wine
- 3 tablespoon teriyaki sauce

Instructions:

1. Add all ingredients into the bowl and mix well and place in refrigerator for 30 minutes.
2. Add marinated chicken in Air Fryer baking pan and cook at 350 - degrees Fahrenheit for 8 minutes. After 8 minutes flip the chicken to other side and Cook 380 – degrees Fahrenheit for 6 minutes. Serve hot and enjoy.

360. Homemade Asian Style Chicken

| **Prep + Cook Time:** 25 minutes | **Servings:** 3 |

Ingredients:

- 1-pound chicken breasts; skinless and boneless
- 3 garlic cloves; minced
- 1 tablespoon grated ginger
- 1/4 teaspoon ground black pepper
- 1/2 cup soy sauce
- 1/2 cup pineapple juice
- 1 tablespoon olive oil
- 2 tablespoon sesame seeds

Instructions:

1. Mix all ingredients in the large bowl. Cut chicken breasts and soak in the marinade. Set aside for at least 30 – 40 minutes.
2. Cook marinated chicken in the Air Fryer at 380 - degrees Fahrenheit for about 10 – 15 minutes. Sprinkle cooked chicken with sesame seeds and serve.

361. Fried Whole Chicken

| **Prep + Cook Time:** 30 minutes | **Servings:** 2 |

Ingredients:

- 1 Pound whole chicken
- 1 fresh lemon juice
- 1 teaspoon lemon zest
- 1 tablespoon soy sauce
- 1 ½ tablespoon honey

Instructions:

1. Add all ingredients into the bowl and mix well and place in refrigerator for 1 hour.
2. Place marinated chicken in baking pan and air fry at 320 – degrees Fahrenheit for 18 minutes. After 18 minutes change temperature to 350 - degrees Fahrenheit for 10 minutes or until chicken is lightly brown.

362. Honey and Garlic Chicken Wings

| **Prep + Cook Time:** 25 minutes | **Servings:** 4 |

Ingredients:

- 16 chicken wings
- 1/2 teaspoon salt
- 3/4 cup potato starch
- 1/4 cup butter; melted
- 4 garlic cloves; minced
- 1/4 cup honey

Instructions:

1. Preheat your Air Fryer to 370 – degrees Fahrenheit.
2. Place the wings in a bowl and coat them with the potato starch.

3. Grease a baking dish with cooking spray.
4. Place the wings in it and air fry for 5 minutes.
5. Meanwhile; whisk together the remaining ingredients. Pour the sauce over the chicken and cook for 10 more minutes.

363. Warm Buffalo Chicken Wings

Prep + Cook Time: 37 minutes   **Servings:** 3

Ingredients:

- 2 pounds chicken wings
- 1 teaspoon salt
- 1/4 teaspoon black pepper
- 1 cup buffalo sauce

Instructions:

1. Wash and dry chicken wings with kitchen towels.
2. Transfer to a large bowl and season with salt and pepper. Stir to combine.
3. Preheat the Air Fryer to 380 – degrees Fahrenheit and cook wings, stirring occasionally.
4. When almost done; remove wings and place to a bowl. Sprinkle with buffalo sauce and mix well.
5. Return to an Air Fryer and cook for another 5 – 6 minutes.

364. Mouthwatering Chicken Meatballs

Prep + Cook Time: 20 minutes   **Servings:** 10

Ingredients:

- 2 chicken breasts
- 1 tablespoon mustard powder
- 1 tablespoon cumin
- 1 tablespoon basil
- 1 tablespoon thyme
- 1 teaspoon chili powder
- 3 tablespoon soy sauce
- 2 tablespoon honey
- 1 onion; diced
- pepper and salt to taste

Instructions:

1. Add chicken into the food processor and process until it forms in minced chicken. Now add all remaining ingredients into the food processor and process until combined.
2. Make small meatballs from mixture and place in Air Fryer basket. Air fry at 350 - degrees Fahrenheit for 15 minutes. Serve the dish hot with sauce.

365. Fried Chicken Legs and Thighs

Prep + Cook Time: 35 minutes   **Servings:** 4

Ingredients:

- 3 chicken legs; bone-in, with skin
- 3 chicken thighs; bone-in, with skin
- 2 cups all-purpose flour
- 1 cup buttermilk
- 1 teaspoon salt
- 1 teaspoon ground black pepper
- 1 teaspoon garhc powder
- 1 teaspoon onion powder
- 1 teaspoon ground cumin
- 2 tablespoon extra virgin olive oil

Instructions:

1. Wash and dry chicken and transfer to a large bowl.
2. Pour in buttermilk and set aside to a fridge for 2 hours.
3. In another mixing bowl combine flour and all seasonings. Mix well.
4. Dip chicken into the flour mixture; then into the buttermilk and again into the flour.
5. Preheat the Air Fryer to 360 - degrees Fahrenheit and place chicken legs and thighs to the fryer basket.

6. Sprinkle with olive oil and cook for about 20 minutes; turning couple times during cooking, until ready and crispy.
7. Serve with fresh vegetables.

366. BBQ Drumsticks

Prep + Cook Time: 45 minutes   **Servings:** 4

Ingredients:

- 4 chicken drumsticks
- 1/2 tablespoon mustard
- 1 clove garlic; crushed
- 1 teaspoon chili powder

- 2 teaspoon brown sugar
- 1 tablespoon olive oil
- freshly ground black pepper

Instructions:

1. Preheat the Air Fryer to 390 – degrees Fahrenheit.
2. Mix the garlic with the brown sugar, mustard, pinch of salt, freshly ground pepper, chili powder and the oil.
3. Rub the drumsticks with the marinade and allow to marinate for at least 20 minutes. Put the drumsticks in the Air Fryer basket and set the timer to 10 minutes.
4. Then lower the temperature to 300 - degrees Fahrenheit and roast the drumsticks for another 10 minutes until done. Serve with French bread and corn salad.

367. Turkey Loaf

Prep + Cook Time: 50 minutes   **Servings:** 4

Ingredients:

- 2/3 cup of finely chopped walnuts
- One Egg
- 1 tablespoon organic tomato paste
- 1 ½ Pounds turkey breast; diced
- 1 tablespoon dijon mustard
- 1/2 teaspoon dried savory or dill
- 1 tablespoon onion flakes

- 1/2 teaspoon ground allspice
- 1 small garlic clove; minced
- 1/2 teaspoon sea salt
- 1/4 teaspoon black pepper
- 1 tablespoon liquid aminos
- 2 tablespoon grated parmesan cheese

Instructions:

1. Preheat Air Fryer to 375 - degrees Fahrenheit.
2. Grease a baking dish using oil. Whisk the egg with dill, tomato paste, liquid aminos, mustard, salt, dill, garlic, pepper and allspice. Mix well and add the diced turkey.
3. Mix again and add in the walnuts, cheese and onion flakes. Pour the mixture into your baking dish and bake in the Air Fryer for 40 minutes.
4. Serve the dish hot.

368. Chicken with Mint Yoghurt

Prep + Cook Time: 20 min. + [1 - 12 hours marinate]   **Servings:** 4

Ingredients:

- 2 ounces. chicken breast
- 3 sprigs of mint; minced
- A few leaves of mint; to serve
- 1+1 tablespoon tandoori paste; separately

- 2+2 tablespoon + 3/4 cup Greek yogurt; separately
- 1 tablespoon olive oil
- 2 serves of cooked basmati rice
- ground pepper to taste.
- sea salt to taste

Instructions:

1. Combine in a bowl 1 tablespoon of Tandoori paste and 2 tablespoons of yogurt.
2. Coat the chicken breast with the mixture completely. You may leave it marinating for 1 – 2 hours, or even overnight for the best results.
3. When you are ready to start cooking; preheat the Air Fryer to 360 - degrees Fahrenheit for 5 minutes.
4. Set the Air Fryer's timer to 15 minutes and start cooking the marinated chicken.
5. Meanwhile; prepare Mint Yogurt sauce: combine the minced mint with 2 tablespoons yogurt. Season it with pepper and salt. Stir well.
6. Prepare Tandoori sauce: heat the olive oil in the pan over a medium heat and sauté 1 tablespoon Tandoori paste for 3 minutes.
7. Then add the remaining 3/4 cup of yogurt and sauté for another 2 minutes.
8. When the main meal is ready; remove it and set aside for 5 minutes.
9. Slice the chicken breast and serve it with basmati rice.
10. Cover the meat with Tandoori sauce and Mint Yogurt sauce on top.
11. Decorate the meal with the leaves of mint.

369. Blackened Chicken

Prep + Cook Time: 20 minutes   **Servings:** 2

Ingredients:

- 2 medium-sized chicken breasts; skinless and boneless
- 1/2 teaspoon salt
- 3 tablespoon cajun spice
- 1 tablespoon olive oil

Instructions:

1. Rub chicken breasts with salt, Cajun spice and sprinkle with olive oil.
2. Preheat the Air Fryer to 370 - degrees Fahrenheit and cook chicken breasts for 7 minutes.
3. Turn to another side and cook for another 3 – 4 minutes.
4. When ready; slice and serve.

370. Homemade Jerk Chicken Wings

Prep + Cook Time: 30 min. + [2h to marinate]   **Servings:** 5

Ingredients:

- 3 pounds chicken wings
- 2 tablespoon olive oil
- 2 tablespoon soy sauce
- 6 cloves garlic; finely chopped
- 1 habanero pepper; ribs and seeds removed [these little guys are super spicy!] and flesh finely chopped
- pinch of allspice
- pinch of cinnamon
- pinch of cayenne pepper
- pinch of white pepper
- 2 tablespoon brown sugar
- 1 tablespoon fresh thyme; finely chopped
- 1 tablespoon fresh ginger; finely grated
- 4 scallions; chopped
- 5 tablespoon lime juice
- 1/2 cup red wine vinegar
- salt to taste

Instructions:

1. Prepare the marinade: in a medium bowl; mix all of the ingredients excluding the chicken. Season with salt.
2. Combine the marinade and chicken wings in a heavy-duty zip-top plastic bag. Seal the bag, removing as much air as possible, and mix the contents well.
3. Marinate in the refrigerator for 2 hours.
4. When you are ready to cook; preheat your Air Fryer to 350 – degrees Fahrenheit.

5. Drain the marinated chicken wings on a paper towel-lined baking sheet and pat dry with more paper towels.
6. Place the chicken in the Air Fryer and cook for 10 minutes.
7. Give the chicken a shake and then cook an additional 10 minutes and serve.

371. Succulent Batter Chicken Thighs

Prep + Cook Time: 4 hours 45 minutes   **Servings:** 4

Ingredients:

- 2 cups buttermilk
- 3 teaspoon salt
- 1 teaspoon cayenne pepper
- 1 tablespoon paprika
- 1 ½ pounds chicken thighs
- 2 teaspoon black pepper
- 2 cups flour
- 1 tablespoon garlic powder
- 1 tablespoon baking powder

Instructions:

1. Place the chicken thighs in a large bowl. In another bowl; combine the buttermilk, salt, cayenne, and black pepper.
2. Pour this mixture over the thighs. Cover the bowl with foil and refrigerate for 4 hours.
3. Preheat your Air Fryer to 400 – degrees Fahrenheit.
4. Combine flour, baking powder, and paprika in a shallow bowl. Line a baking dish with parchment paper.
5. Working in two batches, dip the chicken thighs in the flour mixture and bake for 10 minutes. Flip over and air fry for 8 more minutes.

372. Succulent Chicken Bites

Prep + Cook Time: 30 minutes   **Servings:** 4

Ingredients:

- 1-pound chicken breasts; skinless and boneless
- 1/4 cup blue cheese salad dressing
- 1/4 cup blue cheese; crumbled
- 1/2 cup sour cream
- 1 cup breadcrumbs
- 1 tablespoon olive oil
- 1/2 teaspoon salt
- 1/4 teaspoon black pepper

Instructions:

1. In the large mixing bowl combine salad dressing, sour cream, blue cheese.
2. Stir to combine and set aside.
3. In another bowl combine breadcrumbs, olive oil, salt and pepper.
4. Cut chicken breast to 1 - 2-inch pieces and place to breadcrumbs mixture. Toss to coat.
5. Preheat the Air Fryer to 380 – degrees Fahrenheit and transfer chicken bites to a frying basket.
6. Cook for 12 – 15 minutes; until ready and crispy.
7. Serve with sauce and enjoy.

373. Roasted Chicken with Crispy Potato

Prep + Cook Time: 45 minutes   **Servings:** 2

Ingredients:

- 2 chicken legs
- 2 teaspoon sweet smoked Paprika
- 1/2 teaspoon garlic powder
- 1 teaspoon honey
- salt and pepper to taste

The Rosti:

- 1 sweet potato; peeled and coarsely grated

- 1/4 head of savoy cabbage; shredded
- One Egg
- 1 tablespoon flour
- 1 tablespoon fresh parsley; finely chopped
- salt and pepper to taste
- olive oil for brushing

Instructions:

1. In a small bowl; mix the paprika, garlic, and honey.
2. Score the skin of the chicken to help render the fat, and season the chicken with salt and pepper. Rub all over with the paprika mixture.
3. Briefly preheat your Air Fryer to 350 – degrees Fahrenheit. Place the chicken in the Fryer and cook until the skin is crispy, about 35 min.
4. While the chicken cooks, prepare the rosti. place the grated sweet potato in a clean kitchen towel and wring out as much water as possible.
5. In a large bowl; combine the potatoes, cabbage, egg, flour, and parsley. Season with salt and pepper.
6. Shape the potato mixture into 2 large or 4 small patties.
7. Brush with the olive oil and, after removing the chicken from the Fryer, arrange in the Fryer and cook for 4 minutes.
8. Turn the rosti and cook until golden brown, about 4 more minutes.
9. Serve the chicken alongside the rosti and enjoy.

374. Turmeric & Coconut Fried Chicken

Prep + Cook Time: 45 minutes   **Servings:** 3

Ingredients:

- 3 pcs whole chicken leg [de-skin or with skin is totally up to you!]
- 1.8 ounces. pure coconut paste [alternatively; 1.8 ounces. coconut milk]
- 4 – 5 teaspoon ground turmeric
- 1.8 ounces. old ginger
- 1.8 ounces. galangal [a.k.a. lengkuas]
- 3/4 tablespoon salt [less salt option: 1/2 tablespoon]

Instructions:

1. Pound or blend all the ingredients; except the chicken meat.
2. Cut a few slits on the chicken leg especially on the thick parts [will help the chicken to absorb the flavor when marinating].
3. Preheat the Air Fryer at 375 – degrees Fahrenheit. Air fry the chicken for 20 – 25 minutes and flip over at half-time. The chicken is ready when it turned golden brown.

375. Air Fried Turkey Breast

Prep + Cook Time: 35 minutes   **Servings:** 5

Ingredients:

- 6 – 7 pound turkey breast; skinless and boneless
- 2 teaspoon salt
- 1 teaspoon black pepper
- 1/2 teaspoon dried cumin
- 2 tablespoon olive oil

Instructions:

1. Rub the whole turkey breast with all seasoning and olive oil.

2. Preheat the Air Fryer to 340 – degrees Fahrenheit and cook turkey breast for 15 minutes. When time gone, flip the breast to another side and cook for 10 – 15 minutes more, until ready and crispy.
3. Slice and serve meat with mashed rice or fresh vegetables.

376. Mouthwatering Chicken Wrapped in Bacon

Prep + Cook Time: 25 minutes   **Servings:** 6

Ingredients:

- 6 rashers unsmoked back bacon
- 1 small chicken breast
- 1 tablespoon garlic soft cheese

Instructions:

1. Chop up your chicken breast into six bite-sized pieces.
2. Lay out your bacon rashers and spread them with a layer of cheese.
3. Place chicken on top of the cheese and roll it up.
4. Secure everything with a cocktail stick.
5. Place wrapped chicken pieces in the Air Fryer for 15 minutes on 350 – degrees Fahrenheit.

377. Awesome Buttermilk Chicken

Prep + Cook Time: 30 minutes   **Servings:** 4

Ingredients:

- 1.8 Pound store-bought chicken thighs [skin on; bone in]

Marinade:

- 2 cups buttermilk
- 2 teaspoon salt
- 2 teaspoon black pepper
- 1 teaspoon cayenne pepper [I used paprika powder]
- Seasoned Flour
- 2 cups all-purpose flour
- 1 tablespoon baking powder
- 1 tablespoon garlic powder
- 1 tablespoon paprika powder
- 1 teaspoon salt

Instructions:

1. Rinse chicken thighs to remove any obvious fat and residue, and pat dry with paper towels.
2. Toss together chicken pieces, black pepper, paprika and salt in a large bowl to coat.
3. Pour buttermilk over until chicken is coated. Refrigerated for at least 6 hours or overnight.
4. Preheat Air Fryer at 355 – degrees Fahrenheit.
5. In separate bowl; combine flour, baking powder, paprika and salt and pepper.
6. Remove the chicken 1 piece at a time from the buttermilk and dredge in seasoned flour.
7. Shake off any excess flour and transfer to a plate.
8. Arrange chicken one layer on the fryer basket, skin side up, and slide the basket into the Air Fryer.
9. Set timer and air fry for 8 minutes. Pull out the tray; turn chicken pieces over, and set timer for another 10 minutes.
10. Allow to drain on paper towels and serve.

Tips: Place the chicken pieces with skin side up first is to prevent the skin from sticking to the basket when flip over the chicken.

378. Chicken with Sauce, Rice and Vegetables

Prep + Cook Time: 30 minutes   **Servings:** 4

Ingredients:

- 1-pound chicken breasts; skinless and boneless
- 1/2-pound button mushrooms; sliced
- 1 medium-sized onion; chopped
- 1 package [10 oz] Alfred sauce
- 2 cups cooked rice
- 1/2 teaspoon dried thyme
- 1 tablespoon olive oil
- salt and black pepper; to taste

Instructions:

1. Slice mushrooms; cut chicken breast into 1-inch cubes, chop onions.
2. Mix ingredients in the large bowl; season with salt and dried thyme, combine well.
3. Preheat the Air Fryer to 370 – degrees Fahrenheit and sprinkle the basket with olive oil.
4. Transfer chicken with vegetables to the fryer and cook to 10 – 12 minutes; stirring occasionally until cooked and crispy.
5. Open the Air Fryer and stir in Alfredo sauce. Cook for another 3 – 4 minutes.
6. Serve cooked meat mixture over cooked rice and enjoy.

379. Breadcrumb Turkey Breasts

Prep + Cook Time: 25 minutes   **Servings:** 6

Ingredients:

- 6 turkey breasts
- 1 stick butter; melted
- 1 teaspoon salt
- 2 cups panko breadcrumbs
- 1/2 teaspoon cayenne pepper
- 1/2 teaspoon black pepper

Instructions:

1. Place breadcrumbs, half of the salt, half of the pepper, and the cayenne pepper in a large bowl.
2. Stir to combine. In another bowl; season the melted butter with the remaining salt and pepper.
3. Brush the butter over the turkey breasts. Coat with the seasoned breadcrumbs and place on a lined baking dish.
4. Air fry at 390 - degrees Fahrenheit for 15 minutes.

380. Amazing Chicken Escalope

Prep + Cook Time: 45 minutes   **Servings:** 4

Ingredients:

- 4 chicken breasts [skinless]
- 6 sage leaves
- 1/4 cup breadcrumbs [panko]
- 2 eggs [beaten]
- 1/2 cup flour [plain]
- 1/4 cup cheese [parmesan]
- oil for spray

Instructions:

8. Flatten the chicken breasts by cutting them into thin slices.
9. Mix sage, parmesan in a bowl.
10. Season the mixture with flour, salt and pepper. Dip chicken in the well beaten mixture of flour and eggs.
11. Cover the chicken with breadcrumbs.
12. Spray oil on the pan.
13. Preheat it to 390 – degrees Fahrenheit and cook the chicken in it for 20 minutes; until golden.
14. Serve with fried rice.

381. Turkey with Maple Mustard Glaze

Prep + Cook Time: 70 minutes   **Servings:** 6

Ingredients:

- 5 Pounds. whole turkey breast
- 1 tablespoon olive oil
- 1 teaspoon dried thyme
- 1/2 teaspoon smoked paprika
- 1/2 teaspoon dried sage
- 1 teaspoon sea salt
- 1/2 teaspoon black pepper
- 1 tablespoon unsalted butter; melted
- 2 tablespoon dijon mustard
- 1/4 cup maple syrup

Instructions:

1. Preheat the fryer to 350 - degrees Fahrenheit.
2. Prepare the turkey breast by brushing it with the olive oil.
3. Combine thyme, paprika, sage, salt, and pepper. Cover the turkey breast with this mixture thoroughly.
4. Put the turkey breast into the Air Fryer basket and cook it for 25 minutes. Then turn it the other side down and cook for another 12 minutes.
5. Then turn it for the last time and cook for 12 minutes more. The total cooking time is about 50 minutes.
6. If you have a cooking thermometer, check the inside temperature of the turkey breast at this point. It should be 165 F in the end of the cooking process.
7. While the turkey breast is being cooked, use a small saucepan to mix maple syrup, mustard, and melted butter. Stir well to make a smooth sauce.
8. When the turkey breast is ready; cover it with the sauce prepared in the previous step.
9. Then air-fry it for another 5 minutes to make the turkey browned and crispy.
10. Remove the turkey breast from the Air Fryer and set aside for at least 5 minutes; covering it with aluminum foil.
11. Slice the turkey breast and serve.

382. Flavored Crispy Chicken Wings

Prep + Cook Time: 55 minutes   **Servings:** 4

Ingredients:

- 3 pounds bone-in chicken wings
- 3/4 cup all-purpose flour
- 1 tablespoon old bay seasoning
- 4 tablespoon butter
- couple fresh lemons

Instructions:

1. In the large bowl combine all-purpose flour and Old Bay seasoning.
2. Add chicken wings and toss to combine. Make sure all wings are completely covered with flour mixture.
3. Preheat the Air Fryer to 375 - degrees Fahrenheit.
4. Shake off excess flour from wings and transfer them into Air Fryer. Work in batches and do not overcrowd the basket.
5. Cook for about 30 – 40 minutes until wings are ready and skin crispy. Shake often.
6. Meanwhile; melt butter in a sauté pan over low heat. Squeeze lemon juice from one or two lemons to a melted butter and stir to combine.
7. Serve hot wings and pour butter-lemony sauce on top.

383. Special Mozzarella Turkey Rolls

Prep + Cook Time: 20 minutes   **Servings:** 4

Ingredients:

- 4 slices turkey breast [cold cuts can be used; but best taste is achieved with sliced turkey breast]
- 1 cup sliced fresh mozzarella
- 1 tomato; sliced
- 1/2 cup fresh basil
- 4 chive shoots [for tying the rolls]

Instructions:

1. Preheat your Air Fryer to 390 – degrees Fahrenheit.
2. Place slices of mozzarella, tomato and basil onto each turkey slice.
3. Roll up and tie with a chive shoot [looks like a blade of grass but tastes so much better].
4. Place in the Air Fryer and cook for 10 minutes. Serve with a side salad.

384. Chicken Cheese steak Stromboli

Prep + Cook Time: 45 minutes   **Servings:** 2

Ingredients:

- 14 ounces. pizza dough
- 1/2 cup cheese whiz or any other jarred cheese sauce; warm
- 1 ½ cup grated cheddar cheese
- 2 boneless; skinless chicken breasts; partially frozen
- 1/2 onion; sliced
- 1 tablespoon Worcestershire sauce
- cooking spray or 1 tablespoon olive oil
- salt to taste
- freshly ground black pepper
- ketchup; optional

Instructions:

1. Prepare the chicken breasts: slice them very thin on the bias.
2. Preheat the Air Fryer to 400 – degrees Fahrenheit. When it's hot; grease it with the cooking spray.
3. Add onions and cook for about 8 minutes and stir halfway.
4. Add in chicken and Worcestershire sauce and stir once again. Season with pepper and salt to taste.
5. Cook for another 8 minutes stirring 2 – 3 times during the process. When ready; remove onion and chicken and let the mixture cool.
6. Prepare the surface for making pizza dough - drizzle it with some flour. Then roll or press the dough out into a 13"xll" rectangle, with the long side closest to you.
7. Add the cheese but leave an empty 1-inch border from the edge farthest away from you.
8. Then layer the chicken and onion mixture, cover it with cheese sauce and sprinkle with the remaining cheese.
9. Roll the Stromboli away from you and toward the empty border. The filling should stay tightly tucked inside the roll. Tuck the ends of pizza dough, pinch the seam.
10. Shape Stromboli into a U-shape; the seam side should be down. Make 4 small slits in the top of your dough. Brush the Stromboli with some oil.
11. Prepare the Air Fryer preheating it to 370 – degrees Fahrenheit. Grease the basket with the oil and add the Stromboli.
12. Cook for 6 minutes each side. When ready; remove carefully.
13. Set aside and let it cool for 2 – 3 minutes. Slice Stromboli into 3-inch pieces.
14. Serve with ketchup if desired.

385. Turkey Balls Stuffed with Onion and Sage

Prep + Cook Time: 40 minutes   **Servings:** 2

Ingredients:

- 3.5 ounces. mince [turkey]
- 1/2 onion [small; diced]
- One Egg [medium]
- 1 teaspoon sage
- 1/2 teaspoon garlic [pureed]
- 3 tablespoon breadcrumbs
- salt to taste
- pepper to taste

Instructions:

1. Put all the ingredients in a large bowl and mix the ingredients well.
2. Form the mixture into small ball shapes and put in Air Fryer to cook for 15 minutes at 350 - degrees Fahrenheit. Serve with tartar sauce and mashed potatoes and enjoy the combination.

386. Healthy Turkey Mushroom

Prep + Cook Time: 25 minutes   **Servings:** 4

Servings:

- 4 ingredients
- six eggs
- 1/4 cup cooked turkey; diced
- 4 mushrooms; diced
- 2 onions; chopped
- 1 ¼ cups shredded cheese
- A dash of onion powder
- 12 ounces. spinach
- 1/4 green bell pepper; chopped
- salt and pepper to taste
- A dash of garlic powder

Instructions:

1. Preheat the Air Fryer to 400 - degrees Fahrenheit.
2. Whisk the eggs in a mixing bowl.
3. Add in the bell pepper, garlic powder, salt, pepper, onion powder, onion, mushrooms, and cooked diced turkey.
4. Mix well and add to your casserole dish. Add the spinach on top. Bake in the Air Fryer for about 10 minutes.
5. Serve the dish hot.

387. Mouthwatering Turkey Sausage Patties

Prep + Cook Time: 15 minutes   **Servings:** 6

Ingredients:

- 1 Pound. lean ground turkey
- 1 teaspoon olive oil
- 1 tablespoon chopped chives
- 1 small onion; diced
- 1 large garlic clove; chopped
- 3/4 teaspoon paprika
- Kosher salt and pepper to taste
- A pinch raw sugar
- 1 tablespoon vinegar
- 1 teaspoon fennel seed
- A pinch nutmeg

Instructions:

1. Preheat the air fryer to 375 - degrees Fahrenheit.
2. Add half the oil and the onion and garlic to the air fryer.
3. Air fry for 30 seconds and then add the fennel.
4. Transfer them to a plate. In a mixing bowl add in the ground turkey.
5. Add the sugar, paprika, nutmeg, vinegar, chives and the onion mixture.
6. Mix well and form patties of your desired size.
7. Add the rest of the oil to the air fryer.

8. Add the patties and air fry for about 3 minutes.
9. Serve with lettuce leaves or buns.

388. Chicken Fillet with Brie & Turkey

Prep + Cook Time: 40 minutes   **Servings:** 4

Ingredients:

- 4 slices turkey [cured]
- 2 chicken fillets [large]
- 4 slices brie cheese
- 1 tablespoon chives [chopped]
- pepper and salt to taste

Instructions:

5. Preheat Air Fryer to 360 - degrees Fahrenheit. Cut chicken fillets into 4 pieces and season with salt and pepper.
6. Add chives and brie to it.
7. Add the ingredients onto the plain piece of turkey.
8. Close and wrap Turkey. Hold closed with toothpick. Air fry for 15 minutes, then roast until brown.

389. Fried Chicken with Veggies

Prep + Cook Time: 30 minutes   **Servings:** 4

Ingredients:

- 8 chicken thighs
- 5 ounces. sliced mushrooms
- 1 red onion; diced
- Fresh black pepper; to taste
- 10 medium asparagus
- 1/2 cup carrots; diced
- 1/4 cup balsamic vinegar
- 2 red bell peppers; diced
- 1/2 teaspoon sugar
- 2 tablespoon extra-virgin olive oil
- 1 ½ tablespoon fresh rosemary
- 2 cloves garlic; chopped
- 1/2 tablespoon dried oregano
- 1 teaspoon kosher salt
- 2 fresh sage; chopped

Instructions:

5. Preheat the Air Fryer to 400 - degrees Fahrenheit.
6. Grease a baking tray using oil. Coat the chicken with salt and pepper. In a large bowl; add all the vegetables.
7. Add the sage, oregano, garlic, sugar, vinegar, and mushroom. Mix well and arrange onto your baking tray.
8. Add the chicken thighs as well. Roast in the Air Fryer for about 20 minutes. Serve hot.

Beef Recipes

390. Special Japanese Marinated Flank Steak

Prep + Cook Time: 15 minutes   **Servings:** 4

Ingredients:

- 3/4-pound flank steak
- 1 ½ tablespoons sake
- 1 tablespoon brown miso paste
- 1 teaspoon honey
- 2 garlic cloves; pressed
- 1 tablespoon olive oil

Instructions:

1. Place all the ingredients in a sealable food bag and shake until completely coated and place in your refrigerator for at least 1 hour.
2. Then; spritz the steak with a non-stick cooking spray, make sure to coat on all sides.
3. Place the steak in the Air Fryer baking pan.
4. Set your Air Fryer to cook at 400 – degrees Fahrenheit. Roast for 12 minutes; flipping twice.
5. Serve immediately.

391. Easy Fried Steak

Prep + Cook Time: 15 minutes   **Servings:** 1

Ingredients:

- 3 cm thick beef steak
- pepper and salt to taste

Instructions:

1. Preheat the Air Fryer 400 - degrees Fahrenheit for 5 minutes.
2. Add beef steak in Air Fryer baking tray and season with pepper and salt.
3. Spray beef steak with cooking spray.
4. Cook beef steak in preheated Air Fryer for 3 minutes.
5. Flip steak to other side and cook for another 3 minutes.
6. Serve and enjoy.

392. Homemade Thai Style Meatballs

Prep + Cook Time: 20 minutes   **Servings:** 4

Ingredients:

- 1-pound ground beef
- 1 teaspoon red Thai curry paste
- 1/2 lime; rind and juice
- 1 teaspoon Chinese spice
- 2 teaspoons lemongrass; finely chopped
- 1 tablespoon sesame oil

Instructions:

1. Thoroughly combine all ingredients in a mixing dish.
2. Shape into 24 meatballs and place them into the Air Fryer cooking basket. Cook at 380 - degrees Fahrenheit for 10 minutes.
3. pause the machine and cook for a further 5 minutes; or until cooked through.
4. Serve accompanied by the dipping sauce.

393. Hot Tasty Herbed Crumbed Filet Mignon

Prep + Cook Time: 20 minutes

Servings: 4

Ingredients:

- 1/2-pound filet mignon
- Sea salt and ground black pepper; to taste
- 1/2 teaspoon cayenne pepper
- 1 teaspoon dried basil
- 1 teaspoon dried rosemary
- 1 teaspoon dried thyme
- 1 tablespoon sesame oil
- 1 small-sized egg; well-whisked
- 1/2 cup seasoned breadcrumbs

Instructions:

1. Season the filet mignon with salt, black pepper, cayenne pepper, basil, rosemary, and thyme. Brush with sesame oil.
2. Put the egg in a shallow plate. Now; place the breadcrumbs in another plate.
3. Coat the filet mignon with the egg. then, lay it into the crumbs. Set your Air Fryer to cook at 360 - degrees Fahrenheit.
4. Cook for 10 to 13 minutes or until golden.
5. Serve with mixed salad leaves.

394. Simply Grilled Beef Ribs

Prep + Cook Time: 20 minutes + marinating time

Servings: 4

Ingredients:

- 1-pound meaty beef ribs
- 3 tablespoons apple cider vinegar
- 1 cup coriander; finely chopped
- 1 heaping tablespoon fresh basil leaves; chopped
- 2 garlic cloves; finely chopped
- 1 chipotle powder
- 1 teaspoon fennel seeds
- 1 teaspoon hot paprika
- Kosher salt and black pepper; to taste
- 1/2 cup vegetable oil

Instructions:

1. First of all; rinse the ribs and dry them using paper towels.
2. Place all of the above ingredients in a mixing dish and toss to coat well.
3. Cover and refrigerate for at least 3 hours. Discard the marinade and place your ribs on an Air Fryer grill pan.
4. Now; set your Air Fryer to cook at 360 – degrees Fahrenheit. Cook for 8 minutes.
5. check for doneness and cook for another 3 to 5 minutes.
6. Garnish with the remaining marinade and serve right away!

395. Amazing London Broil Ever

Prep + Cook Time: 30 minutes + marinating time

Servings: 8

Ingredients:

- 2 pounds London broil
- 3 large garlic cloves; minced
- 3 tablespoons balsamic vinegar
- 3 tablespoons whole-grain mustard
- 2 tablespoons olive oil
- Sea salt and ground black pepper; to taste
- 1/2 teaspoon dried hot red pepper flakes

Instructions:

1. Score both sides of the cleaned London broil.

2. Thoroughly combine the remaining ingredients; massage this mixture into the meat to coat it on all sides. Let it marinate for at least 3 hours.
3. Set the Air Fryer to cook at 400 degrees F. Then cook the London broil for 15 minutes.
4. Flip it over and cook another 10 to 12 minutes.

396. Festival Smoked Beef Roast

Prep + Cook Time: 45 minutes   **Servings:** 8

Ingredients:

- 2 pounds roast beef; at room temperature
- 2 tablespoons extra-virgin olive oil
- 1 teaspoon sea salt flakes
- 1 teaspoon black pepper; preferably freshly ground
- 1 teaspoon smoked paprika
- A few dashes of liquid smoke
- 2 jalapeño peppers; thinly sliced

Instructions:

1. Start by preheating the Air Fryer to 330 - degrees Fahrenheit.
2. Then; pat the roast dry using kitchen towels.
3. Rub with extra-virgin olive oil and all seasonings along with liquid smoke.
4. Roast for 30 minutes in the preheated Air Fryer. Then; pause the machine and turn the roast over and roast for additional 15 minutes.
5. Check for doneness using a meat thermometer and serve sprinkled with sliced jalapeños.

397. Vegetables with Hearty Beef Cubes

Prep + Cook Time: 20 minutes + marinating time   **Servings:** 4

Ingredients:

- 1-pound top round steak; cut into cubes
- 2 tablespoons olive oil
- 1 tablespoon apple cider vinegar
- 1 teaspoon fine sea salt
- 1/2 teaspoon ground black pepper
- 1 teaspoon shallot powder
- 3/4 teaspoon smoked cayenne pepper
- 1/2 teaspoon garlic powder
- 1/4 teaspoon ground cumin
- 1/4-pound broccoli; cut into florets
- 1/4-pound mushrooms; sliced
- 1 teaspoon dried basil
- 1 teaspoon celery seeds

Instructions:

1. Firstly; marinate the beef with olive oil, vinegar, salt, black pepper, shallot powder, cayenne pepper, garlic powder, and cumin.
2. Toss to coat well and let it stay for at least 3 hours.
3. Place the beef cubes in the Air Fryer cooking basket and cook at 365 - degrees Fahrenheit for 12 minutes.
4. Pause the machine; check the cubes for doneness and transfer them to a bowl.
5. Now; clean the cooking basket and place the vegetables in, sprinkle them with basil and celery seeds and toss to coat.
6. Set the temperature to 400 degrees F; cook for 5 to 6 minutes or until the vegetables are warmed through.
7. Serve with reserved meat cubes.

398. Kale Omelet and Leftover Beef

Prep + Cook Time: 20 minutes   **Servings:** 4

Ingredients:

- Non-stick cooking spray
- 1/2-pound leftover beef; coarsely chopped
- 2 garlic cloves; pressed
- 1 cup kale; torn into pieces and wilted
- 1 tomato; chopped
- 1/4 teaspoon brown sugar
- four eggs; beaten
- 4 tablespoons heavy cream
- 1/2 teaspoon turmeric powder
- Salt and ground black pepper; to taste
- 1/8 teaspoon ground allspice

Instructions:

1. Spritz the inside of four ramekins with a cooking spray.
2. Divide all of the above ingredients among the prepared ramekins.
3. Stir until everything is well combined.
4. Air-fry at 360 - degrees Fahrenheit for 16 minutes.
5. check with a wooden stick and return the eggs to the Air Fryer for a few more minutes as needed.
6. Serve immediately.

399. Delicious Cheese burgers

Prep + Cook Time: 15 minutes   **Servings:** 4

Ingredients:

- 3/4-pound ground chuck
- 1 envelope onion soup mix
- Kosher salt and freshly ground black pepper; to taste
- 1 teaspoon paprika
- 4 slices Monterey-Jack cheese
- 4 ciabatta rolls
- Mustard and pickled salad; to serve

Instructions:

1. In a mixing dish; thoroughly combine ground chuck, onion soup mix, salt, black pepper, and paprika.
2. Then; set your Air Fryer to cook at 385 - degrees Fahrenheit.
3. Shape the mixture into 4 patties. Air-fry them for 10 minutes.
4. Place the slices of cheese on the top of the warm burgers. Air-fry one minute more.
5. Serve on ciabatta rolls garnished with mustard and pickled salad of choice.

400. Crispy Beef Schnitzel

Prep + Cook Time: 25 minutes   **Servings:** 1

Ingredients:

- 1 thin beef schnitzel
- One Egg; beaten
- 1/2 cup breadcrumbs
- 2 tablespoon olive oil
- pepper and salt to taste

Instructions:

1. Preheat the Air Fryer to 350 - degrees Fahrenheit.
2. In a shallow dish; combine together breadcrumbs, oil, pepper, and salt.
3. In another shallow dish add beaten egg.
4. Dip schnitzel into the egg then coat with breadcrumbs.
5. Place coated schnitzel in Air Fryer basket and air fry for 12 minutes.
6. Serve and enjoy.

401. Beef with Spicy Spaghetti

Prep + Cook Time: 30 minutes   **Servings:** 4

Ingredients:

- 3/4-pound ground chuck
- 1 onion; peeled and finely chopped
- 1 teaspoon garlic paste
- 1 bell pepper; chopped
- 1 small-sized habanero pepper; deveined and finely minced
- 1/2 teaspoon dried rosemary
- 1/2 teaspoon dried marjoram
- 1 ¼ cups crushed tomatoes; fresh or canned
- 1/2 teaspoon sea salt flakes
- 1/4 teaspoon ground black pepper; or more to taste
- 1 package cooked spaghetti; to serve

Instructions:

1. In the Air Fryer baking dish; place the ground meat, onion, garlic paste, bell pepper, habanero pepper, rosemary, and the marjoram.
2. Air-fry, uncovered, for 10 to 11 minutes.
3. stir in the tomatoes along with salt and pepper.
4. cook 17 to 20 minutes.
5. Serve over cooked spaghetti.

402. Amazing Meatloaf

Prep + Cook Time: 30 minutes   **Servings:** 4

Ingredients:

- 1 Pound ground beef
- One Egg; beaten
- 1 mushrooms; sliced
- 1 tablespoon thyme
- 1 small onion; chopped
- 3 tablespoon breadcrumbs
- pepper to taste

Instructions:

1. Preheat the Air Fryer 400 - degrees Fahrenheit.
2. Add all ingredients into the mixing bowl and mix well until combined.
3. Add meatloaf mixture into the loaf pan and place in Air Fryer basket.
4. Cook in preheated Air Fryer for 25 minutes. Cut into slices and serve.

403. Hot Beef Burgers

Prep + Cook Time: 65 minutes   **Servings:** 4

Ingredients:

- 10.5 ounces. beef [minced]
- 1 onion [diced]
- 1 teaspoon garlic [minced/pureed]
- 1 teaspoon tomato [pureed]
- 1 teaspoon mustard
- 1 teaspoon basil
- 1 teaspoon herbs [mixed]
- salt to taste
- pepper to taste
- 1 ounce. cheese [cheddar]
- 4 buns
- Salad leaves

Instructions:

1. Add 1 tablespoon of oil in Air Fryer. Let it warm.
2. Add diced onion into the fryer and let them fry until they are golden brown in color.
3. Add all the seasoning and let it cook for 25 minutes at 390 – degrees Fahrenheit. Now place 2 – 3 rings and slices of onion and tomato between the buns. Than lay out single slice of cheese, followed by the layer of beef.

4. And lastly add salad leaves or any tomatoes if you like.
5. Now serve it with ketchup; cold drink and fresh fries and enjoy the right combination.

404. Brussels Sprouts with Tender Beef Chuck

Prep + Cook Time: 25 minutes + marinating time

Servings: 4

Ingredients:

- 1-pound beef chuck shoulder steak
- 2 tablespoons vegetable oil
- 1 tablespoon red wine vinegar
- 1 teaspoon fine sea salt
- 1/2 teaspoon ground black pepper
- 1 teaspoon smoked paprika
- 1 teaspoon onion powder
- 1/2 teaspoon garlic powder
- 1/2-pound Brussels sprouts; cleaned and halved
- 1/2 teaspoon fennel seeds
- 1 teaspoon dried basil
- 1 teaspoon dried sage

Instructions:

1. Firstly; marinate the beef with vegetable oil, wine vinegar, salt, black pepper, paprika, onion powder, and garlic powder.
2. Rub the marinade into the meat and let it stay at least for 3 hours.
3. Air fry at 390 - degrees Fahrenheit for 10 minutes.
4. Pause the machine and add the prepared Brussels sprouts and sprinkle them with fennel seeds, basil, and sage.
5. Turn the machine to 380 - degrees Fahrenheit. press the power button and cook for 5 more minutes. Pause the machine, stir and cook for further 10 minutes.
6. Next; remove the meat from the cooking basket and cook the vegetables a few minutes more if needed and according to your taste.
7. Serve with your favorite mayo sauce.

405. Spicy Meatballs with Sauce

Prep + Cook Time: 25 minutes

Servings: 8

Ingredients:

- 1 Pound ground beef
- 2 bread slices; crumbled
- 1 small onion; minced
- 1/2 teaspoon garlic salt
- 1 cup tomato sauce
- 2 cups pasta sauce
- One Egg; beaten
- 2 carrots; shredded
- pepper and salt to taste

Instructions:

1. Preheat Air Fryer to 400 - degrees Fahrenheit.
2. In a bowl; add ground beef, egg, carrots, crumbled bread, onion, garlic salt, pepper and salt.
3. Mix well to combine
4. Make small meatballs and place in Air Fryer basket and cook for 7 minutes
5. Place meatballs into oven safe dish and pour tomato sauce over meatballs
6. Place dish into the Air Fryer basket and cook at 320 - degrees Fahrenheit for 5 minutes.

406. Special Beef Schnitzel

Prep + Cook Time: 15 minutes

Servings: 4

Ingredients:

- 4 thin beef schnitzel
- 1 tablespoon sesame seeds
- 2 tablespoons paprika
- 3 tablespoon olive oil

- 4 tablespoon flour
- Two eggs; beaten
- 1 cup breadcrumbs
- pepper and salt to taste

Instructions:
1. Preheat the Air Fryer at 350 – degrees Fahrenheit.
2. Season schnitzel with pepper and salt.
3. In a shallow dish combine together paprika, flour, and salt
4. In another shallow dish add breadcrumbs and sesame seeds. Add beaten eggs in bowl.
5. Dip schnitzel into the flour mixture then in egg and finally coat with breadcrumbs. Place coated schnitzel into the Air Fryer basket and air fry for 12 minutes

407. Quick Steak Total

Prep + Cook Time: 30 minutes   **Servings:** 4

Ingredients:
- 2 Pounds rib eye steak
- 1 tablespoon olive oil
- 1 tablespoon steak rub

Instructions:
1. Preheat the Air Fryer 400 - degrees Fahrenheit for 4 minutes. Season both sides of steak with olive oil and steak rub.
2. Place seasoned steak in Air Fryer basket and cook for 14 minutes. After 14 minutes flip steak to other side and cook for 7 minutes.
3. Serve and enjoy.

408. Tasty Beef Meatloaf

Prep + Cook Time: 30 minutes   **Servings:** 4

Ingredients:
- 3/4-pound ground chuck
- 1/4-pound ground pork sausage
- 1 cup shallot; finely chopped
- Two eggs; well beaten
- 3 tablespoons plain milk
- 1 tablespoon oyster sauce
- 1 teaspoon porcini mushrooms
- 1/2 teaspoon cumin powder
- 1 teaspoon garlic paste
- 1 tablespoon fresh parsley
- Seasoned salt and crushed red pepper flakes; to taste
- 1 cup crushed saltines

Instructions:
1. Simply place all ingredients in a large-size mixing dish; mix until everything is thoroughly combined.
2. Press the meatloaf mixture into the Air Fryer baking dish and set your Air Fryer to cook at 360 - degrees Fahrenheit for 25 minutes.
3. Press the power button and cook until heated through.

409. Tasty Stuffed Bell Pepper

Prep + Cook Time: 25 minutes   **Servings:** 4

Ingredients:
- 4 bell peppers; cut top of bell pepper
- 16 ounces. ground beef
- 2/3 cup cheese; shredded
- 1/2 cup rice; cooked
- 1 teaspoon basil; dried
- 1/2 teaspoon chili powder
- 1 teaspoon black pepper
- 1 teaspoon garlic salt
- 2 teaspoon Worcestershire sauce
- 8 ounces. tomato sauce
- 2 garlic cloves; minced
- 1 small onion; chopped

Instructions:

1. Spray pan with cooking spray and sauté onion and garlic in pan over medium heat.
2. Add beef, basil, chili powder, black pepper, and garlic salt. Mix well and cook until meat brown.
3. Remove pan from heat.
4. Add half cheese, rice, Worcestershire sauce, and tomato sauce in pan and mix well to combine. Stuff beef mixture into the four bell peppers equally.
5. Preheat the Air Fryer 400 - degrees Fahrenheit. Spray Air Fryer basket with cooking spray. Place stuffed bell peppers in Air Fryer basket and cook for 11 minutes.
6. Once timer is off then top bell pepper with remaining cheese and cook for another 2 minutes until cheese is melted.

410. Stylish Asian Beef Burgers

Prep + Cook Time: 20 minutes   **Servings:** 4

Ingredients:

- 3/4-pound lean ground beef
- 1 tablespoon soy sauce
- 1 teaspoon Dijon mustard
- A few dashes of liquid smoke
- 1 teaspoon shallot powder
- 1 clove garlic; minced
- 1/2 teaspoon cumin powder
- 1/4 cup scallions; minced
- 1/3 teaspoon sea salt flakes
- 1/3 teaspoon freshly cracked mixed peppercorns
- 1 teaspoon celery seeds
- 1 teaspoon parsley flakes

Instructions:

1. Mix all of the above ingredients in a bowl; knead until everything is well incorporated.
2. Shape the mixture into four patties.
3. Make a shallow dip in the center of each patty to prevent them puffing up during air-frying.
4. Spritz the patties on all sides using a non-stick cooking spray. Cook approximately 12 minutes at 360 - degrees Fahrenheit.
5. Check for doneness an instant read thermometer should read 160 – degrees Fahrenheit. Serve them on butter rolls with toppings of choice.

411. Easy Cheesy Burger Patties

Prep + Cook Time: 15 minutes   **Servings:** 6

Ingredients:

- 1 Pound ground beef
- 6 cheddar cheese slices
- Pepper and salt to taste

Instructions:

1. Preheat the Air Fryer to 350 - degrees Fahrenheit.
2. Season ground beef with pepper and salt
3. Make six patties from mixture and place in Air Fryer basket
4. Air fry patties in preheated Air Fryer for 10 minutes
5. After 10 minutes place cheese slices over patties and air fry for another 1 minute.
6. Place patties in dinner rolls and serve.

412. Succulent Beef Roll Up

Prep + Cook Time: 30 minutes   **Servings:** 2

Ingredients:

- 2-pound beef flank steak
- 3 teaspoon pesto
- 1 teaspoon black pepper
- 6 slices of provolone cheese

- 3-ounce red bell peppers [roasted]
- 3/4 cup baby spinach
- 1 teaspoon sea salt

Instructions:

1. Spread the pesto evenly on the meat
2. Layer the cheese; roasted red peppers & spinach 3/4 of the way down the meat.
3. Roll up and secure with toothpicks. Season with sea salt and pepper
4. Cook for 14 minutes at 400 - degrees Fahrenheit.
5. Half way through, rotate the meat
6. Let rest 10 minutes.
7. Cut, plate, and serve

413. Fried Spring Rolls

Prep + Cook Time: 35 minutes   **Servings:** 20

Ingredients:

- 1/3 cup noodles
- 1 cup beef minced
- 2 tablespoon cold water
- 1 packet spring rolls
- 1 teaspoon soy sauce
- 1 cup fresh mix vegetables
- 3 garlic cloves; minced
- 1 small onion; diced
- 1 tablespoon sesame oil

Instructions:

1. Add noodles in hot water. Once noodles are soft then drain well and cut into short lengths.
2. Heat oil in pan over medium heat.
3. Add beef minced, soy sauce, mixed vegetables, garlic, and onion in pan and cook until beef minced is completely cooked. Remove pan from heat and add noodles. Mix well and set aside.
4. Place one spring roll sheet the place stuffing on sheet diagonally across.
5. Fold sheet from top point then fold both the sides and final side brush with water before rolling the roll.
6. Preheat the Air Fryer to 350 - degrees Fahrenheit.
7. Brush prepared spring roll with oil and place in preheated Air Fryer. Cook spring roll for 8 minutes. Serve and enjoy.

414. Cheesy Fried Schnitzel

Prep + Cook Time: 30 minutes   **Servings:** 1

Ingredients:

- 1 thin beef schnitzel
- One Egg; beaten
- 1/2 cup breadcrumbs
- 2 tablespoon olive oil
- 3 tablespoon pasta sauce
- 1/4 cup parmesan cheese; grated
- Pepper and salt to taste

Instructions:

1. Preheat the Air Fryer to 350 – degrees Fahrenheit.
2. In a shallow dish combine together breadcrumbs, olive oil, pepper, and salt. In another shallow dish add beaten egg.
3. Dip schnitzel into the egg then coat with breadcrumb mixture and place in Air Fryer basket. Cook schnitzel in preheated Air Fryer for 15 minutes.
4. Once 15 minutes done then add pasta sauce over schnitzel and sprinkle grated cheese. Cook schnitzel for another 5 minutes until cheese is melted.
5. Serve the dish hot.

415. Yummy Beef Schnitzel

Prep + Cook Time: 30 minutes   **Servings:** 1

Ingredients:

- One Egg
- 1 thin beef schnitzel
- 3 tablespoon breadcrumbs
- 2 tablespoon olive oil
- 1 parsley; roughly chopped
- 1/2 lemon; cut in wedges

Instructions:

1. Prepare the Air Fryer: preheat it to the 360 - degrees Fahrenheit.
2. In a bowl combine breadcrumbs and olive oil
3. Stir until mixture is loose and crumbly.
4. Whisk the egg and dip the schnitzel first into the whisked egg and then into oily breadcrumbs mixture. Make sure it is fully covered by it
5. Cook the schnitzel in the Air Fryer for 12 – 14 minutes depending on its thickness Decorate the schnitzel with the lemon wedges and parsley

416. Delicious Meatballs

Prep + Cook Time: 20 minutes   **Servings:** 4

Ingredients:

- One Egg
- 1/2 Pound beef minced
- 1/2 cup breadcrumbs
- 1 tablespoon parsley; chopped
- 2 tablespoon raisins
- 1 cup onion; chopped and fried
- 1/2 tablespoon pepper
- 1/2 teaspoon salt

Instructions:

1. Add all ingredients into the bowl and mix well.
2. Make small meatballs from mixture and place in Air Fryer basket.
3. Air fry meatballs at 350 - degrees Fahrenheit for 15 minutes. Serve with sauce and enjoy.

417. Different Beef Steak

Prep + Cook Time: 15 minutes   **Servings:** 1

Ingredients:

- steak, thickness of 1 inch
- 1 tablespoon olive oil
- black pepper to taste
- sea salt to taste

Instructions:

1. Preheat the Air Fryer with the baking tray inside for about 5 minutes at 390 - degrees Fahrenheit
2. Grease both sides of the steak with the oil.
3. Sprinkle both sides with salt and pepper.
4. Carefully layer the steak on the preheated baking tray
5. Cook for 3 minutes in the Air Fryer.
6. Then turn the steak around and cook for another 3 minutes.
7. When ready; remove and set aside for about 3 minutes and serve

418. Beef and Broccoli

Prep + Cook Time: 25 minutes   **Servings:** 4

Ingredients:

- 1 Pound broccoli; cut into florets
- 3/4 Pound round steak; cut into strips
- 1 garlic clove; minced
- 1 teaspoon ginger; minced
- 1 tablespoon olive oil
- 1 teaspoon cornstarch

- 1 teaspoon sugar
- 1 teaspoon soy sauce
- 1/3 cup sherry wine
- 2 teaspoon sesame oil
- 1/3 cup oyster sauce

Instructions:

1. Add sugar, soy sauce, sherry wine, cornstarch, sesame oil, and oyster sauce in a bowl and mix well.
2. Add steak strips into the bowl mix well and set aside for 45 minutes.
3. Add broccoli in Air Fryer then add marinated steak on top.
4. Add olive oil, garlic and ginger over broccoli and steak mixture.
5. Cook at 350 - degrees Fahrenheit for 12 minutes. Serve the dish hot with rice and enjoy.

419. Mushrooms and Beef

Prep + Cook Time: 3 hours 15 minutes   **Servings:** 1

Ingredients:

- 6 ounces beef
- 1/4 onion; diced
- 1/2 cup mushroom slices

- 2 tablespoon favorite marinade [preferably bulgogi]

Instructions:

1. Cut the beef into strips or cubes, and place them in a bowl
2. Coat the meat with the marinade and cover the bowl and Refrigerate for 3 hours.
3. Place the meat in a baking dish and add the onion and mushrooms
4. Air Fry at 350 - degrees Fahrenheit for 10 minutes.

420. Flavored Meatloaf

Prep + Cook Time: 35 minutes   **Servings:** 4

Ingredients:

- 1 large onion [peeled and diced]
- 2 kilos minced beef
- 1 teaspoon Worcester sauce
- 3 tablespoon tomato ketchup
- 1 tablespoon basil

- 1 tablespoon oregano
- 1 tablespoon mixed herbs
- 1 tablespoon parsley
- breadcrumbs
- salt & pepper to taste

Instructions:

1. In a large mixing bowl; place the mince along with the herbs, Worcester sauce, onion and tomato ketchup
2. Mix thoroughly to distribute flavor evenly.
3. Add the breadcrumbs and mix well again
4. Place in a small dish and cook for 25 minutes in the Air Fryer at 350 – degrees Fahrenheit.

421. Carrot Onion Meatloaf

Prep + Cook Time: 35 minutes

Servings: 6

Ingredients:

- 1 Pound ground beef
- One Egg
- 2 carrots; shredded
- 1/2 onion; shredded
- 1/4 cup milk
- 1/2 cup breadcrumbs
- 1/4 teaspoon pepper
- 1/2 teaspoon salt

Instructions:

1. Preheat the Air Fryer to 400 - degrees Fahrenheit.
2. Add all ingredients into the bowl and mix well to combine
3. Add meatloaf mixture into the loaf pan and place in Air Fryer basket. Cook in preheated Air Fryer for 25 minutes.
4. Cut into slices and serve.

422. Delicious Crispy Beef Cubes

Prep + Cook Time: 30 minutes

Servings: 4

Ingredients:

- 1-pound beef loin
- 1 jar [16 oz] cheese pasta sauce
- 6 tablespoon breadcrumbs
- salt and black pepper; to taste
- 1 tablespoon extra-virgin olive oil

Instructions:

1. Cut beef into 1-inch cubes and transfer to a mixing bowl and coat with pasta sauce.
2. In another bowl combine breadcrumbs, olive oil, salt and pepper. Mix well
3. Place beef cubes to a breadcrumb mixture and coat from all sides.
4. Preheat the Air Fryer to 380 – degrees Fahrenheit
   5. Cook beef cubes for 12 – 15 minutes, stirring occasionally, until ready and crispy.
6. Serve the dish hot.

423. Tangy and Sweet Meatballs

Prep + Cook Time: 30 minutes

Servings: 24

Ingredients:

- 1 Pound beef mince
- 1 tablespoon lemon juice
- 1/4 cup vinegar
- 1 tablespoon Worcestershire sauce
- 1 tablespoon Tabasco
- 3/4 cup tomato ketchup
- 3 gingersnaps cookies; crushed
- 1/2 teaspoon dry mustard
- 1/2 cup brown sugar

Instructions:

1. Add all ingredients into the bowl and mix well to combine
2. Make small meatballs from mixture and place in Air Fryer basket. Air fry meatballs at 370 – degrees Fahrenheit for 15 minutes

424. Tasty Rib Eye Steak

Prep + Cook Time: 30 minutes

Servings: 4

Ingredients:

- 2 pounds rib eye steak
- 2 tablespoon steak rub
- 1 tablespoon olive oil
- salt and black pepper; to taste

Instructions:

1. Preheat the Air Fryer to 390 - degrees Fahrenheit
2. Meanwhile; rub the steak with seasoning, salt and pepper from both sides.
3. Sprinkle frying basket with olive oil and carefully transfer the steak
4. Cook for 7 minutes on one side and then flip the meat and cook for another 7 – 8 minutes from other side.
5. When ready; transfer steak to a serving plate and give a rest for 5 – 10 minutes.
6. Slice and serve

425. Burgers Patties

Prep + Cook Time: 25 minutes   **Servings:** 4

Ingredients:

- 1 ½ Pounds ground beef
- 1 cup cheddar cheese; shredded
- 1/2 cup cheese sauce
- 1 tablespoon Montreal steak seasoning
- 1 tablespoon Worcestershire sauce

Instructions:

1. Preheat the Air Fryer to 370 - degrees Fahrenheit.
2. Add ground beef, Montreal steak seasoning, and Worcestershire sauce in bowl and mix well
3. Make four patties from mixture and place in preheated Air Fryer basket and air fry for 15 minutes
4. Flip patties halfway through.
5. Combine together cheddar cheese and cheese sauce
6. Add cheese mixture over top of patties and cook for another 3 minutes.
7. Serve and enjoy.

426. Teriyaki Halibut Steak

Prep + Cook Time: 70 minutes   **Servings:** 3

Ingredients:

- 1-pound halibut steak

For the Marinade:

- 2/3 cup soy sauce [low sodium]
- 1/2 cup mirin [Japanese cooking wine]
- 1/4 cup sugar
- 2 tablespoon lime juice
- 1/4 cup orange juice
- 1/4 teaspoon crushed red pepper flakes
- 1/4 teaspoon ginger ground
- 1 each garlic clove [smashed]

Instructions:

1. In a sauce pan combine all ingredients for the teriyaki glaze/marinade.
2. Bring to a boil and reduce by half; then cool
3. Once cooled pour half of the glaze/marinade into a resealable bag with the halibut. And Refrigerate for 30 minutes.
4. Preheat the Air Fryer to 390 - degrees Fahrenheit
5. Place marinated halibut into the Air Fryer and cook for 10 – 12 minutes.
6. When finished brush a little of the remaining glaze over the halibut steak.
7. Serve over a bed of white rice with basil/mint chutney.

427. Classic Beef Pot Roast

Prep + Cook Time: 1 hr. 10 minutes   **Servings:** 4

Ingredients:

- 1-pound beef
- 1 teaspoon of paprika
- 2 cardamoms
- 1/2 cup of fresh coriander; chopped
- 1 bay leaf
- 2 tablespoon of ginger garlic paste
- 2 tablespoon of olive oil
- 2 cinnamon sticks
- 4 spring onions
- 1 teaspoon of black pepper
- 1 cup of water
- salt to taste

Instructions:

1. Preheat your Air Fryer to 400 - degrees Fahrenheit.
2. Discard the bones of the beef and cut it into medium chunks
3. In a large mixing bowl add the beef.
4. Add in the onion, ginger garlic paste, cinnamon stick, salt, pepper, oil, bay leaf, coriander, cardamom, paprika and water
5. Mix well and let it marinade for about 1 hour.
6. Add to a casserole dish and roast in the Air Fryer for about 1 hour.
7. Serve the dish hot

428. Beef Stuffed Peppers

Prep + Cook Time: 35 minutes   **Servings:** 2

Ingredients:

- 1/2 medium onion; minced
- 8 ounces. lean ground beef
- 2 ounces. + 2 ounces. shredded cheddar cheese; separately
- 2 medium green peppers; stems and seeds removed
- 1 clove garlic; crushed
- 1 teaspoon Worcestershire sauce
- 1/4 cup + 1/4 cup tomato sauce; separately
- 1/2 teaspoon black pepper
- 1 teaspoon olive oil
- 1/2 teaspoon sea salt

Instructions:

1. Prepare the green peppers: cook them in boiling salted water for 3 minutes.
2. Preheat the Air Fryer to 390 – degrees Fahrenheit
3. Take the nonstick skillet; preferably small. Grease it with oil and sauté onion and garlic until they become golden
4. Then set them aside to cool.
5. Take the medium bowl and mix well ground beef, cooked onion, and garlic, 1/4 cup tomato sauce, 2 ounces. shredded cheese, Worcestershire, pepper, and salt
6. Cut the peppers in halves. Stuff the pepper halves with the beef mixture and top it with the remaining portions of cheese and tomato sauce
7. Place stuffed peppers onto Air Fryer basket and fry for up to 20 minutes or until the ground beef is cooked.

429. Beef Roast

Prep + Cook Time: 65 minutes   **Servings:** 6

Ingredients:

- 2 pounds beef
- 1 tablespoon olive oil
- 1 teaspoon dried rosemary
- 1 teaspoon dried thyme
- 1/2 teaspoon black pepper
- 1/2 teaspoon oregano

- 1/2 teaspoon of garlic powder
- 1 teaspoon salt
- 1 teaspoon onion powder

Instructions:

1. Preheat the Air Fryer to 330 - degrees Fahrenheit.
2. Combine all of the spices in a small bowl
3. Brush the olive oil over the beef. Rub the spice mixture into the meat.
4. Place in the Air Fryer and cook for 30 minutes. Flip it over and cook for 25 more minutes

430. Mouthwatering Tender Beef

Prep + Cook Time: 35 minutes   **Servings:** 4

Ingredients:

- 2-pound beef steak
- 5 – 6 slices cheddar cheese
- 1/2 cup fresh baby spinach
- 4 tablespoon pesto
- 2 tablespoon unsalted butter
- 1 teaspoon salt
- 1/4 teaspoon black pepper
- 1 tablespoon olive oil

Instructions:

1. Open beef steak and spread the butter over the meat. Then cover it with pesto
2. Layer cheese slices; baby spinach and season with salt and pepper.
3. Roll up the meat and secure with toothpicks. Season with salt and pepper again
4. Preheat the Air Fryer to 390 - degrees Fahrenheit and sprinkle frying basket with olive oil.
5. Place beef roll in the Air Fryer and cook for 15 – 20 minutes.
6. turning couple times to roast from all sides
7. Slice beef roll and serve with mashed potatoes or steamed rice.

431. Homemade Chimichurri Skirt Steak

Prep + Cook Time: 50 minutes   **Servings:** 2

Ingredients:

- 1-pound skirt steak

For the Chimichurri

- 1 cup parsley; finely chopped
- 1/4 cup mint; finely chopped
- 2 tablespoon oregano; finely chopped
- 3 garlic cloves; finely chopped
- 1 teaspoon crushed red pepper
- 1 tablespoon ground cumin
- 1 teaspoon cayenne pepper
- 2 teaspoons smoked paprika
- 1 teaspoon salt
- 1/4 teaspoon black pepper
- 3/4 cup olive oil
- 3 tablespoon red wine vinegar

Instructions:

1. Combine the ingredients for the chimichurri in a mixing bowl
2. Cut the steak into 2 - 8-ounce portions and add to a re-sealable bag; along with 1/4 cup of the chimichurri.
3. Refrigerate for 2 hours up to 24 hours
4. Remove from the refrigerator 30 minutes prior to cooking.
5. Preheat the Air Fryer to 390 - degrees Fahrenheit
6. Pat steak dry with a paper towel. Add the steak to the cooking basket and cook for 8 – 10 minutes for medium-rare. Garnish with 2 tablespoons of chimichurri on top and serve

Tip: The time will vary depending upon the size of the steak and the degree of doneness you prefer.

Vegetable Recipes

432. Delicious Vegetables

Prep + Cook Time: 45 minutes   **Servings:** 4

Ingredients:

- 3.5 ounces. radish
- 1/2 teaspoon parsley
- 3.5 ounces. celeriac
- 1 carrot [yellow]
- 1 carrot [orange]
- 1 onion [red]

- 3.5 ounces. pumpkin
- 3.5 ounces. parsnips
- salt to taste
- epaulette pepper to taste
- 1 tablespoon oil [olive]
- 4 garlic cloves [unpeeled]

Instructions:

1. Peel and cut vegetables into 2 to 3 cm sized small pieces
2. Preheat Air Fryer to 390 – degrees Fahrenheit.
3. Warm the oil and add vegetables into it.
4. Add garlic; salt and pepper in the pan.
5. Put in a brisket in Air Fryer to roast for 18 – 20 minutes
6. Sprinkle parsley and serve hot with boiled rice. Enjoy the combination

433. Tasty Potato Chips

Prep + Cook Time: 45 minutes   **Servings:** 4

Ingredients:

- 2 large potatoes; peel and sliced
- 1 tablespoon rosemary

- 3.5 ounces. sour cream
- 1/4 teaspoon salt

Instructions:

1. Add potato slice in water and soak for 30 minutes. After 30 minutes drain potato slice and place in large bowl. Add rosemary, sour cream, and salt in bowl and toss well
2. Preheat the Air Fryer to 320 – degrees Fahrenheit
3. Add coated potato slice in Air Fryer basket and cook for 35 minutes. Serve hot

434. Roasted Corn

Prep + Cook Time: 15 minutes   **Servings:** 4

Ingredients:

- 4 ears of corn; remove husks
- 2 teaspoon olive oil

- pepper to taste
- salt to taste

Instructions:

1. Add corn in Air Fryer basket and drizzle with olive oil
2. Season corn with pepper and salt. Cook corn in Air Fryer at 400 - degrees Fahrenheit for 10 minutes.
3. Serve hot.

435. Easy Brussels Sprouts

Prep + Cook Time: 15 minutes   **Servings:** 2

Ingredients:

- 2 cups Brussels sprouts; sliced in half
- 1 tablespoon balsamic vinegar

- 1 tablespoon olive oil
- 1/4 teaspoon salt

Instructions:

1. Add all ingredients into the bowl and toss well
2. Add Brussels sprouts in Air Fryer basket and air fry at 400 - degrees Fahrenheit for 10 minutes
3. Shake basket halfway through.

436. Crispy Parsley Garlic Potatoes

Prep + Cook Time: 40 minutes   **Servings:** 4

Ingredients:

- 1-pound russet baking potatoes
- 1 tablespoon garlic powder
- 1 tablespoon freshly chopped parsley
- 1/2 teaspoon salt
- 1/4 teaspoon black pepper
- 1 – 2 tablespoon olive oil

Instructions:

1. Wash and dry potatoes with kitchen towels
2. Make holes in each potato with a fork.
3. Transfer potatoes to a large bowl and sprinkle with garlic powder, salt and pepper.
4. Drizzle with the olive oil and stir to combine
5. Preheat the Air Fryer to 360 - degrees Fahrenheit. Cook potatoes for about 30 minutes, shaking couple times during cooking.
6. When ready sprinkle potatoes with chopped parsley and serve.
7. You may also serve with butter, sour cream or another dipping you prefer

437. Healthy Asparagus

Prep + Cook Time: 15 minutes   **Servings:** 4

Ingredients:

- 10 asparagus spears; cut woody end
- 1 garlic clove; minced
- 4 tablespoon olive oil
- pepper to taste
- salt to taste

Instructions:

1. Preheat the Air Fryer 400 - degrees Fahrenheit for 5 minutes.
2. In a bowl; combine together garlic and oil
3. Coat asparagus with oil mixture and place in Air Fryer basket. Season asparagus with pepper and salt. Cook asparagus in preheated Air Fryer for 10 minutes

438. Cheesy Fried Zucchini Chips

Prep + Cook Time: 30 minutes   **Servings:** 2

Ingredients:

- 3 medium zucchini; sliced
- 1 teaspoon parsley; chopped
- 3 tablespoon parmesan cheese; grated
- pepper to taste
- salt to taste

Instructions:

1. Preheat the Air Fryer to 425 – degrees Fahrenheit.
2. Place sliced zucchini on baking paper and Spray with cooking spray.
3. Combine together cheese, pepper, parsley, and salt
4. Sprinkle cheese mixture over sliced zucchini.
5. Place in Air Fryer and cook for 25 minutes or until crisp

439. Sweet Potato Fries

Prep + Cook Time: 45 minutes

Servings: 4

Ingredients:

- 4 large sweet potatoes; peel and cut into strips
- 1/4 cup water
- 3 ½ tablespoon olive oil
- 1/3 cup cornstarch

Instructions:

1. Soak sweet potato strips in water for 20 minutes.
2. Combine together oil, cornstarch, and water in large bowl
3. Add sweet potato strips in bowl and toss well until coated
4. Place coated fries in Air Fryer basket and cook at 400 – degrees Fahrenheit for 30 minutes.
5. Shake basket every 10 minutes

440. Spicy Fried Sweet Potato Wedges

Prep + Cook Time: 25 minutes

Servings: 2

Ingredients:

- 2 large sweet potatoes; cut into wedges
- 1 tablespoon olive oil
- 1 teaspoon chili powder
- 1 teaspoon mustard powder
- 1 teaspoon cumin
- 1 tablespoon Mexican seasoning
- pepper to taste
- salt to taste

Instructions:

1. Preheat the Air Fryer 350 – degrees Fahrenheit.
2. Add all ingredients into the bowl and toss well. Add sweet potato wedges into the Air Fryer basket and air fry for 20 minutes. Shake basket every 5 minutes

441. Yummy Potato Wedges

Prep + Cook Time: 30 minutes

Servings: 4

Ingredients:

- 4 medium potatoes, cut into wedges
- 1 tablespoon cajun spice
- 1 tablespoon olive oil
- pepper to taste
- salt to taste

Instructions:

1. Add potato wedges in Air Fryer basket and drizzle with olive oil. Cook wedges at 370 - degrees Fahrenheit for 25 minutes. Shake basket twice
2. Add cooked wedges in bowl. Season wedges with Cajun spice, pepper, and salt. Toss potato wedges well and serve

442. Delicious Sweet Potato Fries with Curry

Prep + Cook Time: 20 minutes

Servings: 3

Ingredients:

- 1-pound frozen sweet potato fries
- 1/2 cup sour cream
- 1/2 cup mango chutney
- 3 teaspoon curry powder; divided
- 1 tablespoon olive oil
- 1/2 teaspoon salt
- 1/4 teaspoon black pepper

Instructions:

1. In the large mixing bowl combine sour cream, mango chutney, salt, pepper, and 1/2 curry powder. Mix well
2. In another large bowl place frozen sweet potato fries. Sprinkle with olive oil and 1/2 of curry powder. Stir to combine
3. Preheat the Air Fryer to 380 – degrees Fahrenheit and cook potato fries for nearly 10 minutes, until cooked and crispy. Shake the fryer basket couple times during cooking.
4. Serve sweet fries with dipping sauce and enjoy

443. Simple Banana Chips

Prep + Cook Time: 20 minutes   **Servings:** 3

Ingredients:

- 2 large raw bananas; peel and sliced
- 1/2 teaspoon red chili powder
- 1 teaspoon olive oil
- 1/4 teaspoon turmeric powder
- 1 teaspoon salt

Instructions:

1. In bowl add water, turmeric powder and salt. Add sliced bananas in bowl water soak for 10 minutes. Drain well and dry chips with paper towel
2. Preheat the Air Fryer to 350 - degrees Fahrenheit
3. Place banana slices in bowl and toss with olive oil, chili powder and salt. Add in Air Fryer basket and air fry for 15 minutes.

444. Roasted Honey Carrots

Prep + Cook Time: 20 minutes   **Servings:** 4

Ingredients:

- 1 tablespoon honey
- 3 cups of baby carrots or carrots cut into bite-size pieces
- 1 tablespoon olive oil
- sea salt to taste
- ground black pepper to taste

Instructions:

1. Take a bowl and combine carrots, honey, and olive oil. The carrots should be covered completely. Season carrots with salt and ground black pepper
2. Air-fry carrots at 390 - degrees Fahrenheit for 12 minutes. When ready, serve immediately

445. Tasty Lemon Green Beans

Prep + Cook Time: 15 minutes   **Servings:** 2

Ingredients:

- 1 Pound green beans; washed and ends trimmed
- 1/4 teaspoon olive oil
- 1 lemon juice
- pepper to taste
- salt to taste

Instructions:

1. Place green beans in Air Fryer basket and pour 1 lemon juice over the beans. Season with pepper and salt. Drizzle with beans with olive oil
2. Cook beans at 400 - degrees Fahrenheit for 10 minutes.

446. Potato Tots

Prep + Cook Time: 20 minutes   **Servings:** 2

Ingredients:

- 1 large potato; diced
- 1 teaspoon onion; minced
- 1 teaspoon olive oil
- pepper to taste
- salt to taste

Instructions:

1. Add water and potatoes in saucepan and boil over medium-high heat.
2. Drain boiled potatoes and place in bowl. Using masher mash potatoes
3. Add olive oil, onion, pepper and salt in mashed potato and mix well to combine.
4. Make small tots of potato mixture and place in Air Fryer basket. Cook at 380 - degrees Fahrenheit for 8 minutes
5. Shake basket and cook for another 5 minutes.

447. Fried Crispy Zucchini

Prep + Cook Time: 30 minutes   **Servings:** 6

Ingredients:

- 6 medium zucchini; cut into sticks
- 4 tablespoon parmesan cheese; grated
- 4 egg white
- 1/2 teaspoon garlic powder
- 1 cup breadcrumbs
- pepper to taste
- salt to taste

Instructions:

1. Preheat the Air Fryer to 400 – degrees Fahrenheit.
2. In a bowl; beat egg whites with salt and pepper
3. In another bowl combine together breadcrumbs, garlic powder, and parmesan cheese
4. Dip zucchini stick in egg whites then coat with breadcrumbs. Place coated zucchini in Air Fryer basket and cook for 20 minutes

448. Tasty Carrots with Cumin

Prep + Cook Time: 25 minutes   **Servings:** 4

Ingredients:

- 2 cups carrots [peeled; chopped]
- 1 teaspoon cumin seeds
- 1 tablespoon olive oil
- 1/4 cup coriander

Instructions:

1. Coat carrots with cumin and oil. Cook at 390 - degrees Fahrenheit for 12 minutes.
2. Sprinkle coriander. The meal is ready to be served. Enjoy eating

449. Crust Cheese Sticks

Prep + Cook Time: 15 minutes   **Servings:** 4

Ingredients:

- 1 Pound mozzarella cheese
- Two eggs; beaten
- 1 teaspoon cayenne pepper
- 1 cup breadcrumbs
- 1 teaspoon onion powder
- 1 teaspoon garlic powder
- 1 cup plain flour
- 1/2 teaspoon salt

Instructions:

1. Cut mozzarella cheese into 3*1/2-inch sticks.

2. Add beaten eggs in small bowl. In a shallow dish add plain flour
3. In another small bowl combine together breadcrumbs, cayenne pepper, onion powder, garlic powder, and salt
4. Dip strips into beaten egg then dip in flour then return into egg and finally coat with breadcrumbs.
5. Place coated cheese in refrigerator for 20 minutes.
6. Preheat the Air Fryer to 400 - degrees Fahrenheit
7. Spray Air Fryer basket with cooking spray. Place coated cheese stick in Air Fryer basket and cook for 5 minutes. And serve hot

450. Easy Crispy Onion Rings

Prep + Cook Time: 25 minutes   **Servings:** 2

Ingredients:

- 1 large onion; cut into slices
- One Egg; beaten
- 3/4 cup breadcrumbs
- 1 cup milk
- 1 teaspoon baking powder
- 1 1/4 cup plain flour
- 1 teaspoon salt

Instructions:

1. Preheat the Air Fryer for 5 minutes.
2. In a small bowl; combine together baking powder, flour, and salt
3. In another small bowl; whisk together milk and egg
4. Place breadcrumbs in a shallow dish.
5. Coat onion slice with flour then dip in egg mixture and finally coat with breadcrumbs. Place coated onion rings in Air Fryer basket and cook at 350 - degrees Fahrenheit for 10 minutes

451. French Fries

Prep + Cook Time: 40 minutes   **Servings:** 4

Ingredients:

- 4 potatoes; peel and cut into strips
- 1 teaspoon Italian seasoning
- 1 teaspoon onion powder
- 1 teaspoon garlic powder
- 1 teaspoon paprika
- 1 teaspoon pepper
- 2 teaspoon olive oil

Instructions:

1. Add all ingredients into the large bowl and toss well
2. Add in Air Fryer basket and air fry at 400 - degrees Fahrenheit for 30 minutes.
3. Shake basket every 10 minutes
4. Serve hot

452. Mediterranean Veggie Dish

Prep + Cook Time: 30 minutes   **Servings:** 4

Ingredients:

- 1 large zucchini; sliced
- 3 – 4 cherry tomatoes on the vine
- 1 medium carrot; peeled and cubed
- 1 large parsnip; peeled and cubed
- 1 green pepper; sliced
- 1 teaspoon mustard
- 1 teaspoon mixed herbs
- 2 cloves garlic; crushed
- 2 tablespoon honey
- 3+3 tablespoon olive oil; separately
- sea salt to taste
- black pepper to taste

Instructions:

1. Add the slices of zucchini, green pepper, parsnip, carrot and cherry tomatoes on the vine to the bottom of the Air Fryer
2. Cover the ingredients with 3 tablespoons of oil and adjust the time to 15 minutes. Cook at 360 - degrees Fahrenheit.
3. While the ingredients are being cooked, prepare the marinade. For that, combine all the remaining ingredients in the Air Fryer safe baking dish
4. When the veggies are ready; combine the marinade and the vegetables in the baking dish and stir making sure every piece of vegetable is coated with the marinade well.
5. Sprinkle it with pepper and salt.
6. Cook it at 390 – degrees Fahrenheit for 5 minutes and serve hot

453. Tasty and Healthy Tofu

Prep + Cook Time: 20 minutes   **Servings:** 4

Ingredients:

- 15 ounces. extra firm tofu; drain and cut into cubes
- 1 teaspoon chili flakes
- 3/4 cup cornstarch
- 1/4 cup cornmeal
- pepper to taste
- salt to taste

Instructions:

1. In a bowl; add cornmeal, cornstarch, chili flakes, pepper, and salt. Mix well. Add tofu cubes in cornmeal mixture and coat well
2. Preheat Air Fryer at 350 - degrees Fahrenheit.
3. Spray Air Fryer basket with cooking spray. Place coated tofu in Air Fryer basket. Air fry tofu for 8 minutes. Shake basket halfway through

454. Eggplant Fries

Prep + Cook Time: 25 minutes   **Servings:** 2

Ingredients:

- 1 large eggplant; cut into 3-inch slices
- 1/4 cup water
- 1 tablespoon olive oil
- 1/4 cup cornstarch
- 1/4 teaspoon salt

Instructions:

1. Preheat the Air Fryer to 400 - degrees Fahrenheit.
2. In a bowl; combine together water, olive oil, cornstarch, and salt
3. Add sliced eggplant in bowl and coat well. Place coated eggplant slices in Air Fryer basket and air fry for 20 minutes

455. Fired Sweet Potato Bites

Prep + Cook Time: 30 minutes   **Servings:** 2

Ingredients:

- 2 sweet potato; diced into
- 1-inch cubes
- 1 teaspoon red chili flakes
- 2 teaspoon cinnamon
- 2 tablespoon olive oil
- 2 tablespoon honey
- 1/2 cup freshly chopped parsley

Instructions:

1. Preheat Air Fryer at 350 – degrees Fahrenheit
2. Add all ingredients into the bowl and toss well. Place sweet potato mixture into the Air Fryer basket.
3. Cook in preheated Air Fryer for 15 minutes

456. Kale Chips

Prep + Cook Time: 15 minutes   **Servings:** 2

Ingredients:

- 1 head of kale
- 1 tablespoon of olive oil
- 1 teaspoon of soya sauce

Instructions:

1. Remove the center steam of the kale. Tear the kale up into 1 1/2" pieces. Wash clean and dry thoroughly
2. Toss with the olive oil and soya sauce.
3. Fry in the Air Fryer at 390 - degrees Fahrenheit for 2 to 3 minutes; tossing the leaves halfway through

457. Roasted Vegetables

Prep + Cook Time: 40 minutes   **Servings:** 4

Ingredients:

- 15 ounces. yellow squash; slices
- 15 ounces. zucchini; slices
- 8 ounces. carrots; slices
- 1 tablespoon oregano; chopped
- 1 tablespoon thyme leaves
- 2 tablespoon olive oil
- 1/2 teaspoon pepper
- 1/2 teaspoon salt

Instructions:

1. In a bowl; add slice zucchini, squash and carrots toss well. Add oil, oregano, and thyme in bowl. Season with pepper and salt. Toss well
2. Place bowl mixture into the Air Fryer basket and cook at 400 – degrees Fahrenheit for 30 minutes. Shake the basket half way through

458. Tasty Stuffed Tomatoes

Prep + Cook Time: 30 minutes   **Servings:** 4

Ingredients:

- 4 large tomatoes; without tops, seeds, and pith
- 1 clove garlic; crushed
- 1 onion; cubed
- 1 cup frozen peas
- 2 cups cooked rice; cold
- 1 tablespoon soy sauce
- 1 carrot; cubed
- 1 tablespoon olive oil
- parsley to taste; roughly chopped
- cooking spray

Instructions:

1. Prepare fried rice: take a pan; grease it with the olive oil and heat over the low heat.
2. Add cubed onion, carrots, crushed garlic, and frozen peas. Cook for 2 minutes stirring a few times.
3. Then add soy sauce and rice; toss well and turn off the heat.
4. Preheat the fryer to 360 - degrees Fahrenheit
5. Meanwhile; fill the tomatoes with rice and vegetable mixture
6. Put it into the Air Fryer and adjust the cooking time to 20 minutes.
7. When it's cooked; decorate stuffed tomatoes with chopped parsley and serve

459. Spicy Mix Nuts

Prep + Cook Time: 15 minutes   **Servings:** 8

Ingredients:

- 2 cup mix nuts
- 1 teaspoon chipotle chili powder
- 1 teaspoon ground cumin
- 1 tablespoon butter; melted
- 1 teaspoon pepper
- 1 teaspoon salt

Instructions:

1. In a bowl; add all ingredients toss well to coat.
2. Preheat Air Fryer at 350 - degrees Fahrenheit for 5 minutes
3. Add mix nuts in Air Fryer basket and roast for 4 minutes. Shake basket halfway through

460. Cheesy Potatoes

Prep + Cook Time: 20 minutes   **Servings:** 4

Ingredients:

- 11 ounce. potatoes [diced; boiled]
- One Egg yolk
- 2 tablespoon flour
- 3 tablespoon cheese [parmesan]
- 3 tablespoon breadcrumbs [with oil]
- pepper to taste
- nutmeg to taste
- salt to taste

Instructions:

1. Mash potatoes and add all ingredients except breadcrumbs in a bowl. Mix the ingredients well and make into medium size balls
2. Coat the balls with breadcrumbs.
3. Preheat Air Fryer at 390 – degrees Fahrenheit and cook for 4 minutes.
4. Serve with fish

461. Onion Mushroom Frittata

Prep + Cook Time: 60 minutes   **Servings:** 4

Ingredients:

- six eggs
- 4 cups button mushrooms; cleaned
- 1 red onion
- 2 tablespoon olive oil
- 6 tablespoon feta cheese; crumbled
- 1 pinch salt

Instructions:

1. Peel and slice a red onion into 1/4-inch thin slices. Clean button mushrooms; then cut into 1/4-inch thin slices.
2. In a sauté pan with olive oil, sweat onions and mushrooms under a medium flame until tender
3. Remove from heat and place on a dry kitchen towel to cool
4. Preheat the Air Fryer to 330 - degrees Fahrenheit. In a mixing bowl crack six eggs and whisk thoroughly and vigorously, adding a pinch of salt. In an 8-inch. heat resistant baking dish, coat the inside and bottom with a light coating of pan spray
5. Pour eggs into the baking dish; then the onion and mushroom mixture and then the cheese.
6. Place the baking dish in the cooking basket and cook in the
7. Air Fryer for 27 to 30 minutes.
8. The frittata is done when you can stick a knife into the middle, and the knife comes out clean

462. Baked Parsley Garlic Potatoes

Prep + Cook Time: 45 minutes   **Servings:** 3

Ingredients:

- 3 idaho or russet baking potatoes; washed
- 2 cloves garlic; crushed
- 1 tablespoon olive oil
- 1 tablespoon sea salt
- parsley; roughly chopped
- sour cream to taste

Instructions:

1. Prepare the potatoes and make the holes using a fork.
2. Season potatoes with salt and cover with garlic puree and olive oil
3. Layer potatoes in the Air Fryer basket and cook at 390 - degrees Fahrenheit. Set the timer for 35 - 40 minutes. It is ready when it is fork tender.
4. You may add your favorite toppings at the end of cooking time, but lean recommend fresh parsley and sour cream

463. Yummy Fried Potato Gratin

Prep + Cook Time: 25 minutes   **Servings:** 4

Ingredients:

- 3 potatoes; peeled and sliced
- 1/4 cup milk
- 3 tablespoon cheddar cheese; grated
- 1/4 cup coconut cream
- 1/4 teaspoon nutmeg
- 1/4 teaspoon pepper

Instructions:

1. Preheat Air Fryer to 400 - degrees Fahrenheit.
2. Add milk and cream in bowl and season with pepper, salt, and nutmeg
3. Coat the potato slices in milk and cream mixture. Arrange potato slices in oven safe dish and pour remaining cream on top of potato slices
4. Sprinkle grated cheese over potato slices. Place dish in Air Fryer basket and cook for 15 minutes until lightly browned.

464. Crunchy Baby Corn

Prep + Cook Time: 20 minutes   **Servings:** 4

Ingredients:

- 8 ounces. baby corns; boiled
- 1 cup plain flour
- 1 teaspoon garlic powder
- 1/2 teaspoon carom seeds
- 1/4 teaspoon chili powder
- pinch of baking soda
- salt to taste

Instructions:

1. In a bowl; add flour, chili powder, garlic powder, cooking soda, salt and carom seed. Mix well. Pour little water in bowl and make nice consistency batter
2. Dip boiled baby corns in batter and coat well.
3. Preheat the Air Fryer at 350 – degrees Fahrenheit
4. Line Air Fryer basket with aluminum foil then place coated baby corns on foil. Cook baby corns in preheated Air Fryer for 10 minutes.

465. Homemade French Potatoes Fries

Prep + Cook Time: 25 minutes

Servings: 4

Ingredients:

- 1-pound russet potatoes
- 1 teaspoon salt
- 1/2 teaspoon black pepper
- 1 tablespoon olive oil

Instructions:

1. Heat the water in a pan and blanch potatoes until tender. Let cool and then cut into fries.
2. Transfer to a large bowl and toss sprinkle with olive oil, salt and pepper
3. Preheat the Air Fryer to 390 - degrees Fahrenheit and cook French fries for about 15 minutes, shake periodically while cooking. Serve and garnish with freshly chopped herbs if desired

466. Tasty Tawa Veggies

Prep + Cook Time: 30 minutes

Servings: 4

Ingredients:

- 1/4 cup okra
- 1/4 cup eggplant
- 1/4 cup potato
- 1/4 cup taro root
- 1 teaspoon amchur powder
- 1 teaspoon red chili powder
- 2 teaspoon garam masala
- salt according to taste
- oil for brushing

Instructions:

1. Cut potato and taro root into fries and soak in salt water for 10 minutes
2. Cut okra and eggplant into four pieces in a way that it is attached at one end. Rinse potatoes and taro root and pat them dry
3. Add spices over the potatoes, taro roots, okra and egg plants. Brush the pan with oil.
4. Preheat to 390 - degrees Fahrenheit and cook the mixture for 10 minutes.
5. Lower heat to 355 – degrees Fahrenheit and cook for 15 minutes. And Serve with rice

467. Simple Roasted Corn

Prep + Cook Time: 15 minutes

Servings: 8

Ingredients:

- 4 fresh ears of corn
- 2 to 3 teaspoon vegetable oil
- salt and pepper to taste

Instructions:

1. Remove husks from corn, wash and pat dry. You may need to cut the corn to fit in your basket. If you need to do so, cut the corn
2. Drizzle vegetable oil over the corn. Try to cover the corn well. Season with salt and pepper.
3. Cook at 400 - degrees Fahrenheit for about 10 minutes

468. Delicious Vegetable Spring Rolls

Prep + Cook Time: 35 minutes

Servings: 10

Ingredients:

- 2 cups cabbage; shredded
- 1 large carrot; cut into thin matchsticks
- 2 large onions; cut into thin matchsticks
- 1/2 bell pepper; cut into thin matchsticks - any color will work
- 2-inch piece ginger; grated
- 8 cloves garlic; minced

- 2 tablespoon of cooking oil plus more for brushing
- A few pinches sugar
- A few pinches salt
- 1 teaspoon soy sauce
- 1 tablespoon black pepper
- 2 – 3 green onions; thinly sliced
- 10 spring roll wrappers
- 2 tablespoon cornstarch
- water

Instructions:

1. Prepare the filling: in a large bowl; combine the cabbage, carrot, onion, bell pepper, ginger, and garlic.
2. In a medium sauté pan; heat 2 tablespoon oil over high heat. Add the filling mixture, stirring in a few pinches of sugar and salt [the sugar helps the vegetables maintain their color].
3. Cook for 2 – 3 min; add the soy sauce and black pepper, mix well, and remove from heat. Stir in the green onions and set aside
4. In small bowl; combine the cornstarch and enough water to make a creamy paste.
5. Fill the rolls: place a tablespoon or so of filling in the center of each wrapper and roll tightly, dampening the edges with the cornstarch paste to ensure a good seal
6. Repeat until all the wrappers and filling are used. Alternatively; cut the wrappers into smaller sizes and make mini spring rolls - fun!
7. Briefly preheat your Air Fryer to 350 – degrees Fahrenheit.
8. Brush the rolls with oil, arrange in the Fryer, and cook until crisp and golden, about 20 min, flipping once at the halfway point

Notes: When preparing the vegetables for the filling; take care to cut them all to a uniform size, as this will ensure even cooking and allow for a more attractive presentation.

469. Zucchini Fries and Garlic Aioli

Prep + Cook Time: 30 minutes   **Servings:** 4

Roasted Garlic Aioli Ingredients:
- 2 tablespoon olive oil
- 1 teaspoon roasted garlic; pureed
- 1/2 lemon; juiced
- 1/2 cup mayonnaise
- sea salt to taste
- black pepper to taste

Zucchini Fries Ingredients:
- Two eggs; beaten
- 1/2 cup all-purpose flour
- 1 cup breadcrumbs
- 1 large zucchini; cut into 1/2-inch sticks
- 1 tablespoon olive oil
- cooking spray
- sea salt to taste
- pepper to taste

Instructions:

1. Take three shallow dishes. In the first one com-bine and stir well flour, pepper, and salt.
2. Beaten eggs should be in the second dish. The third dish is for breadcrumbs combined with some salt and pepper
3. Take the zucchini sticks and dip them first in the flour, then in the eggs and crumbs consequently. After this shake the dish with the breadcrumbs and pat them on the sticks.
4. Set the sticks aside for about 10 minutes.
5. Preheat the Air Fryer to 400 – degrees Fahrenheit
6. Cover the sticks with the cooking spray, layer them in the basket. There should be two layers, first one pointing at one direction, and the second layer pointing in the opposite direction.
7. Set timer to 12 minutes. Rotate and turn the fries halfway done and use some more cooking spray
8. Meanwhile; prepare roasted garlic aioli: take a medium bowl and combine mayonnaise, olive oil, pureed roasted garlic, and lemon juice. Stir in some more pepper and salt.
9. When zucchini fries are ready, serve it with roasted garlic aioli

470. Roasted Honey Carrots

Prep + Cook Time: 20 minutes   **Servings:** 2

Ingredients:

- 1 tablespoon olive oil
- 3 cups of baby carrots or carrots cut into large chunks
- 1 tablespoon honey
- salt and pepper to taste

Instructions:

1. In a bowl; mix your carrots with your honey and the olive oil. Ensure carrots are well covered. Season with salt and pepper
2. Cook in Air Fryer set to 390 – degrees Fahrenheit for 12 minutes. Serve while hot

471. Fried Kale Chips

Prep + Cook Time: 10 minutes   **Servings:** 2

Ingredients:

- 1 head kale; tear into
- 1 ½ -inch pieces
- 1 tablespoon olive oil
- 1 teaspoon soy sauce

Instructions:

1. Wash kale pieces and dry well with paper towel. Add kale in a bowl and toss with soy sauce and oil
2. Add in Air Fryer and cook at 400 - degrees Fahrenheit for 3 minutes. Toss halfway.

472. Orange Cauliflower

Prep + Cook Time: 30 minutes   **Servings:** 2

Ingredients:

- 1/2 lemon; juiced
- 1 head cauliflower
- 1/2 tablespoon olive oil
- 1 teaspoon curry powder
- sea salt to taste
- ground black pepper to taste

Instructions:

1. Prepare the cauliflower: wash it and remove the leaves and core.
2. Slice into florets of similar size
3. Grease the Air Fryer with the oil and heat it for about 2 minutes selecting 390 - degrees Fahrenheit
4. Combine fresh lemon juice and curry powder. Stir and add the cauliflower florets. Season it with pepper, salt and stir well again.
5. Cook the meal for 20 minutes and serve warm

473. Lemon Green Beans

Prep + Cook Time: 20 minutes   **Servings:** 4

Ingredients:

- 1 lemon
- 1 Pound. green beans; washed and destemmed
- 1/4 teaspoon extra virgin olive oil
- sea salt to taste
- black pepper to taste

Instructions:

1. Preheat the Air Fryer to 400 – degrees Fahrenheit
2. Place the green beans into your Air Fryer basket. Squeeze the lemon over the beans. Season it with pepper and salt. Cover the ingredients with oil and toss well
3. Cook the green beans for 10 – 12 minutes. Serve Warm.

474. Air Roasted Broccoli Florets

Prep + Cook Time: 20 minutes   **Servings:** 4

Ingredients:

- 1 Pound broccoli; cut into florets
- 1 tablespoon lemon juice
- 1 tablespoon olive oil
- 1 tablespoon sesame seeds
- 3 garlic cloves; minced

Instructions:

1. Add all ingredients to the bowl and toss well. Add broccoli into the Air Fryer basket and air fry at 400 - degrees Fahrenheit for 13 minutes

475. Amazing Avocado Fries

Prep + Cook Time: 20 minutes   **Servings:** 4

Ingredients:

- 1/2 cup panko
- 1/2 teaspoon salt
- 1 whole avocado
- 1 ounce. aquafaba

Instructions:

1. Toss together the panko and salt in a shallow bowl. Pour the aquafaba into another shallow bowl.
2. Dredge the avocado slices in the aquafaba and then in the panko
3. Arrange the slices in a single layer in your Air Fryer basket. The single layer is important. Air fry for 10 minutes at 390 – degrees Fahrenheit

476. Asian Spinach Samosa

Prep + Cook Time: 45 minutes   **Servings:** 2

Ingredients:

- 3/4 cup of boiled and blended spinach puree
- 1/4 cup of green peas
- 1/2 teaspoon sesame seeds
- Ajwain, salt, chaat masala, chili powder to taste
- 2 teaspoon of olive oil
- 1 teaspoon of chopped fresh coriander leaves
- 1 teaspoon of garam masala
- 1/4 cup of boiled and cut potatoes
- 1/2 1 cup of refined flour
- 1/2 teaspoon of cooking soda

Instructions:

1. Mix Ajwain, flour, cooking soda and salt in a bowl to make the dough. Add 1 tablespoon of oil. Add spinach puree and mix the dough until it smoothens
2. Put it in the fridge for twenty minutes. Add 1 tablespoon of oil into a pan then add potato and peas and allow them to cook for 5 minutes.
3. Add sesame seeds, coriander, and any other spices as you stir. Kneading the dough again, make the small ball with the help of a rolling pin.
4. From the balls make cone shapes which are then filled with the stuffing that is not yet cooked.
5. Make sure the flour sheets are well sealed. Get the Air Fryer preheated to 390 - degrees Fahrenheit. Place the samosa in the Air Fryer basket and allowed them to cook in there for 10 minutes
6. serve the samosa with sauce.

477. Tomatoes & Herbs

Prep + Cook Time: 30 minutes   **Servings:** 2

Ingredients:

- 2 large tomatoes; washed and cut into halves
- herbs; such as oregano, basil, thyme, rosemary, sage to taste
- cooking spray
- pepper to taste
- parmesan; grated [optional]
- parsley; minced [optional]

Instructions:

1. Take the halves of tomatoes and spray its bottoms with a small amount of cooking spray. Then turn the tomatoes cut side up. Spray that side as well
2. Season tomatoes with pepper and dried or fresh herbs as you prefer
3. Layer tomatoes in the basket cut-side up. Set 320 – degrees Fahrenheit without preheating. Adjust the time to 20 minutes.
4. After the end of cooking; check the tomatoes for readiness, cook for another minute or two if necessary. Serve hot; or room temperature, or chilled as a summer side dish or covered with grated Parmesan and minced parsley

478. Peppery Crispy Vegetable Fritters

Prep + Cook Time: 15 minutes   **Servings:** 4

Ingredients:

- 1 cup bell peppers; deveined and chopped
- 1 teaspoon sea salt flakes
- 1 teaspoon cumin
- 1/4 teaspoon paprika
- 1/2 cup shallots; chopped
- 2 cloves garlic; minced
- 1 ½ tablespoons fresh chopped cilantro
- One Egg; whisked
- 3/4 cup Cheddar cheese; grated
- 1/4 cup cooked quinoa
- 1/4 cup self-rising flour

Instructions:

1. Mix all the Ingredients until everything is well incorporated. Shape into balls, then, slightly flatten each ball.
2. Spritz the patties with a cooking spray.
3. Place the patties in a single layer in your Air Fryer cooking basket.
4. Cook at 340 degrees for 5 minutes and flip them over and cook another 5 minutes.

479. Delicious Pineapple Sticks With Yoghurt Dip

Prep + Cook Time: 25 minutes   **Servings:** 2

Ingredients:

- 1/4 cup desiccated coconut
- 1/2 pineapple

Yogurt dip ingredients:

- 1 cup vanilla yogurt
- fresh mint

Instructions:

1. Preheat your Air Fryer to 390 - degrees Fahrenheit. Cut the pineapple into sticks.
2. Take the desiccated coconut and dip the pineapple sticks in it. Put the sticks covered with desiccated coconut in the Air Fryer basket and cook for 10 minutes

3. Meanwhile; prepare the yogurt dip. Dice the mint leaves and combine it with the vanilla yogurt stirring well.
4. Serve the pineapple sticks on a large plate and the yogurt dip in the small bowls separately for each person

480. Tasty Onion Pakova

Prep + Cook Time: 25 minutes   **Servings:** 6

Ingredients:

- 1 cup graham flour
- 1/4 cup rice flour
- 2 teaspoon vegetable oil
- 4 onions; finely chopped
- 2 green chili peppers; finely chopped
- 1 tablespoon fresh coriander; chopped
- 1/4 teaspoon carom
- 1/8 teaspoon chili powder
- turmeric
- salt to taste

Instructions:

1. In a large bowl; combine the flours and oil. Mix well; adding water as necessary to create a thick, dough-like consistency
2. Add the onions, peppers, coriander, carom, chili powder, and turmeric. Season with salt and mix well
3. Briefly preheat your Air Fryer to 350 - degrees Fahrenheit. Roll the vegetable mixture into small balls, arrange in the Fryer, and cook until browned, about 6 minutes, serve with hot sauce and enjoy!

481. Butternut Pumpkin with Nuts

Prep + Cook Time: 30 minutes   **Servings:** 4

Main Ingredients:

- 2 ½ tablespoon toasted pine nuts
- 1 butternut pumpkin; cut into 1-inch slices
- 1 ½ tablespoon olive oil
- 1/4 a bunch thyme
- sea salt to taste
- black pepper to taste

Vinaigrette ingredients:

- 6 tablespoon olive oil
- 1 tablespoon Dijon mustard
- 2 tablespoon balsamic vinegar
- sea salt to taste
- black pepper to taste

Instructions:

1. Preheat your Air Fryer to 390 - degrees Fahrenheit for 5 minutes
2. Take the slices of a pumpkin and cover it with 1 ½ tablespoons of olive oil and season it with thyme, salt, and pepper.
3. When the Air Fryer is hot; adjust the time to 20 minutes
4. Put the seasoned pumpkin into the Air Fryer basket and cook. The pumpkin is ready when it's soft and tender. In the meantime; prepare the vinaigrette. For that, simply combine all the vinaigrette ingredients in a bowl and stir well
5. Serve the pumpkin covered with the vinaigrette. Sprinkle it with toasted pine nuts and sprigs of thyme

482. Zucchini Roll Ups

Prep + Cook Time: 15 minutes   **Servings:** 3

Ingredients:

- 3 zucchinis; sliced thinly lengthwise [with a mandolin or very good knife]
- 1 tablespoon olive oil
- 1 cup goat cheese
- 1/4 teaspoon black pepper

Instructions:

1. Preheat your Air Fryer to 390 – degrees Fahrenheit.
2. Brush each zucchini strip with a bit of olive oil [use a food brush] Mix the sea salt and black pepper with the goat cheese
3. Spoon a bit of goat cheese into the middle of each strip of zucchini. Roll up each zucchini and fasten with a toothpick. Place in the Air Fryer and cook for 5 minutes
4. The cheese will be warm and the zucchini slightly crispy. Top with tomato sauce or enjoy as is for a light lunch or snack

483. Chili Cumin Squash

Prep + Cook Time: 45 minutes   **Servings:** 4

Ingredients:

- 1 butternut squash [medium]
- 2 teaspoon cumin seeds
- 1 bunch coriander
- 1/4 cup pine nuts
- 1 pinch chili flakes
- 1 tablespoon olive oil
- 2/3 yoghurt [Greek]
- salt and pepper to taste

Instructions:

1. Slice squash and cut into small chunks
2. Mix with spices and oil pan. Roast squash at 380 - degrees Fahrenheit for 20 minutes in the pan.
3. Toast nuts and serve with yoghurt; sprinkle coriander

484. Mary's Charred Shishito Pepper

Prep + Cook Time: 20 minutes   **Servings:** 4

Ingredients:

- 20 shishito peppers [about 6 ounces]
- 1 teaspoon vegetable oil
- coarse sea salt
- 1 lemon

Instructions:

1. Pre-heat the Air Fryer to 390 - degrees Fahrenheit.
2. Toss the shishito peppers with the oil and salt. You can do this in a bowl or directly in the Air Fryer basket
3. Air fry at 390 – degrees Fahrenheit for 5 minutes; shaking the basket once during cooking.
4. Turn the peppers out into a bowl. They should be a little charred in places. Squeeze some lemon juice on them and season them with coarse sea salt
5. These should be served as finger foods. Pick the pepper up by the stem and eat the whole pepper, seeds and all. Watch for that hot one!

485. Curried Cauliflower Florets

Prep + Cook Time: 15 minutes   **Servings:** 4

Ingredients:

- 1/4 cup sultanas or golden raisins
- 1/2 cup olive oil
- 1/4 cup pine nuts
- 1 head cauliflower; broken into bite-size florets
- 1 tablespoon curry powder
- 1/4 teaspoon salt

Instructions:

1. Soak the sultanas in 1 cup of boiling water to plump them.

2. Briefly preheat your Air Fryer to 350 – degrees Fahrenheit
3. Add the oil and pine nuts to the Fryer and toast for a minute or so.
4. Toss the cauliflower with the curry powder and salt and add to the fryer; mixing well. Cook for 8 – 10 minutes
5. Depending upon the capacity of your Air Fryer; you make need to cook the cauliflower in two batches.
6. Drain the sultanas; toss with the cauliflower, and serve

486. Homemade Special Samosas

Prep + Cook Time: 55 minutes   **Servings:** 4

Ingredients:

- 2 russet potatoes; peeled and cubed
- 1/2 cup of green peas
- 2 teaspoon garam masala powder
- 1 teaspoon ginger-garlic paste
- 1 teaspoon chili powder
- 1 teaspoon turmeric
- salt to taste

- 1/2 teaspoon cumin seed
- vegetable oil for frying and brushing
- 2 cups all-purpose flour
- 1 teaspoon carom seed
- 1 – 2 teaspoon ghee [melted butter will also work]

Instructions:

1. Prepare the crust: in a medium bowl; combine the flour, carom seed, ghee, and as much water as necessary to make a smooth dough.
2. Knead the dough briefly and chill in the refrigerator for 30 min.
3. While the dough chills, prepare the filling: in a medium saucepan, cover the potatoes with water and bring to a boil
4. Add the peas and continue to boil until the vegetables are tender. Drain and mash them well.
5. Add the garam masala, ginger- garlic paste, chili powder, and turmeric to the potato mixture. Season with salt to taste and mix well
6. In a small sauté pan; heat 2 tablespoons of oil over medium heat.
7. Add the cumin seeds and toast until aromatic and sizzling. Add the cumin to the potato mixture, mix well again, and set aside
8. Remove the dough from the refrigerator, roll out on a counter, and cut into several squares approximately 3 – 4 in. across
9. Place a spoonful of filling in each square and fold the samosa to resemble the photograph above, carefully sealing the edges
10. Briefly preheat your Air Fryer to 350 – degrees Fahrenheit.
11. Brush the samosas with oil, place in the Fryer, and cook until golden, 18 – 20 min

487. Awesome Semolina Cutlets

Prep + Cook Time: 25 minutes   **Servings:** 2

Ingredients:

- 5 cups milk
- 1 ½ cups of your favorite vegetables [I like a combination of cauliflower, carrot, peas, green beans, and bell pepper]
- 1 cup semolina
- salt and pepper to taste
- oil for frying

Instructions:

1. In a medium saucepan; heat the milk over medium heat
2. When hot; add the vegetables and cook until softened, 2- 3 minutes. Season with salt and pepper.
3. Add the semolina to the milk mixture, continuing to cook until thickened, about 10 minutes.
4. Remove from heat; spread in a thin layer on a parchment-lined baking sheet, and chill in the refrigerator until firm, 3 – 4 hours
5. When ready to cook; remove the baking sheet from the refrigerator, and cut the semolina mixture into cutlets using a sharp knife.
6. Alternatively; use cookie cutters to make fun shapes if you will be serving the cutlets to children.
7. Briefly preheat your Air Fryer to 350 - degrees Fahrenheit
8. Brush the cutlets with oil, arrange in the Fryer, and bake until golden, about 10 minutes. Serve with hot sauce!

488. Sweet Potato Chips

Prep + Cook Time: 20 minutes   **Servings:** 2

Ingredients:

- 2 large sweet potatoes; thinly sliced with a mandoline.
- 2 tablespoon olive oil
- salt to taste

Instructions:

1. Briefly preheat your Air Fryer to 350 - degrees Fahrenheit
2. In a large bowl or zip-top plastic bag, toss the sweet potato slices with the oil.
3. Arrange in the Air Fryer and cook until crispy; about 15 minutes

Desserts

489. Delicious Banana Chocolate Cake

Prep + Cook Time: 30 minutes   **Servings:** 10

Ingredients:

- 1 stick softened butter
- 1/2 cup caster sugar
- One Egg
- 2 bananas; mashed
- 3 tablespoons maple syrup
- 2 cups self-rising flour
- 1/4 teaspoon anise star; ground
- 1/4 teaspoon ground mace
- 1/4 teaspoon ground cinnamon
- 1/4 teaspoon crystallized ginger
- 1/2 teaspoon vanilla paste
- A pinch of kosher salt
- 1/2 cup cocoa powder

Instructions:

1. Firstly; beat the softened butter and sugar until well combined. Then; whisk the egg, mashed banana and maple syrup. Now, add this mixture to the butter mixture and mix until pale and creamy
2. Add in the flour, anise star, mace, cinnamon, crystallized ginger, vanilla paste, and the salt. now, add the cocoa powder and mix to combine
3. Then; treat two cake pans with a non-stick cooking spray.
4. Press the batter into the cake pans. Air-bake at 330 - degrees Fahrenheit for 30 minutes. To serve, frost with chocolate butter glaze

490. Tasty Lemon Butter Pound Cake

Prep + Cook Time: 2 hours 20 minutes   **Servings:** 8

Ingredients:

- 1 stick softened butter
- 1/3 cup muscovado sugar
- 1 medium-sized egg
- 1 ¼ cups cake flour
- 1 teaspoon butter flavoring
- 1 teaspoon vanilla essence
- A pinch of salt
- 3/4 cup milk
- Grated zest of 1 medium-sized lemon

For the Glaze:

- 1 cup powdered sugar
- 2 tablespoons fresh squeezed lemon juice

Instructions:

1. In a mixing bowl; cream the butter and sugar. Now; fold in the egg and beat again.
2. Add the flour, butter flavoring, vanilla essence, salt and mix to combine well
3. Afterward; add the milk and lemon zest and mix on low until everything's incorporated.
4. Evenly spread a thin layer of melted butter all around the cake pan using a pastry brush. Now; press the batter into the cake pan
5. Bake at 350 – degrees Fahrenheit for 15 minutes. After that; take the cake out of the Air Fryer and carefully run a small knife around the edges and invert the cake onto a serving platter.
6. Allow it to cool completely.
7. To make the glaze; mix powdered sugar with lemon juice.
8. Drizzle over the top of your cake and allow hardening for about 2 hours

491. Jenny's Fried Pineapple Rings

Prep + Cook Time: 10 minutes

Servings: 6

Ingredients:

- 2/3 cup all-purpose flour
- 1/3 cup rice flour
- 1/2 teaspoon baking powder
- 1/2 teaspoon baking soda
- A pinch of kosher salt
- 1/2 cup water
- 1 cup rice milk
- 1/2 teaspoon ground cinnamon
- 1/4 teaspoon ground anise star
- 1/2 teaspoon vanilla essence
- 4 tablespoons caster sugar
- 1/4 cup unsweetened flaked coconut
- 1 medium-sized pineapple; peeled and sliced

Instructions:

1. Mix all of the above Ingredients; except the pineapple.
2. Then; coat the pineapple slices with the batter mix, covering well
3. Air-fry them at 380 – degrees Fahrenheit for 6 to 8 minutes.
4. Drizzle with maple syrup, garnish with a dollop of vanilla ice cream, and serve

492. Amazing Hazelnut Brownie Cups

Prep + Cook Time: 30 minutes

Servings: 12

Ingredients:

- 6 ounces' semisweet chocolate chips
- 1 stick butter; at room temperature
- 1/2 cup caster sugar
- 1/4 cup brown sugar
- 2 large-sized eggs
- 1/4 cup red wine
- 1/4 teaspoon hazelnut extract
- 1 teaspoon pure vanilla extract
- 3/4 cup all-purpose flour
- 2 tablespoons cocoa powder
- 1/2 cup ground hazelnuts
- A pinch of kosher salt

Instructions:

1. Microwave the chocolate chips with butter.
2. Then; whisk the sugars, eggs, red wine, hazelnut and vanilla extract. Add to the chocolate mix.
3. Stir in the flour, cocoa powder, ground hazelnuts, and a pinch of kosher salt
4. Mix until the batter is creamy and smooth. Divide the batter among muffin cups that are coated with cupcake liners.
5. Air-bake at 360 - degrees Fahrenheit for 28 to 30 minutes
6. Bake in batches and serve topped with ganache if desired

493. Classic Swirled German Cake

Prep + Cook Time: 25 minutes

Servings: 8

Ingredients:

- 1 cup flour
- 1 teaspoon baking powder
- 1 cup white sugar
- 1/8 teaspoon kosher salt
- 1/4 teaspoon ground cinnamon
- 1/4 teaspoon grated nutmeg
- 1 teaspoon orange zest
- 1 stick butter; melted
- Two eggs
- 1 teaspoon pure vanilla extract
- 1/4 cup milk
- 2 tablespoons unsweetened cocoa powder

Instructions:

1. Lightly grease a round pan that fits into your Air Fryer.
2. Combine the flour, baking powder, sugar, salt, cinnamon, nutmeg, and orange zest using an electric mixer. Then; fold in the butter, eggs, vanilla, and milk
3. Add 1/4 cup of the batter to the baking pan, leave the remaining batter and stir the cocoa into it.
4. Drop by spoonful over the top of white batter. Then, swirl the cocoa batter into the white batter with a knife
5. Bake at 360 – degrees Fahrenheit approximately 15 minutes. Let it cool for about 10 minutes.
6. Finally; turn the cake out onto a wire rack.

494. Oaty Apple and Plum Crumble

Prep + Cook Time: 20 minutes   **Servings:** 6

Ingredients:

- 1/4-pound plums; pitted and chopped
- 1/4-pound Braeburn apples; cored and chopped
- 1 tablespoon fresh lemon juice
- 2 ½ ounces golden caster sugar
- 1 tablespoon honey
- 1/2 teaspoon ground mace
- 1/2 teaspoon vanilla paste
- 1 cup fresh cranberries
- 1/3 cup oats
- 2/3 cup flour
- 1/2 stick butter; chilled
- 1 tablespoon cold water

Instructions:

1. Thoroughly combine the plums and apples with lemon juice, sugar, honey, and ground mace.
2. Spread the fruit mixture onto the bottom of a cake pan that is previously greased with non-stick cooking oil
3. In a mixing dish; combine the other Ingredients until everything is well incorporated.
4. Spread this mixture evenly over the fruit mixture.
5. Air-bake at 390 – degrees Fahrenheit for 20 minutes or until done

495. Chocolate Chip Cookies

Prep + Cook Time: 25 minutes   **Servings:** 9

Ingredients:

- 1 1/4 cup self-rising flour
- 2/3 cup chocolate chips; any kind or bakers chocolate
- 1/3 cup brown sugar
- 1/2 cup butter
- 4 tablespoon honey
- 1 tablespoon milk
- high quality cooking spray

Instructions:

1. Start by preheating your Air Fryer to 320 - degrees Fahrenheit for about 10 minutes.
2. In the meantime; use a large mixing bowl to cream the butter until it is soft.
3. Add the sugar and cream together and blend until they are light and fluffy
4. Once the mix has reached your desired texture, mix in the honey.
5. Slowly fold in the flour until it has all been added. If you are using baker's chocolate, use a rolling pin to smash it up to give yourself chunks of all different sizes. If you are using chocolate chips, skip this step
6. Add the chocolate to your cookie dough and blend well so they are evenly distributed throughout the dough.
7. Pour in the milk and thoroughly stir the mixture. Lightly spray your Air Fryer basket with a high-quality cooking spray
8. Dump or spoon the entire cookie dough mixture into it. cook the dough for 20 minutes.
9. Cut into 9 portions and serve immediately or store in an air tight container for up to 3 days.

496. Delicious Cupcakes with Buttercream Icing

Prep + Cook Time: 25 minutes   **Servings:** 6

Ingredients:

For the Cupcakes:

- 1/2 cup all-purpose flour
- 1/2 teaspoon baking soda
- 1 baking powder
- 1/8 teaspoon salt
- 1/4 teaspoon ground anise star
- 1/4 teaspoon grated nutmeg
- 1 teaspoon cinnamon

- 3 tablespoons caster sugar
- 1/2 teaspoon pure vanilla extract
- One Egg
- 1/4 cup plain milk
- 1/2 stick melted butter
- 1/2 cup Sultanas

For the Buttercream Icing:

- 1/3 cup butter; softened
- 1 ½ cups powdered sugar
- 1 teaspoon vanilla extract

- 1/8 teaspoon salt
- 2 tablespoons milk
- A few drop food coloring

Instructions:

1. Take two mixing bowls. Thoroughly combine the dry Ingredients for the cupcakes into the first bowl
2. In another bowl; whisk the vanilla extract, egg, milk, and melted butter.
3. To form a batter; add the wet milk mixture to the dry flour mixture
4. Fold in Sultanas and gently stir to combine. Ladle the batter into the prepared muffin pans.
5. Air-bake at 390 – degrees Fahrenheit for 15 minutes.
6. Meanwhile; to make the Buttercream Icing, beat the butter until creamy and fluffy.
7. Gradually add the sugar and beat well
8. Then; add the vanilla, salt, and milk, and mix until creamy. Afterward, gently stir in food coloring. Frost your cupcakes and enjoy!

497. Homemade Coconut Banana Treat

Prep + Cook Time: 20 minutes   **Servings:** 6

Ingredients:

- 2 tablespoons coconut oil
- 3/4 cup breadcrumbs
- 2 tablespoons coconut sugar
- 1/2 teaspoon cinnamon powder

- 1/4 teaspoon ground cloves
- 6 ripe bananas; peeled and halved
- 1/3 cup rice flour
- 1 large-sized well-beaten egg

Instructions:

1. Preheat a non-stick skillet over a moderate heat and stir the coconut oil and the breadcrumbs for about 4 minutes
2. Remove from the heat; add coconut sugar, cinnamon, cloves and set it aside
3. Coat the banana halves with the rice flour, covering on all sides. Then, dip them in beaten egg. Finally, roll them over the crumb mix.
4. Cook in a single layer in the Air Fryer basket at 290 - degrees Fahrenheit for 10 minutes. Work in batches as needed
5. Serve warm or at room temperature sprinkled with flaked coconut if desired.

498. Delicious Chocolate Muffins

Prep + Cook Time: 25 minutes   **Servings:** 12

Ingredients:

- 2 1/8 cups caster sugar
- 2 cups self-rising flour
- 1/2 cup butter
- 1/8 cup milk chocolate; chips or broken up chunks of baker's chocolate
- 5 tablespoon milk
- 2 tablespoon cocoa powder
- 1/2 teaspoon vanilla extract
- two eggs; medium
- water

Instructions:

1. Start by preheating your Air Fryer to 350 - degrees Fahrenheit for about 10 minutes. In a large mixing bowl; combine the sugar and cocoa until it is completely mixed.
2. Cut in the butter by cutting it into small chunks and putting it in the sugar and cocoa mixture. Rub it in until the entire mixture has the consistency of breadcrumbs
3. In a small mixing bowl; crack the eggs in and beat them together. Pour in the milk and then mix it into the eggs until they are thoroughly mixed.
4. Add the egg and milk mixture into the sugar mixture and blend the two together until they are completely combined
5. Add the vanilla extract and mix the batter. If it is too thick, add some water, a little bit at a time, until it creates a cake batter consistency.
6. If you are using baker's chocolate or another large piece of chocolate, smash it under a rolling pin to create small chunks. If you are using chocolate chips, skip this step. Mix the chocolate into the batter until it is evenly distributed
7. Give the muffin batter a final mix to make sure everything is combined.   Spoon the batter into small, pre-greased bun cases until they are about 80% full.
8. Put the bun cases in the preheated Air Fryer and bake for 9 minutes. Reduce the temperature to 320 - degrees Fahrenheit and bake for an additional 6 minutes.
9. Serve hot with a side of vanilla ice cream or fresh fruit. Alternatively; store in an air tight container in the fridge for up to 3 days

499. Amazing Mini Strawberry Pies

Prep + Cook Time: 15 minutes   **Servings:** 8

Ingredients:

- 1/2 cup powdered sugar
- 1/4 teaspoon ground cloves
- 1/8 teaspoon cinnamon powder
- 1 teaspoon vanilla extract
- 1 [12-ounce] can biscuit dough
- 12 ounces strawberry pie filling
- 1/4 cup butter; melted

Instructions:

1. Thoroughly combine the sugar, cloves, cinnamon, and vanilla
2. Then; stretch and flatten each piece of the biscuit dough into a round circle using a rolling pin.
3. Divide the strawberry pie filling among the biscuits.
4. Roll up tightly and dip each biscuit piece into the melted butter and cover them with the spiced sugar mixture
5. Brush with a non-stick cooking oil on all sides.
6. Air-bake them at 340 - degrees Fahrenheit for approximately 10 minutes or until they're golden brown
7. Let them cool for 5 minutes before serving.

500. Tasty Coconut Brownies

Prep + Cook Time: 15 minutes   **Servings:** 8

Ingredients:

- 1/2 cup coconut oil
- 2 ounces dark chocolate
- 1 cup sugar
- 2 ½ tablespoons water
- 4 whisked eggs
- 1/4 teaspoon ground cinnamon
- 1/2 teaspoon ground anise star
- 1/4 teaspoon coconut extract
- 1/2 teaspoon vanilla extract
- 1 tablespoon honey
- 1/2 cup cake flour
- 1/2 cup desiccated coconut
- Icing sugar; to dust

Instructions:

1. Microwave the coconut oil along with dark chocolate.
2. Stir in sugar, water, eggs, cinnamon, anise, coconut extract, vanilla, and honey
3. After that; stir in the flour and coconut and mix to combine thoroughly.
4. Press the mixture into a lightly buttered baking dish. Air-bake at 355 - degrees Fahrenheit for 15 minutes
5. Let your brownie cool slightly. then, carefully remove from the baking dish and cut into squares.
6. Dust with icing sugar

501. Banana and Vanilla Pastry Puffs

Prep + Cook Time: 15 minutes   **Servings:** 8

Ingredients:

- 1 package [8-ounce] crescent dinner rolls; refrigerated
- 1 cup of milk
- 4 ounces instant vanilla pudding
- 4 ounces cream cheese; softened
- 2 bananas; peeled and sliced
- One Egg; lightly beaten

Instructions:

1. Unroll crescent dinner rolls and cut into 8 squares.
2. Combine the milk and the pudding; whisk in the cream cheese
3. Divide the pudding mixture among the pastry squares. Top with the slices of banana.
4. Now; fold the dough over the filling, pressing the edges to help them seal well.
5. Brush each pastry puff with the whisked egg.
6. Air-bake at 355 - degrees Fahrenheit for 10 minutes

502. Christmas Double Chocolate Cake

Prep + Cook Time: 45 minutes   **Servings:** 8

Ingredients:

- 1/2 cup caster sugar
- 1 ¼ cups cake flour
- 1 teaspoon baking powder
- 1/3 cup cocoa powder
- 1/4 teaspoon ground cloves
- 1/8 teaspoon freshly grated nutmeg
- A pinch of table salt
- One Egg
- 1/4 cup soda
- 1/4 cup milk
- 1/2 stick butter; melted
- 2 ounces bittersweet chocolate; melted
- 1/2 cup hot water

Instructions:

1. Take two mixing bowls. Thoroughly combine the dry Ingredients in the first bowl.

2. In the second bowl; mix the egg, soda, milk, butter, and chocolate.
3. Add the wet mix to the dry mix and pour in the water and mix well
4. Butter a cake pan that fits into your Air Fryer. Pour the mixture into the baking pan.
5. Loosely cover with foil and bake at 320 - degrees Fahrenheit for 35 minutes.
6. Now; remove foil and bake for further 10 minutes. Frost the cake with buttercream if desired

503. Yummy Banana Oats Cookies

Prep + Cook Time: 20 minutes   **Servings:** 6

Ingredients:
- 2 cups quick oats
- 1/4 cup milk
- 4 ripe bananas; mashed
- 1/4 cup coconut shredded

Instructions:
1. Preheat the Air Fryer to 350 – degrees Fahrenheit. Add all ingredients into the bowl and mix well to combine.
2. Spoon cookie dough onto baking sheet and place in Air Fryer basket. Bake cookies in preheated Air Fryer for 15 minutes

504. Sugar Butter Fritters

Prep + Cook Time: 30 minutes   **Servings:** 16

Ingredients:

For the dough:
- 4 cups fine cake flour
- 1 teaspoon kosher salt
- 1 teaspoon brown sugar
- 3 tablespoons butter; at room temperature
- 1 packet instant yeast
- 1 ¼ cups lukewarm water

For the Cakes:
- 1 cup caster sugar
- A pinch of cardamom
- 1 teaspoon cinnamon powder
- 1 stick butter; melted

Instructions:
1. Mix all the dry Ingredients in a large-sized bowl; add the butter and yeast and mix to combine well.
2. Pour lukewarm water and stir to form soft and elastic dough
3. Lay the dough on a lightly floured surface, loosely cover with greased foil and chill for 5 to 10 minutes.
4. Take the dough out of the refrigerator and shape it into two logs, cut them into 20 slices.
5. In a shallow bowl; mix caster sugar with cardamom and cinnamon.
6. Now; brush with melted butter and coat the entire slice with sugar mix, repeat with the remaining Ingredients.
7. Treat the Air Fryer basket with a non-stick cooking spray. Air-fry at 360 - degrees Fahrenheit for about 10 minutes, flipping once during the baking time. To serve, dust with icing sugar and enjoy!

505. Pear and Apple Crisp with Walnuts

Prep + Cook Time: 25 minutes   **Servings:** 6

Ingredients:
- 1/2-pound apples; cored and chopped
- 1/2-pound pears; cored and chopped
- 1 cup all-purpose flour
- 1/3 cup muscovado sugar
- 1/3 cup brown sugar
- 1 tablespoon butter

- 1 teaspoon ground cinnamon
- 1/4 teaspoon ground cloves
- 1 teaspoon vanilla extract
- 1/4 cup chopped walnuts
- Whipped cream; to serve

Instructions:

1. Arrange the apples and pears on the bottom of a lightly greased baking dish.
2. Mix the remaining Ingredients without the walnuts and the whipped cream, until the mixture resembles the coarse crumbs
3. Spread the topping onto the fruits. Scatter chopped walnuts over all. Air-bake at 340 – degrees Fahrenheit for 20 minutes or until the topping is golden brown
4. Check for doneness using a toothpick and serve at room temperature topped with whipped cream

506. Sweet and Crisp Bananas

Prep + Cook Time: 20 minutes   **Servings:** 4

Ingredients:

- 4 ripe bananas
- 1 tablespoon almond meal
- 1 tablespoon cashew; crush
- One Egg; beaten
- 1 ½ tablespoon coconut Oil
- 1/4 cup corn flour
- 1 ½ tablespoon cinnamon sugar
- 1/2 cup breadcrumbs

Instructions:

1. Heat coconut oil in pan over medium heat and add breadcrumbs in pan and stir for 4 minutes
2. Remove pan from heat and place breadcrumbs in bowl.
3. Add almond meal and crush cashew in breadcrumbs and mix well. Peel bananas and cut into half pieces
4. Dip banana half in corn flour then in beaten egg and finally coat with breadcrumbs.
5. Place coated banana in Air Fryer basket. Sprinkle bananas with Cinnamon Sugar.
6. Air fry at 350 – degrees Fahrenheit for 10 minutes

507. Shortbread Fingers

Prep + Cook Time: 20 minutes   **Servings:** 10

Ingredients:

- 1 ½ cups butter
- 1 cup plain flour
- 3/4 cup caster sugar
- high quality cooking spray

Instructions:

1. Start by preheating your Air Fryer to 350 – degrees Fahrenheit.
2. In a medium bowl; combine the flour and sugar
3. Cut the butter into the mix by cutting it into small chunks and putting the chunks in the flour and sugar mixture.
4. Using the back of a fork; rub the butter into the mixture until it is well combined.
5. Using your hands; knead the mixture until it is smooth and evenly combined
6. Make the shortbread dough into 10 evenly sized finger shapes. If you desire; you can decorate them with fork markings.
7. Lightly spray the Air Fryer basket with high quality cooking spray and carefully line each of the 10 cookies in so that they are not touching each other
8. Bake the shortbread cookies for 12 minutes. Allow to cool slightly and then serve, or store in an air tight container and eat within' 3 days

508. Coconut and Bananas Cake

Prep + Cook Time: 1 hour 15 minutes   **Servings:** 5

Ingredients:

- 2/3 cup coconut sugar; shaved
- 2/3 cup unsalted butter
- three eggs
- 1 ¼ cup self-raising flour
- 1 ripe banana; mashed
- 1/2 teaspoon vanilla extract
- 1/8 teaspoon baking soda
- sea salt to taste

Topping Ingredients:

- coconut sugar to taste; shaved
- walnuts to taste; roughly chopped
- bananas to taste; sliced

Instructions:

1. Preheat the Air Fryer to 360 - degrees Fahrenheit.
2. Combine and mix flour, baking soda, and a pinch of sea salt. Set the flour mixture aside.
3. In another bowl mix butter, vanilla extract and coconut sugar with the help of an electrical mixer or a blender. Make the mixture fluffy and beat in eggs one by one
4. Add the half of flour mixture to this mixture and stir well. Add mashed banana and stir well again. Finally, add the remaining flour mixture and make a perfectly smooth batter.
5. Pour the batter into the baking tray and layer the banana slices on top. Sprinkle it with chopped walnuts and cover with shaved coconut sugar. Then cover the tray with the foil and poke the holes in it
6. Put the covered tray into the Air Fryer. Adjust the time to 48 minutes and decrease the temperature to 320 - degrees Fahrenheit.
7. When the cooking time ends, remove the foil. Cook for another 10 minutes
8. The cake is ready when golden brown.
9. Check the cake with the skewer, if it comes out clean - the cake is ready to be served

509. Healthy Roasted Pumpkin Seeds with Cinnamon

Prep + Cook Time: 35 minutes   **Servings:** 2

Ingredients:

- 1 cup pumpkin raw seeds
- 1 tablespoon ground cinnamon
- 2 tablespoon brown sugar
- 1 cup water
- 1 tablespoon olive oil

Instructions:

1. Add pumpkin seeds, cinnamon and water in a sauté pot
2. Stir to combine and heat the mixture over high heat. Boil for 2 - 3 minutes.
3. Drain water and transfer seeds to a kitchen towel.
4. Dry for 20 - 30 minutes
5. In the mixing bowl combine sugar, dried seeds, a pinch of cinnamon and 1 tablespoon of olive oil. Mix well.
6. Preheat the Air Fryer to 340 – degrees Fahrenheit and transfer seed mixture to the fryer basket.
7. Cook for 15 minutes; shaking couple times. Enjoy

510. Pineapple Sticks

Prep + Cook Time: 20 minutes   **Servings:** 4

Ingredients:

- 1/2 fresh pineapple; cut into sticks
- 1/4 cup desiccated coconut

Instructions:

1. Preheat the Air Fryer to 400 - degrees Fahrenheit. Roll pineapple sticks into the desiccated coconut and place in Air Fryer basket
2. Air fry in preheated Air Fryer for 10 minutes.

511. Amazing Sponge Cake

Prep + Cook Time: 50 minutes   **Servings:** 8

Ingredients:

- 9 ounces sugar
- 9 ounces butter
- three eggs
- 9 ounces self-rising flour
- 1 teaspoon vanilla extract
- zest of 1 lemon
- 1 teaspoon baking powder

Frosting:

- juice of 1 lemon
- zest of 1 lemon
- 1 teaspoon yellow food coloring
- 7 ounces caster sugar
- 4 egg whites

Instructions:

1. Preheat your Air Fryer to 320 – degrees Fahrenheit.
2. Beat all of the cake ingredients with an electric mixer
3. Grease two round cake pans. Divide the batter between them.
4. Cook the cakes; one at a time, for 15 minutes
5. Meanwhile; beat together all of the frosting ingredients. Spread the frosting over one cake and top with the other

512. Apple Wedges

Prep + Cook Time: 25 minutes   **Servings:** 4

Ingredients:

- 4 large apples
- 2 tablespoon olive oil
- 1/2 cup dried apricots; chopped
- 1 – 2 tablespoon brown sugar
- 1/2 teaspoon ground cinnamon

Instructions:

1. Peel apples and cut each one into quarters. Remove and discard cores.
2. Cut each apple quarter in half to make 2 even wedges [each whole apple is cut into 8 even wedges]
3. Cover apple wedges with the oil. Cook in the Air Fryer for 12 - 15 minutes at 350 - degrees Fahrenheit.
4. Add the apricots and cook for another 3 minutes
5. Mix together sugar and cinnamon and top cooked apples with the sugar mixture.

513. Yummy Easy Chocolate Lava Cake

Prep + Cook Time: 20 minutes   **Servings:** 4

Ingredients:

- 1 cup dark cocoa candy melts
- 1 stick butter
- Two eggs
- 4 tablespoons superfine sugar
- 1 tablespoon honey

- 4 tablespoons self-rising flour
- A pinch of kosher salt
- A pinch of ground cloves
- 1/4 teaspoon grated nutmeg
- 1/4 teaspoon cinnamon powder

Instructions:

1. Firstly; spray four custard cups with non-stick cooking oil.
2. Put the cocoa candy melts and butter into a small microwave-safe bowl and set the microwave on high for 30 seconds to 1 minute.
3. In a mixing bowl; whisk the eggs along with sugar and honey until frothy. Add it to the chocolate mix
4. After that; add the remaining Ingredients and mix to combine well. You can whisk the mixture with an electric mixer.
5. Spoon the mixture into the prepared custard cups. Air-bake at 350 - degrees Fahrenheit for 12 minutes
6. Take the cups out of the Air Fryer and let them rest for 5 to 6 minutes.
7. Lastly; flip each cup upside-down onto a dessert plate and serve with some fruits and chocolate syrup

514. English Lemon Tarts

Prep + Cook Time: 30 minutes   **Servings:** 4

Ingredients:

- 1/2 cup butter
- 1/2-pound plain flour
- 2 tablespoon sugar

- 1 large lemon [juice and zest taken]
- 2 tablespoon lemon curd
- A pinch of nutmeg

Instructions:

1. In a large mixing bowl combine butter, flour and sugar.
2. Mix well until the mixture will be like breadcrumbs
3. Then add lemon zest and juice, a pinch of nutmeg and mix again. If needed, add couple tablespoons of water to make really soft dough
4. Take little pastry tins and sprinkle with flour. Add dough and top with sugar or lemon zest.
5. Preheat the Air Fryer to 360 – degrees Fahrenheit and cook mini lemon tarts for 15 minutes, until ready

515. Yummy Blueberry Pancakes

Prep + Cook Time: 20 minutes   **Servings:** 4

Ingredients:

- 1/2 teaspoon vanilla extract
- 2 tablespoon honey
- 1/2 cup blueberries
- 1/2 cup sugar
- 2 cups plus

- 2 tablespoon flour
- three eggs; beaten
- 1 cup milk
- 1 teaspoon baking powder
- pinch of salt

Instructions:

1. Preheat the Air Fryer to 390 – degrees Fahrenheit
2. Combine all of the dry ingredients in a bowl.

3. Add the wet ingredients and whisk until the mixture becomes smooth
4. Fold in the blueberries; making sure not to color the dough. You can do that by coating the blueberries with some flour before adding them to the dough.
5. Grease a baking dish. Drop the batter onto the dish, ensuring that the pancakes have some space between the
6. Do it in two batches if you have too much batter. Bake for about 10 minutes.

516. Simple Pumpkin Cake

Prep + Cook Time: 50 minutes   **Servings:** 4

Ingredients:

- 1 large egg
- 1/2 cup skimmed milk
- 7 ounces. all-purpose flour
- 2 tablespoon brown sugar
- 5 ounces. pumpkin puree
- A pinch of salt
- A pinch of cinnamon [if desired]
- cooking spray

Instructions:

1. Mix pumpkin puree and brown sugar in a bowl. Add one egg and whisk until smooth.
2. Stir in flour and salt. Pour milk and combine again. Take the baking tin and coat with cooking spray. Pour the batter into the baking tin
3. Preheat the Air Fryer to 350 - degrees Fahrenheit.
4. Put the baking tin to the Air Fryer basket and set the timer for 15 minutes

517. Mix Berry Puffed Pastry

Prep + Cook Time: 20 minutes   **Servings:** 3

Ingredients:

- 3 pastry dough sheets
- 1/2 cup mixed berries; mashed
- 1 tablespoon honey
- 2 tablespoon cream cheese
- 3 tablespoon chopped walnuts
- 1/4 teaspoon vanilla extract

Instructions:

1. Preheat your Air Fryer to 375 - degrees Fahrenheit.
2. Spread the cream cheese over the pastry. Combine the berries with vanilla extract and honey. Line a baking sheet with parchment paper
3. Divide the filling between the pastry dough. Make sure to place the filling in the middle. Top the filling with chopped walnuts. Close the pastry and seal the edges with the back of a fork.
4. Place the baking sheet in the Air Fryer and cook for about 15 minutes

518. Cherry Pie

Prep + Cook Time: 35 minutes   **Servings:** 8

Ingredients:

- 1 tablespoon Milk
- 2 Store-Bought Pie Crusts
- 21 ounces. Cherry Pie Filling
- 1 Egg Yolk

Instructions:

1. Preheat the Air Fryer to 310 – degrees Fahrenheit.
2. Grease a pie pan and place one of the pie crusts in it. Poke holes with a fork. Add the pie filling and spread it evenly
3. Cut the other crust into strips and arrange them over the pie filling to give the pie a more authentic look. Air Fry for 15 minutes

519. Small Apple Pie

Prep + Cook Time: 25 minutes   **Servings:** 7

Ingredients:

- 2 large apples
- 1/2 cup plain flour
- 2 tablespoon unsalted butter
- 1 tablespoon sugar
- 1/2 teaspoon cinnamon

Instructions:

1. Preheat the Air Fryer to 360 - degrees Fahrenheit
2. In the large mixing bowl combine flour and butter. Stir to combine. Add sugar and mix well.
3. Add couple tablespoons of water and prepare nice dough. Mix until you get a smooth texture.
4. Take small pastry tins and cover with butter. Fill tins with pastry
5. Peel and core apples. Dice them. Place diced apples over the pastry and sprinkle with sugar and cinnamon.
6. Transfer pastry tins to an Air Fryer and cook for 15 - 17 minutes, until ready. Serve with whipped cream or ice cream

520. Amazing Chocolate Molten Lava Cake

Prep + Cook Time: 25 minutes   **Servings:** 4

Ingredients:

- 3 ½ ounces. butter; melted
- 3 ½ tablespoon sugar
- 3 ½ ounces chocolate; melted
- 1 ½ tablespoon flour
- Two eggs

Instructions:

1. Preheat the Air Fryer to 375 - degrees Fahrenheit.
2. Grease 4 ramekins
3. Beat together the eggs and butter. Stir in the chocolate. Gently fold in the flour.
4. Divide the mixture between the 4 ramekins. Place them in the Air Fryer and cook for 10 minutes
5. After 2 minutes; invert them onto serving plates

521. Tasty Pineapple Cake

Prep + Cook Time: 40 minutes   **Servings:** 4

Ingredients:

- 2 cups self-raising flour
- 1/4-pound butter
- 1/4 cup sugar
- 1/2-pound pineapple; chopped
- 1/2 cup pineapple juice
- 1 ounce. dark chocolate; grated
- 1 large egg
- 2 tablespoon skimmed milk

Instructions:

1. Preheat the Air Fryer to 370 – degrees Fahrenheit and grease a cake tin.
2. In the mixing bowl combine butter and flour
3. Mix well until the mixture will be like breadcrumbs
4. Add sugar, diced pineapple, juice, and crushed dark chocolate. Mix well.
5. In another bowl mix egg and milk. Pour to the flour mixture and prepare a soft pastry.
6. Transfer the mixture to a greased tin and place to an Air Fryer
7. Cook for about 35 - 40 minutes, then serve and enjoy.

522. Yummy Glazed Donuts

Prep + Cook Time: 25 minutes   **Servings:** 3

Ingredients:

- 1 can [8 oz] refrigerated croissant dinner rolls.
- non-stick cooking spray
- 1 can [16 oz] vanilla frosting

Instructions:

1. Slice croissant dough into 1-inch rounds. Tear hole in the center to make a donut shape. Place five donuts in the basket, do not overcrowd, and spritz with nonstick spray.
2. Put the basket and pan into the Air. Set temperature to 400 - degrees Fahrenheit and adjust the timer to 5 minutes
3. After 2 minutes; flip donuts over and cook for the remaining time. Once cooking is complete, remove and place on paper plate. Repeat with remaining rolls
4. Microwave 1/2 cup of frosting in a microwave-safe dish for 30 seconds. Drizzle donuts with glaze and serve.

523. Tasty Apple Dumplings

Prep + Cook Time: 40 minutes   **Servings:** 2

Ingredients:

- 2 tablespoon sultanas
- 2 sheets puff pastry
- 2 tablespoon butter; melted
- 2 tiny apples
- 1 tablespoon brown sugar

Instructions:

1. Preheat your Air Fryer to 350 - degrees Fahrenheit
2. Peel and core the apples.
3. In a bowl; mix the brown sugar and the sultanas
4. Place each small apple on one of the pastry sheets and then fill the core with the sugar and sultanas. Fold the pastry around the apple, so it is entirely covered. Place the apple dumplings on a small sheet of foil. Brush the dough with the melted butter
5. Place in you Air Fryer and set the timer for 25 minutes and bake the apple dumplings until golden brown and the apples are soft

524. Cinnamon Rolls with Cream Cheese Glaze

Prep + Cook Time: 45 minutes   **Servings:** 8

Ingredients:

- 1-pound frozen bread dough; thawed
- 1/4 cup butter; melted and cooled
- 3/4 cup brown sugar
- 1 ½ tablespoon ground cinnamon

Cream Cheese Glaze:

- 4 ounces cream cheese; softened
- 2 tablespoon butter; softened
- 1 ¼ cups powdered sugar
- 1/2 teaspoon vanilla

Instructions:

1. Let the bread dough come to room temperature on the counter. On a lightly floured surface roll the dough into a 13-inch by 11-inch rectangle.
2. Position the rectangle so the 13-inch side is facing you. Brush the melted butter all over the dough, leaving a 1-inch border uncovered along the edge farthest away from you.

3. Combine the brown sugar and cinnamon in a small bowl. Sprinkle the mixture evenly over the buttered dough, keeping the 1-inch border uncovered
4. Roll the dough into a log starting with the edge closest to you. Roll the dough tightly, making sure to roll evenly and push out any air pockets.
5. When you get to the uncovered edge of the dough, press the dough onto the roll to seal it together.
6. Cut the log into 8 pieces; slicing slowly with a sawing motion so you don't flatten the dough. Turn the slices on their sides and cover with a clean kitchen towel.
7. Let the rolls sit in the warmest part of your kitchen for 1 ½ to 2 hours to rise.
8. To make the glaze, place the cream cheese and butter in a microwave-safe bowl. Soften the mixture in the microwave for 30 seconds at a time until it is easy to stir.
9. Gradually add the powdered sugar and stir to combine. Add the vanilla extract and whisk until smooth. Set aside
10. When the rolls have risen; pre-heat the Air Fryer to 350 - degrees Fahrenheit.
11. Transfer 4 of the rolls to the Air Fryer basket. Air-fry for 5 minutes.
12. Turn the rolls over and air-fry for another 4 minutes. Repeat with the remaining 4 rolls.
13. Let the rolls cool for a couple of minutes before glazing. Spread large dollops of cream cheese glaze on top of the warm cinnamon rolls, allowing some of the glaze to drip down the side of the rolls

525. Air Fried Bananas with Ice Cream

Prep + Cook Time: 25 minutes   **Servings:** 2

Ingredients:

- 2 large bananas
- 1 tablespoon butter
- 1 tablespoon brown sugar
- 2 tablespoon breadcrumbs
- Vanilla ice cream for serving

Instructions:

1. Melt butter in the Air Fryer basket in one minute at 350 - degrees Fahrenheit
2. Mix sugar and bread crumbs in a bowl. Cut bananas into 1-inch slices and add to sugar mixture. Mix well
3. Put covered bananas into Air Fryer and cook for 10 – 15 minutes. Serve warm and add ice cream

526. Raspberry Muffins

Prep + Cook Time: 35 minutes   **Servings:** 10

Ingredients:

- One Egg
- 1 cup frozen raspberries coated with some flour
- 1 ½ cups flour
- 1/2 cup sugar
- 1/3 cup vegetable oil
- 2 teaspoon baking powder
- yogurt; as needed
- 1 teaspoon lemon zest
- 2 tablespoon lemon juice
- pinch of sea salt

Instructions:

1. Preheat the Air Fryer to 350 – degrees Fahrenheit
2. Combine the dry ingredients in a bowl. Beat the egg and combine it with the oil and lemon juice in a cup. Fill the rest of the cup with yogurt. Combine the dry and wet ingredients. Stir in lemon zest and raspberries
3. Grease 10 muffin tins. Divide the mixture between the muffin tins. You will probably need to do it in batches. Cook for 10 minutes

527. Tasty Pecan Pie

Prep + Cook Time: 1 hour 10 minutes   **Servings:** 4

Ingredients:

- 1 8-inch pie dough
- 1/2 teaspoon cinnamon
- 3/4 teaspoon vanilla extract
- Two eggs
- 3/4 cup maple syrup
- 1/8 teaspoon nutmeg
- 2 tablespoon almond butter
- 1 tablespoon butter; melted
- 2 tablespoon brown sugar
- 1/2 cup chopped pecans

Instructions:

1. Preheat the Air Fryer to 370 - degrees Fahrenheit
2. Combine the melted butter and pecans in a small bowl; and coat them well.
3. Toast the mix in the Air Fryer for about 10 minutes. Place the pie dough in a greased 8-inch pie pan and top with the pecans
4. Combine the remaining ingredients together in a bowl; and pour the mixture over the pecans. Bake for 25 minutes

528. Easy Cinnamon Rolls

Prep + Cook Time: 40 minutes   **Servings:** 8

Ingredients:

- 3/4 cup brown sugar
- 1 ½ tablespoon ground cinnamon
- 1 Pound. frozen bread dough; thawed, room temperature
- 1/4 cup butter; melted and cooled

Cream Cheese Glaze:

- 2 tablespoon butter; softened
- 1/2 teaspoon vanilla
- 4 ounces. cream cheese; softened
- 1 ¼ cups powdered sugar

Instructions:

1. Dust your work surface with some flour and roll the dough into a 13"xl 1" rectangle. The wider side should face you
2. Melt the butter and grease the dough with it, leaving a 1-inch border uncovered along the edge farthest away from you.
3. Combine brown sugar and cinnamon. Then cover the dough with this mixture and leave the same 1-inch border uncovered
4. Roll the dough tightly into a log, starting with the side that is the closest to you. Make sure it has no air pockets.
5. Once you get to the uncovered part - press the dough onto the roll to seal it together tightly.
6. Cut the log into 8 pieces without flattening the dough. Turn the pieces on their sides and place them in the warmest part of the kitchen covering them with a towel.
7. Let them rest and rise for about 2 hours
8. Prepare the glaze: take the microwave-safe bowl and put in cream cheese and butter. Heat it in the microwave for 30 seconds. Now you can easily stir the mixture.
9. Gradually add in powdered sugar stirring well. Then add in vanilla extract and stir once again to make a smooth cream cheese glaze.
10. Check the rolls: if they rose already; preheat the Air Fryer to 350 - degrees Fahrenheit.
11. Layer four rolls in the basket and cook for 5 minutes once the Air Fryer pre heated. When time is up, flip them and cook for another 4 minutes.
12. Repeat this with the other four rolls as well
13. When ready; remove the rolls from the Air Fryer and set them aside to cool.
14. Cover cinnamon rolls with the cream cheese glaze generously and serve

529. Orange Carrot Cake

Prep + Cook Time: 30 minutes   **Servings:** 8

Ingredients:

- 2 large carrots; peeled and grated
- 1 and 3/4 cup self-raising flour
- 3/4 cup brown sugar
- two eggs
- 10 tablespoon olive oil
- 2 cups icing sugar
- 1 teaspoon mixed spice
- 2 tablespoon milk
- 4 tablespoon melted butter
- 1 small orange; rind and juice

Instructions:

1. Preheat the Air Fryer to 360 – degrees Fahrenheit for 10 minutes
2. Use a baking sheet for the tin. Meanwhile; combine flour, sugar, grated carrots, mixed spice and stir well.
3. Then add in milk, beaten eggs, and olive oil into the center of the batter and stir everything thoroughly once again
4. Place the mixture in the tin and cook in the preheated Air Fryer for 5 minutes.
5. Reduce the temperature to 320 - degrees Fahrenheit and cook for another 5 minutes
6. In the meantime; make the frosting: combine melted butter, orange juice, rind, and icing sugar. Beat everything until smooth.
7. When the cake is ready; let it cool for several minutes Top it with the frosting and serve

530. Choco Chip Cookies

Prep + Cook Time: 30 minutes   **Servings:** 8

Ingredients:

- 3 ounces brown sugar
- 4 ounces butter
- 1 tablespoon honey
- 6 ounces self-rising flour
- 1 ½ tablespoon milk
- 2 ounces chocolate chips

Instructions:

1. Preheat the Air Fryer to 350 - degrees Fahrenheit
2. Beat the sugar and butter with an electric mixer; until fluffy.
3. Beat in the rest of the ingredients; except the chocolate chips
4. Fold in the chocolate chips. With a spoon, drop cookies onto a lined baking sheet.
5. Cook for 18 minutes

531. Yummy Butter Cake

Prep + Cook Time: 25 minutes   **Servings:** 2

Ingredients:

- One Egg
- 1 ½ cup plain flour
- 7 tablespoon butter; room temperature
- 6 tablespoon milk
- 6 tablespoon caster sugar
- 1 pinch sea salt
- cooking spray
- icing sugar to sprinkle

Instructions:

1. Preheat the Air Fryer to 360 - degrees Fahrenheit. Take a small ring cake tin and grease it with the cooking spray.
2. Blend butter and sugar thoroughly. Then whisk in the egg and continue blending until smooth and fluffy. Sift in the flour
3. Add the milk and a pinch of salt. Blend well until you get perfect cake batter.

4. Place this batter into the tin and level the surface using a spoon
5. Cook for 15 minutes. Insert the toothpick to check whether the cake is ready - the toothpick should come out cleanly.
6. When it's cooked; set the cake aside to cool and serve

532. Fried Banana Mores

Prep + Cook Time: 20 minutes   **Servings:** 4

Ingredients:

- 3 tablespoon mini peanut butter chips
- 3 tablespoon mini semi-sweet chocolate chips
- 3 tablespoon graham cracker cereal
- 3 tablespoon mini marshmallows
- 4 unpeeled bananas

Instructions:

1. Preheat the Air Fryer to 400 – degrees Fahrenheit.
2. Prepare bananas leaving them unpeeled: slice them lengthwise along the inside of the curve, but do not slice through the bottom of the peel
3. Shape the pocket by slightly opening the banana
4. Add into this pocket chocolate chips, peanut butter chips, and mini marshmallows.
5. Then add graham cracker cereal.
6. Take the basket and place the bananas in it. Make sure the filling is facing up
7. Cook for 6 minutes when bananas are soft and chocolate and marshmallows are melted.
8. Let it cool for 3 minutes and eat spooning out the filling

533. Delicious Chocolate Mug Cake

Prep + Cook Time: 15 minutes   **Servings:** 1

Ingredients:

- 1 tablespoon cocoa powder
- 3 tablespoon coconut oil
- 1/4 cup self-raising flour
- 3 tablespoon whole milk
- 5 tablespoon powdered sugar

Instructions:

1. Mix all the ingredients very thoroughly and pour it into not a very tall mug
2. Place the mug into your Air Fryer and set the timer to 10 minutes with the temperature 390 - degrees Fahrenheit.
3. Serve at the end of cooking

534. Special Dough Dippers with Chocolate Almond Sauce

Prep + Cook Time: 45 minutes   **Servings:** 5

Ingredients:

- 3/4 cup sugar
- 1 Pound. bread dough, defrosted
- 1 cup heavy cream
- 12 ounces. good quality semi-sweet chocolate chips
- 1/2 cup butter; melted
- 2 tablespoon almond extract

Instructions:

1. Preheat the Air Fryer to 350 – degrees Fahrenheit. Grease its basket with a little amount of melted butter
2. Prepare the dough: roll it into two 15-inch logs. Then cut the logs into 20 pieces.
3. Cut each of these pieces into halves and twist these halves 3 to 4 times.

4. Take the cookie sheet; add place the twisted dough on it. Cover it with some more melted butter and drizzle with sugar.
5. Air-fry cookies in batches. Place 10 – 12 pieces of twisted dough in the basket at once. Cook for 5 minutes
6. Turn the dough twists, and grease it with more butter. Cook for another 3 minutes.
7. Repeat until you run out of dough twists.
8. Meanwhile; prepare the chocolate almond sauce. Bring to a simmer the heavy cream over the medium heat
9. Place the chocolate chips into a large bowl and pour in simmering cream. Whisk the chocolate chips well to get completely smooth consistency. Stir in 2 tablespoons of almond extract.
10. When the cookies are ready; place them into a shallow dish, cover with the remaining melted butter and drizzle with sugar.
11. Sprinkle with chocolate almond sauce and serve

535. Easy Peach Crumble

Prep + Cook Time: 35 minutes   **Servings:** 6

Ingredients:

- 1 ½ pounds peeled and chopped peaches
- 2 tablespoon lemon juice
- 1 cup flour
- 1 tablespoon water
- 1/2 cup sugar
- 5 tablespoon cold butter
- pinch of sea salt

Instructions:

1. Using a fork, slightly mash the peaches, ensuring that there are chunks left.
2. Combine them with 2 tablespoons sugar and lemon juice
3. In a bowl; combine flour, salt, and sugar. Add a tablespoon of water and rub the cold butter into the mixture, until it becomes crumbed
4. Place the berries at the bottom of a greased baking dish
5. Place the crumbs over it. Air Fry for 20 minutes at 390 - degrees Fahrenheit

536. Banana Walnut Cake

Prep + Cook Time: 55 minutes   **Servings:** 6

Ingredients:

- 16 ounces. bananas [mashed]
- 8 ounces. flour [self-raising]
- 6 ounces. sugar [caster]
- 3.5 ounces. walnuts [chopped]
- 2.5 ounces. butter
- two eggs
- 1/4 teaspoon baking soda

Instructions:

1. Grease baking dish with oil.
2. Preheat Air Fryer to 355 – degrees Fahrenheit
3. Whisk sugar, butter, egg, flour and soda. Stir the ingredients well. Add bananas and walnuts into the mixture. Pour the mixture into the pan. Let it cook for 10 minutes
4. Lower temperature to 330 - degrees Fahrenheit and cook for an additional 15 minutes. Serve while hot. Enjoy the yummy taste.

537. Cheesy Lemon Cake

Prep + Cook Time: 60 minutes   **Servings:** 6

Ingredients:

- 17.5 ounces. cheese [ricotta]
- 5.4 ounces. sugar
- three eggs
- 3 tablespoon corn flour

- 1 lemon [juice; zest]
- 2 teaspoon vanilla extract [optional]

Instructions:

1. Mix all the ingredients until they present a creamy texture. Pour the mixture in a dish and form cake out of it.
2. Preheat Air Fryer to 320 – degrees Fahrenheit; cook the cakes for 25 minutes. Serve the cake when it is cold enough and enjoy the combination

538. Mouthwatering Chocolate Brownies with Caramel Sauce

Prep + Cook Time: 45 minutes   **Servings:** 4

Ingredients:

- 1/2 cup butter plus more for greasing the pan
- 1 and 3/4 ounces. unsweetened chocolate
- 1 cup brown sugar
- 2 medium eggs; beaten
- 1 cup self-rising flour
- 2 teaspoon vanilla
- 1/2 cup caster sugar
- 2 tablespoon water
- 2/3 cup milk

Instructions:

1. In a medium saucepan; melt the butter and chocolate over medium heat. Remove from heat and add the brown sugar, eggs, flour, and vanilla, mixing well
2. Briefly preheat your Air Fryer to 350 – degrees Fahrenheit.
3. Grease a baking dish with butter and pour the batter into the prepared dish. Bake in the Fryer for 15 minutes
4. While the brownies bake; make the caramel sauce in a small saucepan, combine the caster sugar with water and bring to a boil over medium heat
5. Continue cooking until the mixture is light brown, about 3 minutes. Reduce the heat and, after two minutes, add the remaining butter bit by bit. Let the caramel cool.
6. Cut the brownies into squares, top with caramel sauce, and serve
7. Bonus points if you add some sliced banana

539. Pumpkin Cinnamon Pudding

Prep + Cook Time: 25 minutes   **Servings:** 4

Ingredients:

- 3 cups pumpkin puree
- 3 tablespoon honey
- 1 tablespoon ginger
- 1 tablespoon cinnamon
- 1 teaspoon clove
- 1 teaspoon nutmeg
- 1 cup full fat cream
- two eggs
- 1 cup brown sugar

Instructions:

1. Preheat your Air Fryer to 390 - degrees Fahrenheit. Mix together all of the ingredients.
2. Place in a greased heat safe small dish; Cook for 15 minutes. Serve topped with whipped cream.

540. Special Banana Walnut Bread

Prep + Cook Time: 40 minutes   **Servings:** 1 loaf

Ingredients:

- 7 ounces. self-rising flour
- 1/4 teaspoon baking powder
- 2.5 ounces. butter
- 5.5 ounces. caster sugar
- 2 medium eggs
- 14 ounces. bananas [weight after peeling]
- 2.8 ounces. chopped walnuts

Instructions:

1. Preheat the Air Fryer to 350 – degrees Fahrenheit. Grease a tin that will slot into the Air Fryer. Mix the baking powder with the flour
2. In a separate bowl cream sugar and butter until fluffy and pale. Little at a time, add in flour and egg and stir. Add in walnuts and remaining flour and stir until even.
3. Peel the bananas and mash them up and add them to your mixture. Stir. Place the banana bread mix into the tin and cook for 10 minutes

541. Sugared Dough Dippers with Chocolate Amaretto Sauce

Prep + Cook Time: 35 minutes   **Servings:** 10

Ingredients:

- 1-pound bread dough; defrosted
- 1/2 cup butter; melted
- 3/4 to 1 cup sugar
- 1 cup heavy cream
- 12 ounces. good quality semi-sweet chocolate chips
- 2 tablespoon Amaretto liqueur [or almond extract]

Instructions:

1. Roll the dough into two 15-inch logs. Cut each log into 20 slices.
2. Cut each slice in half and twist the dough halves together 3 to 4 times
3. Place the twisted dough on a cookie sheet, brush with melted butter and sprinkle sugar over the dough twists.
4. Pre-heat the Air Fryer to 350 – degrees Fahrenheit
5. Brush the bottom of the Air Fryer basket with melted butter. Air-fry the dough twists in batches.
6. Place 8 to 12 [depending on the size of your Air Fryer] in the Air Fryer basket.
7. Air-fry for 5 minutes. Turn the dough strips over and brush the other side with butter.
8. Air-fry for an additional 3 minutes
9. While dough is cooking; make the chocolate amaretto sauce. Bring the heavy cream to a simmer over medium heat.
10. Place the chocolate chips in a large bowl and pour the hot cream over the chocolate chips. Stir until the chocolate starts to melt.
11. Then switch to a wire whisk and whisk until the chocolate is completely melted and the sauce is smooth. Stir in the Amaretto.
12. Transfer to a serving dish
13. As the batches of dough twists are complete, place them into a shallow dish. Brush with melted butter and generously coat with sugar, shaking the dish to cover both sides.
14. Serve the sugared dough dippers with the warm chocolate Amaretto sauce on the side

542. Appetizing Peach Slices

Prep + Cook Time: 40 minutes   **Servings:** 4

Ingredients:

- 4 cups peaches; sliced
- 2 – 3 tablespoon sugar
- 2 tablespoon all-purpose flour
- 1/3 cup oats
- 2 tablespoon unsalted butter
- 1/4 teaspoon vanilla extract
- 1 teaspoon cinnamon

Instructions:

1. In a large mixing bowl mix peach slices, sugar, vanilla extract, and cinnamon. Transfer to a baking pan
2. Place baking pan to an Air Fryer and cook for 20 minutes on 290 - degrees Fahrenheit. Meanwhile in another bowl mix oats, flour, and unsalted butter. Stir to combine
3. When peach slices cooked; open the lid and top peaches with butter mixture

4. Close the fryer and cook for 10 minutes more on 300 - 310 - degrees Fahrenheit.
5. When ready; set aside for 5 - 10 minutes to become crispy. Serve with ice-cream.

543. Easy Vanilla Soufflé

Prep + Cook Time: 50 minutes   **Servings:** 6

Ingredient:

- 1/4 cup all-purpose flour
- 1/4 cup butter; softened
- 1 cup whole milk
- 1/4 cup sugar
- 2 teaspoon vanilla extract
- 1 vanilla bean
- 5 egg whites
- 4 egg yolks
- 1 ounce sugar
- 1 teaspoon cream of tartar

Instructions:

1. Mix the flour and butter until it is a smooth paste. In a sauce pan heat the milk and dissolve the sugar. Add the vanilla bean and bring to a boil
2. Add the flour and butter mixture to the boiling milk. With a wire whisk; beat vigorously to ensure there are no lumps. Simmer for several minutes until the mix thickens. Remove from the heat, discard the vanilla bean and cool for 10 minutes in an ice bath
3. While the mix is cooling, take 6 3-ounce ramekins or soufflé dishes. Coat with butter and sprinkle with a pinch of sugar. In another mixing bowl quickly beat the egg yolks and vanilla extract and combine with the milk mixture.
4. Separately beat the egg whites; sugar and cream of tartar until the egg whites form medium stiff peaks. Fold the egg whites into the soufflé base and pour into the prepared baking dishes and smooth off the tops
5. Preheat the Air Fryer to 330 - degrees Fahrenheit. Place 3 soufflé dishes into the cooking basket and cook for 14 – 16 minutes. Repeat the cooking process with the next 3 ramekins. Serve with powdered sugar on top of the soufflé and with chocolate sauce on the side.

544. Butter Marshmallow Fluff Turnovers

Prep + Cook Time: 35 minutes   **Servings:** 4

Ingredients:

- 4 sheets filo pastry; defrosted
- 4 tablespoon chunky peanut butter
- 4 teaspoon marshmallow fluff
- 2 ounces. butter; melted
- 1 pinch sea salt

Instructions:

1. Preheat the Air Fryer to 360 – degrees Fahrenheit. Brush 1 sheet of filo with butter.
2. Place a second sheet of filo on top of the first and also brush with butter
3. Repeat until you have used all 4 sheets. Cut the filo layers into 4 3-inch x 12-inch strips.
4. Place 1 tablespoon of peanut butter and 1 teaspoon of marshmallow fluff on the underside of a strip of filo
5. Fold the tip of the sheet over the filling to form a triangle and fold repeatedly in a zigzag manner until the filling is fully wrapped
6. Use a touch of butter to seal the ends of the turnover.
7. Place the turnovers into the cooking basket and cook for 3 – 5 minutes; until golden brown and puffy. Finish with a touch of sea salt for a sweet and salty combination.

545. Holiday Chocolate Soufflé

Prep + Cook Time: 30 minutes   **Servings:** 2

Ingredients:

- 4 tablespoon butter
- two eggs; separated
- 1/2 teaspoon vanilla extract
- 3 ounces. semi-sweet chocolate; chopped
- 2 tablespoon all-purpose flour
- 3 tablespoon sugar
- 1 tablespoon powdered sugar
- heavy cream to taste for serving

Instructions:

1. Prepare two 6-oz. ramekins: grease them with butter and cover with small amount of sugar. Remove the excess of sugar that did not stick
2. Use the microwave to melt the butter and the chocolate combined together in a dish.
3. Beat egg yolks in a bowl and add sugar, vanilla extract, melted chocolate, and butter mixture step by step.
4. Stir each time you add a new ingredient. Then add in flour and stir well until the batter contains no lumps
5. Preheat your Air Fryer to 330 - degrees Fahrenheit
6. Take the bowl and whisk egg whites very well. The whites should reach the soft peak stage [they should almost stand up on the end of the whisk].
7. Gradually add these whites to the chocolate mixture.
8. Add the batter to the ramekins. Leave 1/4 -inch empty at the top. Place the ramekins into the Air Fryer and cook for 14 minutes.
9. When time is up; make sure the soufflés rose nicely and its top is brown. Other-wise, cook for a couple minutes more
10. Sprinkle the ramekins with the powdered sugar and serve adding heavy cream on top

546. Amazing Apple Fries with Caramel Cream Dip

Prep + Cook Time: 30 minutes   **Servings:** 8

Ingredients:

- 3 Pink Lady or Honey crisp apples; peeled, cored and cut into 8 wedges
- 1/2 cup flour
- three eggs; beaten
- 1 cup graham cracker crumbs
- 1/4 cup sugar
- 8 ounces. whipped cream cheese
- 1/2 cup caramel sauce; plus more for garnish

Instructions:

1. Toss the apple slices and flour together in a large bowl.
2. Set up a dredging station by putting the beaten eggs in one shallow dish, and combining the crushed graham crackers and sugar in a second shallow dish
3. Dip each apple slice into the egg, and then into the graham cracker crumbs.
4. Coat the slices on all sides and place the coated slices on a cookie sheet
5. Pre-heat the Air Fryer to 380 - degrees Fahrenheit. Spray or brush the bottom of the Air Fryer basket with oil
6. Air-fry the apples in batches. Place one layer of apple slices in the Air Fryer basket and spray lightly with oil. Air-fry for 5 minutes.
7. Turn the apples over and air-fry for an additional 2 minutes.
8. While apples are cooking make caramel cream dip. Combine the whipped cream cheese and caramel sauce, mixing well.
9. Transfer the Caramel Cream Dip into a serving bowl and drizzle additional caramel sauce over the top
10. Serve the apple fries hot with the caramel cream dip on the side. Enjoy!

547. Blackberry Apricot Crumble

Prep + Cook Time: 30 minutes   **Servings:** 6

Ingredient:

- 18 ounces. fresh apricots; halved and stones removed
- 6 ounces. blackberries
- 2 tablespoon fresh lemon juice
- 1/2 cup sugar; divided

- 1 cup all-purpose flour
- pinch of salt
- 5 tablespoon cold butter plus more for greasing the pan

Instructions:

1. Dice the apricots and combine them with the blackberries, lemon juice, and 2 tablespoons of the sugar in a large bowl
2. Mix well and transfer to a buttered baking dish.
3. To make the crumble topping, combine the remaining sugar, flour, salt, butter, and 1 tablespoon cold water in a medium bowl
4. Mix until crumbly in texture and sprinkle on top of fruit mixture.
5. Briefly preheat your Air Fryer to 350 - degrees Fahrenheit. Bake the crumble until golden brown, about 20 minutes

548. Cherry Pound Chocolate Cake

Prep + Cook Time: 40 minutes   **Servings:** 2

Ingredients:

- three eggs
- 1 cup and 2 tablespoons plain flour
- 12 cherries; halved and deseeded
- 1/2 teaspoon baking powder
- 10 tablespoons [5 oz] unsalted butter; melted

- 6+1 tablespoon castor sugar; separately
- 1 tablespoon lemon juice
- 1 lemon; zested
- sea salt to taste
- 1/4 cup dark chocolate chips; optional

Instructions:

1. Preheat the Air Fryer to 320 - degrees Fahrenheit.
2. Combine and blend 6 tablespoons of castor sugar, melted butter, and lemon zest
3. Add the eggs one at a time. Keep blending until you get light and fluffy batter
4. Add in sieved flour mixtures: flour, baking powder, and salt. Pour in lemon juice and blend until there are no traces of flour. Then add dark chocolate chips, if desired.
5. Take mini disposal loaf pan, add batter and top it with the cherries
6. Place this loaf pan into the Air Fryer basket and put it into the Air Fryer
7. Cook for 25 minutes. Check the readiness with the help of a skewer - insert it in the middle of the cake and if it comes out clean, the cake is ready
8. Sprinkle it with additional castor sugar before your serve

549. Almond Cookies with White Chocolate

Prep + Cook Time: 35 minutes   **Servings:** 8

Ingredients:

- 1/3 cup brown sugar
- 2 tablespoon honey
- 1 ½ cup self raising flour
- 7 tablespoon butter; melted

- 2 tablespoon whole milk
- 2 ounces. white chocolate; melted
- 2 – 4 tablespoon almonds to taste; chopped

Instructions:

1. First; whisk or blend the melted butter with sugar
2. The mixture you get should be fluffy. Add in flour, honey, melted white chocolate, and milk. Stir the ingredients thoroughly
3. Add in almonds and stir well. Preheat the Air Fryer to 360 - degrees Fahrenheit
4. Shape the mixture into the cookie shapes. Place them in the Air Fryer basket and put it in the fryer. Air-fry for 18 minutes and serve warm or at room temperature

550. Cranberry Muffins

Prep + Cook Time: 25 minutes   **Servings:** 12

Ingredients:

- 1/4 cup salted butter; softened
- 1/2 cup granulated sugar
- 1 medium egg
- 1/2 tablespoon of vanilla
- 3/4 cup milk

- 1 ¼ cups all-purpose flour
- 1/2 teaspoon baking powder
- 1/2 teaspoon baking soda
- 1/3 cup dried cranberries [or more as you desire]

optional: up to 1/2 cup walnuts, cashews, or almonds

Instructions:

1. Using an electric mixer; cream the butter and sugar in a large bowl until fluffy and pale in color. Beat in the egg and then the vanilla. Sift the flour, baking powder, and baking soda together in a medium bowl
2. Working in batches, beat the milk and flour mixture into the butter mixture alternating liquid and dry ingredients. Fold the cranberries and nuts [if using] into the batter
3. Briefly preheat your Air Fryer to 350 - degrees Fahrenheit.
4. While the Fryer preheats; fill 12 cupcake liners ⅔ full. [You will need sturdy liners that can stand on their own when filled with batter.] Bake the muffins for 15 minutes, let cool slightly, and serve

Made in the USA
San Bernardino, CA
14 March 2018